The Sixth Sense

Accelerating Organizational Learning with Scenarios

Kees van der Heijden

Ron Bradfield

George Burt

George Cairns

George Wright

JOHN WILEY & SONS, LTD

CONTENTS

ABOUT THE AUTHORS   x

INTRODUCTION   1
The Quest for a Clear Vision of the Future   1
The Significance of Scenario Thinking   2
Developing the Sixth Sense – the Approach to Scenario Thinking   5
How this Book is Organized   6

1. PREPARING FOR THE FUTURE   11
Understanding Organizational Success   12
Success and Failure are Inevitable   12
Understanding success by understanding failure   13
Explaining the Sharpbenders Research: Why Organizations Fail   14
Maintaining Organizational Performance: Problems   19
Sustaining Competitive Advantage – the Battle of Canon and Xerox   19
Yahoo! – Competing in Fast-moving Markets   23
Building a Colourful New Future Brick by Brick – the Story of Lego 26
Success Stories   28
Providing Customer Value – the Rise of Tetra Pak   28
Entering New Markets and Maintaining Growth – Nokia Answers
the Call   32
Barriers to Strategic Success   34
Lessons Learned   34
Creating Value – The Difference Between Success and Failure   36
Value is Created in a Domain of Scarcity   37
Summary: Understanding the Barriers to Scenario Planning   37

2. HOW MANAGERS THINK ABOUT THE FUTURE   41
Understanding Management Thinking   42

Routines in Management Thinking   43
Over-reliance on Routines: Success Formulas and Managerial
    Thinking   44
Biases in thinking   46
  The Relevance of Framing Flaws   46
  How a Failed Product Launch Actually Boosted Sales: the Sparkle
      of New Coke   47
  Confirmation Bias   50
  Hindsight Bias   51
  The Problem of Overconfidence   52
The Limitations of Judgemental Forecasting   53
Decision Avoidance   54
  Escalation of Commitment   54
  Bolstering, Procrastination and Buck-Passing   57
  Example of a Management Team Facing a Decision Dilemma   58
  Thinking Flaws: A Synthesis   61
Overcoming Strategic Inertia: the Potential Benefits of Scenario
  Planning   63
A Scenario is not a Forecast of the Future   63
Scenarios Focus on Key Uncertainties *and* Certainties About the Future 63
Scenarios Help Identify Information to Anticipate How the Future
    will Unfold   64
  Typical Outcomes of the Scenario Planning Process   65
Summary: Overcoming Thinking Flaws with Scenario Planning   65
  Summary Checklist – the Limits to Managerial Thinking   65

3. **HOW ORGANIZATIONS THINK ABOUT THE FUTURE**   69
    Flaws in Organizational Thinking   70
      Communication Difficulties   71
      Group-think in Organizations   72
      Fragmentation in Organizations   73
    Limitations Imposed by Identity   75
      Balancing Change and Constancy   75
      Overcoming the Limits of Organizational Identity: the Example
          of IBM   77
    Organizational Lock-in   78
      Understanding Organizational Lock-in   78
      The Consequences of Organizational Feedback Loops and Lock-in   79

Behavioural flaws   80
  Learning and Action   80
  An Organizational Dilemma   81
  Management and Action   82
Overcoming the Pathologies of Organizational Life   84
  Using Organizational Processes   84
  The Benefits of Scenario Planning Interventions   85
Summary: How Organizations Think About the Future   85

4.   THE IMPACT OF CULTURE AND CULTURAL
    ASSUMPTIONS ON STRATEGY   89
Understanding the Impact of Cultural Issues   90
  The Significance to Strategy of Globalization and Cultural Issues   91
  From Mickey Mouse to The Lion King: the Tale of Disney in France   92
Defining Culture for Pragmatic Purposes   96
  Recognizing Differences in Others   96
  The Value of Scenarios in Assessing the Impact of Cultural Factors   97
National Cultural Differences and the Role of Scenario Thinking   98
  Global Organizations and Local Service Offerings: IKEA Shelve
    Their Universal Approach   98
  How Can We Explore Differences in National Cultures?   100
Differences in Organizational Cultures   103
  A Clash of Personality: The Merger of Daimler-Benz and Chrysler   103
  Organizational Culture and the External Environment   105
Differences in Professional Cultures Within Organizations   106
  The Call of the Wild: How Varying Interpretations of Management
    Intent Divided Senior Executives in an ITC Business   106
Moving Beyond Cultural Preconceptions and Stereotypes   108
  Understanding Cultures Across Boundaries   108
  Language, Meaning and Overcoming Ambiguity   109
  Increasing Diversity in a World of Similarity   109
  The Starting Point for Cultural Appraisal   110
  Developing Multiple Perspectives   110
The Application of Scenario Thinking to Cultural
  Understanding   111
  Applying the Defining Factors of Organizational Culture to Your
    Organization   111

Developing a Scenario Culture   112
Key Questions   114

5. SHAPING THE FUTURE: THE EMERGENCE OF MODERN
    SCENARIO TECHNIQUES   117
Scenario Planning: the Human Dimension   118
    Bringing the Future into the Present: The Story of
        Margareta Lonnberg   118
    Memories of the Future: Scenarios Filter What We Perceive   119
    Scenarios: A Cornerstone of Human Thought   120
Scenario Thinking and War Games   121
    Uncertainty and Crisis   121
    War Game Preparations   122
    A Natural Scenario Planner: Field Marshal Lord Alanbrooke   123
    Crisis Management Training   124
The Era of Possibility: the Makeable Post-war World   124
    The Age of Forecasting and Systems Engineering   124
    The US Perspective   125
    The Rand Corporation: the Emergence of Scenario Techniques   126
    The Impact of Herman Kahn and the Hudson Institute   127
    The French Perspective   128
Challenging Established Thinking: the Development of
    Scenarios in the 1970s   129
    The Club of Rome   129
Royal Dutch/Shell and the Problem of Predictability   131
The Development of Scenarios and Strategy During the 1980s   134
    Factors Affecting the Use of Scenario Techniques in Business 135
    Scenarios Become Popular   135
    Scenario Planning and Other Strategic Approaches   136
The 1990s: Scenario Planning and Organizational Learning   138
    The Age of Complexity, the Limits of Certainty – and the Rise
        of Scenario Planning   138
    Organizational Learning   139
    The World of Identity, Experience and Change   140
Summary: the Benefits of Scenario Planning   142
    Enhanced Perception   142
    Integration of Corporate Planning   142

Making People Think   143
A Structure for Dealing with Complexity   143
A Communications Tool   143
A Management Tool   144
Summary Checklist – Building an Understanding of Scenario
    Thinking in Your Organization   144

6.   DEVELOPING THE SKILLS FOR LONG-TERM SURVIVAL
    AND SUCCESS: PRINCIPLES OF THE SCENARIO PROCESS   147
The Need for a Scenario Process   148
Scenarios and Scenario-based Organizational Learning   150
Rationalistic Decision-making   150
Cause and Effect Thinking   152
Systems Thinking   154
Mental Models and their Limitations   158
The Strategic Conversation   161
How Scenarios Tackle the Problems of Organizational Thinking   162
Surfacing Mental Models   163
Eliciting the Agenda   164
Activating and Integrating Intuitive Knowledge   166
Analysing Driving Forces   169
Scenario Telling   170
Organizational Learning   171
The Process of Organizational Learning   172
Scenario Planning as a Way Towards Adaptive Organizational
    Learning   174
Memories of the Future – Creating the Jolt   175
From Scenarios to Adaptive Behaviour   178
Making it Happen   180
Summary: Developing the Skills of Survival   184

7.   SCENARIO PLANNING IN THE ORGANIZATIONAL
    CONTEXT   187
Introducing the Scenario Method   188
Scenarios for the Future of e-Government and the Impact of
    Information and Communications Technologies (ICT)   190
Background   190

The Story of the 'People's Kailyard'   191
Stage 1: Structuring the Scenario Process   192
Identifying Knowledge Gaps   192
Building the Scenario Team   193
Timing for the Scenario Project   194
Stage 2: Exploring the Scenario Context   195
Interviewing Key Players and Widening the Conversation   195
Setting the Scenario Agenda   199
Setting the Scenario Agenda: the Northshire Example   200
The Role of the Remarkable Person   201
Stage 3: Developing the Scenarios   202
Determining the Driving Forces and Testing the Outcomes   202
Clustering the Driving Forces: the Northshire Example   204
Dealing with Impact and Uncertainty   206
Scoping the Scenarios   209
Setting the 'Limits of Possibility' for Alternative Futures:
    the Northshire Example   210
Fleshing out the Storylines   213
Beyond the Kailyard   215
Stage 4: Stakeholder Analysis   216
Stage 5: Systems Thinking   219
Stage 6: Impacting Organizational Thinking and Action   220
Looking for the Organizational Jolt   220
Identifying the Early Indicators   220
Action Planning from the Future to the Present: the Northshire
    Example   221
Summary: Effective Scenario Planning   223
Summary Checklist – Implementing a Scenario Planning Process   224

8. **SCENARIO PLANNING: TAKING CHARGE OF
    THE FUTURE**   229
The Energetic Problem Solver   230
Observation – the Cornerstone of Strategic Success   231
Purposeful Scenario Work   232
Project 1: Making Sense of a Puzzling Situation   234
The Analytical Approach   234
The Limitations of Analysis   235

Purposeful Analysis and How Scenarios Steer Attention   236
Combining Intuition with Rational Analysis: the Iterative Scenario
   Approach   236
Facing the Important Questions   238
Project 2: Developing Strategy   239
Defining Strategy   239
The Stakeholder Game   239
Strategic Aims   240
The Business Idea   242
Friction Forces and Barriers to Entry   244
Developing Distinctiveness   246
The Role of the Business Idea in Strategy   247
Business Idea and Operations   250
The Strategic Journey   252
Project 3: Improving Organizational Anticipation   255
Multiple World Views – The Limits of the Rationalistic Approach   255
The Mont Fleur Story   258
The Role of Scenarios in Strategic Conversation   260
Creating the Scenario-based Strategic Conversation   264
Project 4: Building an Adaptive Learning Organization   266
Action and Experiential Learning   266
The Strategic Journey of Project 2 Revisited   266
What is Adaptive Organizational Learning?   268
Building a Scenario Culture   270
Team Empowerment   272
The Across-team Strategic Conversation   273

SUMMARY   276
Rethinking the Future – the Value of Scenarios in Developing
   Competitive Advantage   276
Developing The Sixth Sense   277

GLOSSARY   279

REFERENCES   293

INDEX   299

ABOUT THE AUTHORS

Kees van der Heijden is director of the Centre of Scenario Planning and Future Studies at University of Strathclyde Graduate School of Business (GSB). Together with the coauthors of this book – all principals of the centre – he works with private and public sector organizations to enable them to negotiate a successful course for their organizations in the face of uncertainty.

Director and cofounder of the Global Business Network (GBN), Professor of General and Strategic Management at Strathclyde University and visiting professor at Nyenrode University, Kees was formerly head of the Business Environment Division in Group Planning at Royal Dutch/Shell, London. His groundbreaking book, *Scenarios: the Art of Strategic Conversation* (John Wiley & Sons, 1996), was runner up for the World Business Book Prize and numerous articles on his work in scenario planning and strategy have been published in a range of books and journals worldwide.

Ron Bradfield, lectures in management at GSB, he is also the director of the school's international MBA programmes in Asia, and has held visiting academic positions at institutions in Poland, Switzerland and Singapore. Prior to his academic career, Ron spent 15 years in senior management positions in industry in the UK, USA and Canada. In addition to his academic activities, Ron is an active scenario planning practitioner and has led a number of large-scale scenario projects with a range of organizations in Asia and the UK. Resident in Shanghai, Ron represents GBN in Asia.

George Burt is a lecturer in strategic management and scenario planning at GSB. He has recently completed doctoral research into the role of scenario thinking to bring about strategic change in organizations. His research identifies and describes the process of reconceptualization of the business during the scenario process as the key to transition and change. George is a qualified chartered accountant, working internationally with one of the 'big five' accountancy firms, prior to taking up a career in academia.

George Cairns, senior lecturer in management at GSB, has over 20 years' experience in a range of business and academic posts. He has previously worked at the University of York and the Department of Architecture and Building Science at the University of Strathclyde. A fellow of the British Institute of Facilities Management, George's interest lies in the understanding of the relationship between the business, social, physical and technological environments of the workplace.

George Wright is a professor at GSB. Previously, he held faculty positions at the London Business School and the University of Leeds Business School and was recently a visiting professor at the Athens University of Economics and Business. Founder and editor of the *Journal of Behavioural Decision Making* and author of a number of books on forecasting and decision making, including *Strategic Decision Making: A Best Practice Blueprint* (John Wiley & Sons, 2001), George is a psychologist with knowledge of the way managers make decisions. He is a GBN associate.

THE QUEST FOR A CLEAR VISION OF THE FUTURE

Unknown Variables, Uncertain Future

A famous scene in the film *Lawrence of Arabia* illustrates the typical managerial response often observed when companies face an unknown or changing situation. While Lawrence and a fellow traveller rest in the desert, a tiny dot becomes visible on the horizon, growing larger as it approaches. At this stage, the horizon seems far away, but they do not know what the spectre is and their curiosity holds them. They watch, and wait. They hardly speak, they just stand there, not knowing what to do about the approaching phenomenon. Eventually, the unknown object is recognized: a man approaching on a camel. Still, the uncertainty continues, as the man's identity is a mystery. They remain fixed, not knowing who it is or what they should do. Finally, Lawrence's fellow traveller, suspecting that something terrible is about to happen, reaches for his revolver. Before he can lift it, the unknown man shoots him. Walking over to the body, he says: 'He's dead.'

Lawrence replies: 'Yes . . . why?'

In this illustration, having identified an approaching dot on the horizon, the two men try to relate it meaningfully to their known world. Various hypotheses are considered. However, it is not clear how these can be explored. Resources for gathering additional data are extremely limited. Nothing much is done to respond while they attempt to develop a theory to assess what the future will bring. A degree of understanding is needed in order to work out what needs to be done. As the 'dot on the horizon' develops, new data is taken in and parts of the old incomplete theory are discarded. While trying to simply keep up with the dynamics of the situation, paralysis sets in, as no theory is durable enough to be used for decision-making. Their intuition is their undoing. Unfortunately, the situation continues to evolve, leaving little time to develop or implement an effective solution. Further inaction intuitively feels intolerable. The need to do something – anything – becomes overwhelming; there is no more time left for thinking. Panic sets in. The first action that presents itself is pursued, with disastrous consequences. And when it is all over you can only wonder: 'Why?'

The Significance of Scenario Thinking

The focus of this book, and of scenario planning, is the capability of organizations to perceive what is going on in their business environments, to think through what this means for them, and then to act upon this new knowledge. It is the need to understand the dots on the horizon, perceiving, thinking and taking action, before it is too late. We have called this *Adaptive Organizational Learning*. We believe, with Arie de Geus[1], that being skilful in this constitutes the ultimate competitive advantage, in that most sources of competitive advantage which are normally put forward can be traced back to this basic quality and capability. We propose that most organizations manifest a significant deficit in this capability, compared to what is possible. There is huge potential for development in this area for most organizations, and those that see this first will move well ahead in the competitive race for success, taking control and ensuring their future position.

The scenario process provides this capability, and if confirmation were needed, it is worth considering the example of Royal Dutch/Shell, the Anglo-Dutch energy giant that remains one of the world's leading multinational companies after nearly a century of growth. The scenario-planning process enables executives to take control of the adaptation process, providing them with the skills needed to manoeuvre their organization, over time, and creating huge process gains for their organizations. On the other hand, using scenario thinking to achieve Adaptive Organizational Learning is nothing new; it has been around for ages. So why is it not being picked up as a matter of course?

Based on our experience and research, we propose that the bottleneck is not so much in the availability of the process, but in the lack of realization of 'below potential' performance in organizations. Many people have become so used to the constraints under which they operate that they are simply not aware of these anymore. Managers become locked into a mode of thinking that acts as a filter, restricting the information they are able to perceive. They do not recognize that they are locked into a systemic loop, and this is reinforced by the dynamics occurring within the organization.

> **The significance of scenario thinking lies in its ability to help overcome thinking limitations by developing multiple futures.**

Personal biases and routines imprison the individual manager within a world of recipes and business-as-usual assumptions. Human psychology, as well as the environment, conspire to keep them there. In this book, we will show how most roads that people take to deal with their day-to-day issues lead to inertia. Organizations can also be the subjects of sub-optimal behaviour, driving towards the pathological states of fragmentation or group-think that subvert effective organizational perception and action, leading many organizations to their demise. And beyond that there are the assumptions we all inherit from our cultural environment, that lead so many cross-cultural projects to dismal failure.

The crux of the matter is a serious lack of awareness of these impediments to success. One reason for this is that, although many thinking traps are individual, they happen within ongoing interactions where people are under the influence of many others. That makes it extremely difficult for them to think their way out of the problem. This is why we propose that the situation needs to be tackled by 'process gain', working on the dominant group in the organization. We believe that the scenario approach helps managers and organizations to overcome these flaws – an assertion based on reasoning, real world observations and a long track record of scenario-based methods. Many years of practice have shown overwhelmingly how scenarios can produce such process gain.

Not all experience with scenarios is positive. Poorly-executed scenario work leaves managers feeling that not much has been achieved. One common problem is that people often focus on the scenarios themselves, while the benefit needs to derive from the process gain. All emphasis must be on the quality of the 'strategic conversation'. This means that scenario work should always be a customized activity. In our experience and research we have come to the conclusion that a lack of such purposefulness is the most common problem with less than professional scenario work. Scenario work is not particularly difficult, and many have used it to great advantage. What is often lacking is a sense of purpose.

The ultimate purpose is to achieve adaptive organizational learning skills in the organization at large. That is a big objective, and while one may work towards this over time, individual projects need to be made purposeful by ambitions that constitute steps along the way. At the beginning of the road is the objective of rehearsing the future, which does not mean that scenarios seek to predict the future. The complex nature of change means that predicting events is impossible, and is quite likely to be dangerous, as it implies inflexibility and a need to become locked into one specific prophecy. Of much greater value is the ability to recognize 'dots on the horizon' – the signs of change that inevitably affect every organization – and to understand their significance and how the organization should adapt. This is much more valuable than trying to predict the exact nature of these dots even before they arrive. The benefit of this approach is that it enables managers to give consideration and priority to the important issues that have not been on the agenda so far.

Moving on from there, the ultimate aspiration of adaptive organizational learning can be reached via the goals of 'sense making', 'strategy development' and 'anticipation', while keeping the organization away from fragmentation and group-think. Being very clear where you are on this road and designing the work accordingly is the first step towards process gain. But in the long run honing the skills of perception and thinking, while crucially important, is not enough. There must be a link with action to realize adaptive organizational learning. The link with action raises many issues around motivation, inertia, identity, history, rewards and, most importantly, coherence in leadership from the top. The reasons for resistance to change have to surface and be dealt with. Scenario thinking can help in all these areas. While the project as a whole is wider, there are few tools around like scenario methods that can make a contribution over such a wide area.

At the end of the road there is the state of adaptive organizational learning, where the loop from action to perception to thinking and back to action is closed. At that stage, it is clear that these three crucial skills are heavily interrelated. Action determines what we see, as much as perception determines action. The same applies for thinking: the puzzles of complexity cannot be comprehended by thinking alone but require experimentation. The process has to be seen as one system. In organizations where scenario thinking has become a culture perception, thinking and action are always considered in each other's contexts.

The alternative is for the organization to remain stuck within blockages and defensive routines that create inertia and paralysis. These not only lead to the perils of complacency and flawed thinking, but to a failure to maximize potential opportunities. Where an organization is blocked or defensive, success, if it is achieved at all, is perilous – achieved more by luck than judgement, and impossible to sustain.

The process gain we want starts from acknowledging that the organization is full of complexity, uncertainty and paradoxes, and that a comprehensive approach is needed to help understand and manage these puzzles. In this book, we develop and outline a holistic approach that encapsulates all three aspects of adaptive organizational learning, namely perception, thinking and action.

Developing the Sixth Sense – the Approach to Scenario Thinking

Exactly how this can be achieved is introduced in Chapter 6, and detailed in Chapters 7 and 8. We will describe the modern approach to scenario planning, which has grown out of ongoing practice over time. The necessary steps that organizations need to take to overcome the inertia and pitfalls of traditional thinking are explained. It is worth noting that a major feature (and benefit) of this approach is its ability to deliberately induce a high degree of turbulence and conversation. This is necessary in order to become aware of the many different perspectives to complex and ambiguous business challenges. What is valuable here is the ability to accept diversity of opinion and belief, and to understand how these different views might affect the organization's future. By challenging their own perspectives on the way the world is organizations can understand and develop an ongoing awareness of the ambiguous and complex nature of the world, leading to greater structural insights into the nature of possible futures – and their implications.

We re-emphasize that this is a practical, proven framework for action. It frees thinking, promotes action, and breaks the constraints that bind traditional strategic processes. Moreover, the method has proven to be effective in organizations of all sizes, types and locations, facing different opportunities and threats, both apparent and unnoticed. The approach is inclusive, enabling strategic conversations to take place with diverse groups of stakeholders. The richness of multiple perspectives is opened up, resulting in a deeper, broader perspective of the business environment and possible strategies.

The approach described generates ownership of the process by stakeholders. Clearly, the thinking must have value and relevance to the organization and its members. It needs to be acceptable – even motivational – for stakeholders; it needs to be innovative and competitive, challenging people as well as their concept of business-as-usual.

In this way, scenarios are invaluable for recognizing signs of change, understanding them and their implications, and providing the motivation for action. A crucial part of this is creating the strategic conversation. In order to succeed and be truly effective, scenario thinking needs to be understood in a wider strategic and organizational learning framework.

Scenarios offer a powerful and unique method of harnessing organizational insights, enabling organizations to adapt to change, by exploiting adaptive organizational learning, including perception, thinking and action. Doing this in a superior way drives the organization way ahead of its competitors. This unique source of advantage and rent, a sixth sense for organizations, is the real power of scenario thinking.

HOW THIS BOOK IS ORGANIZED

This book provides a guide to scenario thinking: what it means, why it is valuable and how it benefits organizations – and keeps the people within them focused on delivering better performance. Scenario planning is central to the tasks of developing an effective strategy and building a learning organization capable of delivering this strategy. However, as the first four chapters highlight, there are significant barriers confronting organizations.

Chapter 1, *Preparing for the Future*, analyses the causes of organizational success and failure. The concept of scenario planning and its role in strategy development are introduced. The business environment is not a static arena; in fact, it is said that its only constant is an ever-increasing rate of change. Establishing an ongoing, scenario-based process for strategic thinking enables an organization to plan for change, achieving optimum performance. In particular, the first chapter examines how traditional, business-as-usual approaches to strategy are flawed, undermining success. Flaws in thinking at three levels undermine traditional approaches to strategy: individual, organizational and community; these are introduced. In Chapters 2, 3 and 4, these are then explored in detail. We explain how scenario thinking improves reaction times and adaptability, and how it adds value to established recipes and formulas for success. We will also highlight the range of opportunities where strategic thinking is forged, introducing the cultural issues that promote an efficient, ground-breaking level of debate. A key element in this chapter is an examination of why organizations fail, and this is explained with reference to an important research study known as 'Sharpbenders'.

Chapter 2, *How Managers Think about the Future*, focuses on individual thinking flaws and their effects on strategy development. It addresses the fact that commonly held management assumptions tend to be ones that preserve organizational coherence, filtering in signals and failing to detect signals. Personal techniques and belief systems also set the context in which decisions will be made, and often these are guided by a view of the past, more than a vision of the future. As a result, it is valuable to have an understanding of the *psychological* context in which managers approach the future and make decisions. The complexities of management thinking are examined, including the problems that result from cognitive inertia; the importance of framing; the need to debate and challenge individual assumptions about success formulas, and the way that managers approach decisions. The impact of scenario thinking on these issues is explained.

In Chapter 3, *How Organizations Think about the Future*, this theme is developed further. Discussion of the ways that individuals think about the future and make decisions broadens, so that we can discover how organizations as a whole can improve their decision-making processes, overcoming problems of lock-in on business-as-usual thinking by becoming effective observers of change. The need for organizations to continuously adapt to change is outlined, together with the limitations of much current management thinking in organizations and the consequences of inertia and business-as-usual tendencies.

Having introduced the topic of scenario thinking and explained the effects of individual and organizational approaches to strategy development, Chapter 4 turns its attention to *The Impact of Culture and Cultural Assumptions on Strategy*. The types of problems that arise due to conflicting organizational cultures and what can be done (using a scenario-based approach) to resolve them are explored in this chapter. Chapter 4 examines the issue of culture at a macro-level, where differences are perceived across national cultures, as well as at the micro-, organizational level, highlighting how conflicting cultures cause obstacles for strategy development. The application of a scenario-based approach is explained, along with how this can enable the exploration of different potential cultural responses.

Scenario methods are neither difficult nor new and in Chapter 5, *Shaping the Future: the Emergence of Modern Scenario Techniques*, we will show how scenarios have been around for hundreds of years. The reason why people stop short of using the obvious tools for the development of future strategy is not in their availability, but in the *thinking flaws* that stop them from engaging in this exploratory activity. This chapter explains that scenario thinking is an ongoing approach leading to adaptive organizational learning. The factors that have driven the development of scenario thinking are explored, as these serve to inform modern thinking about the benefits of scenarios. Scenario thinking has an established and successful heritage, with deep roots in the development of decision-making. Chapter 5 explains how making the unthinkable a part of current thinking has shaped policy. It has enabled people, organizations and countries to better direct and control their fortunes, learning to cope with changing conditions. Arguably, people are natural scenario planners: it is how we make sense of the world and how we decide on which course of action to take. Also in an institutional context, identifying and harnessing the intricacies of situations is the true intellectual measure of potential.

Chapter 6, *Developing the Skills for Long-term Survival and Success: Principles of the Scenario Process*, develops the themes outlined earlier and explores how the scenario process overcomes the flaws and problems identified. The issue of *how* organizations can adopt the scenario approach to enable them to recognize and react to change before competitors do is the focus of this chapter. This is significant because successful organizations need to be aware of change and react to their changing business environment before their competitors. In particular, successful organizations need to develop superior organizational learning skills. This chapter explains how scenario thinking provides people with a purposeful organizational learning approach, helping them to safely navigate the shifting business landscape.

In Chapter 7, *Scenario Planning in the Organizational Context*, we explore the specific processes involved in scenario thinking, helping organizations to overcome many of the problems that severely limit the development and implementation of an effective strategy, in a detailed and operational step-by-step way. This proven guide to the scenario approach is modern and up-to-date, but based on this type of thinking's long history. Building on the belief that scenarios provide unique insights, harnessing knowledge, skills and distinctive competencies to drive organizations forward, we outline five key areas. These are the need to: structure the scenario process; explore the scenario context; build the scenarios, identify the driving forces in the environment; undertake a stakeholder analysis, and understand the impact on organizational thinking and action.

Chapter 8 broadens the scope and considers scenario activity in the wider context of problem solving, strategy and organizational learning. It is titled *Scenario Planning: Taking Charge of the Future*. No other strategic approach satisfies the fundamental business need for meeting and successfully handling external environmental drivers. We will also explain why scenario-based continuous learning is essential for all organizations and individuals. The next steps organizations take to integrate scenario processes and culture into the organization are crucial to ensure a successful future.

Throughout the book, we have used case histories to illustrate issues. For example, organizations typically seem unable to anticipate changes in customer values and are vulnerable to the future. In the following chapters, we document the causes of business-as-usual thinking (the enemy of creativity, learning and development) and show how scenario thinking can overcome these causes. This enables people and organizations to understand the nature of the future, so that the organizational response is aligned with reality.

The perspective adopted throughout is that of the scenario planner – but for us, the scenario planner is not an offline professional, thinking in splendid isolation on behalf of the organization. Rather, she is an active manager personally involved in the day-to-day running of the organization and determined to build its strength, competitive advantage and success, now and in the future.

Currently, the traditional mindset that is formulating and guiding a great deal of business strategy is woefully inadequate, embedded in conventional business practice and thinking, and presenting a formidable challenge to companies wishing to maximize strategic effectiveness. The solution is scenario thinking.

In essence, it is possible for managers now to see things that others cannot. This book will explain how: the Sixth Sense.

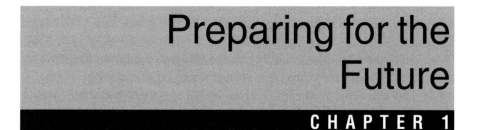

Preparing for the Future

In this chapter, we introduce scenario thinking: what it means, why it is valuable, and how it enables organizations and the people within them to focus on achieving sustained competitive advantage.

Overview

This chapter is concerned with preparing for the future, introducing the concept of scenario thinking and its potential value in delivering a world-beating strategy. Understanding how best to achieve competitive advantage, in a world where the only constant is an ever-increasing rate of change, is the key attribute of profitable, market-leading organizations. As the pace and scope of change quickens, the urgency of finding the best, most competitive approach grows. In this context, the core tool to deliver continued success is the development of a new approach to strategic thinking. Tomorrow's successful companies will overturn strategic inertia and business-as-usual thinking, avoiding complacency and finding new, scarce sources of value.

In this chapter we will:

- **Assess the drivers both of organizational success and failure** – understanding that both are inevitable, dynamic and closely tied together.
- **Explain the Sharpbenders research into why organizations fail** – this research highlights problems in store for organizations that are inherently unable to detect or respond to change.

CONTINUED... Overview

- Use case examples to outline the problems in maintaining organizational performance – knowing where organizations go wrong, how and why, is essential in forming an approach that will deliver sustained competitive advantage.

- Highlight the factors that are critical to achieving success – explaining how the barriers to success can be overcome, notably by creating lasting value.

The business environment is not a static arena. Establishing an ongoing, scenario-based strategic thinking process enables a business to plan for change, achieving optimum performance. These concepts are introduced in this chapter using several case study examples: Xerox and Canon, Yahoo!, Lego, Tetra Pak and Nokia.

UNDERSTANDING ORGANIZATIONAL SUCCESS

Success and Failure are Inevitable

This book is ultimately about organizational success. Organizational success is inevitable: there will always be successful organizations. Equally, organizational failure is inevitable. Organizations operating in the world are like football clubs playing in a competition: they cannot all win and they cannot all lose. Success and failure go together like the positive and the negative poles of a magnet; you can't have one without the other.

Most managers work towards the objective of making their own organization successful. Right from the start we know that they cannot all end up where they want to be. That thought has aspects that are both depressing and uplifting. We know that, however hard they try, some managers are going to be disappointed, and each of us should wonder: 'Could I be that manager?' On the other hand, knowing that everything is relative helps us to realize that the task ahead is not impossible. We do not have to be perfect, only better than the competition.

Success and failure are dynamic notions
If there is one thing we can all agree on, it is that the world around us is subject to constant and considerable change. It is clear that organizations operating success-

fully one day may fail totally the next. No matter how illustrious an organization's history might be, all rely on their *future* business. The game does not remain the same. Winning means changing the way one plays over time. Organizations that want to survive have to adapt. The challenge is that the way that the game is changing remains uncertain until it is played. This is fundamental: without uncertainty everyone could do the same calculation, or act in the same way. However, it is important to remember that not everyone can win at the same time: there are winners because there is uncertainty or, to put it in a more positive way, without uncertainty there can

> There are winners because there is uncertainty; without uncertainty, there can be no winners. Therefore, instead of seeing uncertainty as a problem, we should start viewing it as the basic source of our future success.

be no winners. Instead of seeing uncertainty as a problem, therefore, we had better start learning to love it as the basic source of our future success.

This is highly relevant to this book. We will explain how organizations that lose show poor performance due to thinking and behavioural flaws that can be improved by the use of scenario thinking. Certainly, everyone can discover this for himself, and if we were ever to reach a stage where this had become clear to all managers and every one of them was a scenario planner, there wouldn't be much competitive advantage left in it! At that stage it would have become a qualifier; something no organization could do without. But the fact is, we are far from that state of affairs. Meanwhile, as managers and organizations are slow to discover the fundamental importance of scenario thinking, early adopters can gain huge advantages.

Understanding success by understanding failure

Understanding that success and failure exist together, in close relation to each other, means that the study of organizational success starts with the study of organizational failure. Remembering that the quality of performance is relative, we will try to identify what people and organizations do that makes them end up on the losing side. Understanding weaknesses will help us to turn them into relative strengths.

In this chapter, we analyse what creates failure. This will lead to the notion of 'flaws', which we find at the level of individual thinking, organizational behaviour and community thinking, based on shared cultural beliefs and assumptions. In Chapters 2, 3 and 4 we will analyse flaws at these three levels in some detail.

We will approach the analysis from the perspective of the scenario planner, who for us is the practising manager. It is our belief that scenarios are the most powerful tools that managers have at their disposal today to move their organization to the winning side. In order to make that case, we need to understand the flaws and how they come about. In order to get us there we will first analyse organizational failure.

Explaining the Sharpbenders Research: Why Organizations Fail

In this section, we are going to make use of a body of interesting research highlighting the problems for organizations that are inherently unable to detect or respond to change. This is known as the Sharpbenders research[2]. The people who undertook the research had the bright idea of concentrating on companies that had been failing, as manifest in a stock value that had been slipping against the market average, but which had been able to turn things around. That is where the word *Sharpbenders* came from – a slipping stock value followed by a recovery. The idea was that these companies, having been able to turn things around, would be able to articulate what had gone wrong and why this had happened. After all, if they had managed to turn things around they must have made a successful diagnosis of what went on during the downward part of their history. Having identified such companies from stock market records, the researchers then interviewed many of them and thus produced what is effectively a list of what can go wrong.

The outcomes of the Sharpbenders research
The findings highlight the key causes of relative decline in five categories:

- adverse development in market demand or increased competition;
- high cost structure;
- poor financial controls;
- failure of big projects;
- acquisition problems.

Later, we will analyse these results in more detail. But before we do this we need to introduce a few basic concepts that will help us to navigate this territory.

The difference between hygiene factors and the business idea
The causes of failure identified by the Sharpbenders research can be divided into two categories: *hygiene factors* and *business idea factors*. What do we mean by this?

As we discussed earlier, organizations have always been trying to discover ways of outsmarting the competition. This book is an example of that. Not all ideas that are developed are equally effective, but some stick out as clearly being successful. Initially some organizations develop significant competitive advantage by exploiting these ideas but, over time, others see the beneficial effects and will start to copy the ideas in their own organizations. They can be learned from studying organizations deemed as 'best in class', through a benchmarking process. They will be codified in textbooks and taught to managers. Once an idea reaches this point it has become a *hygiene factor*, something that is generally recognized as fundamental in running any healthy organization. Without hygiene factors, professional management knows in advance that the organization will not have a chance to play in the competitive game.

Most hygiene factors are about the need to ensure sound and efficient business processes, critical to ensure that the organization remains a going concern. These business processes are the generally accepted basics for running any organization; they are qualifiers, allowing you to play. However, winning the game requires much more: additional, distinctive factors and capabilities that will distinguish the winner from the losers. These additional, distinctive factors and capabilities that are not yet generally codified and available only to one organization are summarized in what we call its *business idea*.

The business idea

An organization's business idea (BI) can be described as its success formula in the competitive game. We look at three fundamental factors to judge the strength of a BI:

- A BI must be capable of explaining how value will be created for stakeholders of the organization. Without value creation, no organization will be able to survive. We know that value is being created if the BI addresses a scarcity somewhere in society, by filling it or by alleviating its effect. This is what prompts customers to come to the store to buy its products.
- An organization that wants to be able to meet a scarcity in society must have something unique to offer. If nothing is unique in what the

> ## CONTINUED . . . **The business idea**
>
> organization does, it cannot engage in unique activities and therefore, by definition, not address any scarcity. A BI has to clarify the system of uniqueness that the organization brings to bear on its activities.
>
>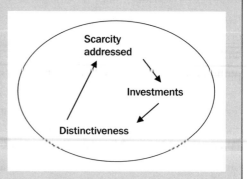
>
> • Once an organization makes a unique contribution and creates value it can charge a price for its efforts and in that way generate resources to invest in its survival. A success formula cannot be effective forever. Anything that is unique will eventually be copied, or its value may disappear because people's interests move elsewhere. Therefore, an organization must be able to show how it invests on an ongoing basis in its distinctiveness.
>
> The three factors operate in a loop, which feeds on itself and stands for the survival capability of the formula. We return to the notion of the business idea in more detail in Chapter 8.

Returning to the Sharpbenders research, the first striking observation is that most failures are due to hygiene factors. The following causes are highlighted:

- **Poor controls** in areas such as credit, working capital, budgets, costs, cash flow or quality. This is often due to inadequate management accounts, leading to infrequent and incomplete reports that are late, too complex, too voluminous, irrelevant or incorrect.
- **Immature management style**. Typical examples include an inflexible CEO (chief executive officer), excessive caution, authoritarianism, ineffective delegation and coordination and over-centralization.
- **Failure to create and communicate purpose and the business idea**, both between the top and middle management, and with the workforce.

Another hygiene factor and one crucial business process that frequently gets pushed into the background is a systemic approach to sensing or responding to external change, based on maintaining sound and efficient relationships with all stakeholders. Maintaining relationships with stakeholders – such as shareholders, suppliers and customers – is vital for all organizations, as any of these groups have the power to threaten its existence. Shareholders can decide to invest elsewhere, customers may 'vote with their feet'; the government can pass unfavourable legislation, and so on. These vital groups have to be kept on board. Their conflicting expectations need to be identified and reconciled.

This book is not about hygiene factors. That does not mean that it is not important to recognize their existence as qualifiers in the race. Indeed, often they are not looked after sufficiently, notwithstanding the fact that professional managers know what needs to be done. Unfortunately, in real life things often slip due to lack of time or attention. If this results in poor performance, the manager has to create a 'sharp bend' by applying well-known codified management knowledge. For example, where management accounts are found to be inadequate, effort on getting these up to standard pays significant dividends. Similarly, inadequate internal communications leading to a poorly motivated workforce will offer significant scope for improving results with a relatively modest and obvious upgrading project. There are many examples where hygiene factors have to be considered and addressed with the application of codified knowledge in order to ensure success.

This knowledge is available, for example, in business schools and in textbooks, and help is at hand from the many consultants who offer their services in these areas. In this book, however, we will concentrate on where winning business ideas come from. Our focus here is on longer-term strategy.

Looking after hygiene factors should be seen, therefore, as a minimum requirement to play, a qualifier for being in the game. However, the ultimate aim is to try to win. For this, the organization needs a unique business idea. The Sharpbenders research shows interesting failures in this area as well.

The Sharpbenders business idea failures

The strategic reasons for failure identified in the Sharpbenders research include:

- A lack of recognizable strategies in such areas as functional policies, corporate strategy and environmental monitoring.

- Poor execution or timing of responses to developments such as declining market demand or increasing competition.
- Inappropriate risk-taking, in terms of projects that are too large in relation to the size of the organization taking them on, or acquisitions that are assessed too optimistically.

In considering these causes of decline, we see clear evidence of organizational inability to understand and adapt to change in their environment. In retrospect, people identify changes in the marketplace that passed unnoticed at the time. Typical examples include new products and new substitutes coming on the market, changes in product technology, demographic changes, changes in income distribution, changes in fashion, and a cyclical fall in demand that wasn't taken seriously.

Similarly, increased competition often went unnoticed, while in retrospect the signals were obvious, such as technological change lowering rivals' costs, threats from substitutes keeping prices low, political changes related to loosening of regulations, trade barriers and purchasing policy, removal of protection and other barriers to entry, a significant new entry, high exit costs keeping competition intense in the face of falling sales, a lack of strong product differentiation or strong cost advantage, or falling switching costs for customers.

Turning things around

The Sharpbenders research findings also show the managerial actions that were successful in reversing a decline in organizational performance. The business idea-related strategic factors that were identified in the research included:

- An emphasis on customers and their dynamic value systems.
- A strong marketing focus.
- A clear product focus with a deliberate concentration on what the organization can do best.
- Regular reviews of strategy (the danger of formalizing this process tends to increase with the size of the business).
- A forward-looking approach which invests in the future through plant, equipment, research and development (R & D) and training.

Several themes stand out from these issues. First, there is a *lack of exploration of the environment* and its potential or actual impact is not sufficiently recognized.

Second, there is a *lack of understanding of how the wider environment is impacting customers, their needs and value systems,* and whether the organization's products or services continue to create value for them. Let's consider a number of examples where these forces can be seen at work.

MAINTAINING ORGANIZATIONAL PERFORMANCE: PROBLEMS

Sustaining Competitive Advantage – the Battle of Canon and Xerox

Background [3]

Consider the example of Xerox, who in the early 1970s held a *95% market share* of the global photocopier industry. Its target customers were large corporations and its concept of customer value was that of centrally controlled photocopying. Xerox focused on manufacturing and leasing complex high-speed photocopiers, using its own manufacturing and sales force to provide a complete package to those who leased its machines. Then came along Canon – who competed head-to-head for Xerox's large corporate customer base. The case below sets out what happened, and the key question to consider is this: why didn't Xerox appreciate the nature of the threat and respond earlier than it did to Canon's attack?

In 1956 Chester Carlson, inventor of the electrostatic process that led to the birth of the copier industry, sold his patents to the Haloid Corporation which changed its name to Xerox in 1961. The 914 copier (named because of its ability to copy documents 9″ × 14″ in size) was introduced in 1959 and heralded Xerox's emergence as the dominant force in the copier industry. The first of its kind to make both multiple copies and the fastest number of copies per minute, the 914 opened up the era of mass copying. Xerox seized the initiative by inventing a business idea targeted at large corporations requiring high-volume copying. The results were spectacular: by 1961, only two years after the introduction of the 914, Xerox became a Fortune 500 company. *Business Week* displayed the 914 on its cover and *Fortune* magazine declared the 914 to be 'the most successful product ever marketed in America'. In 1968, Xerox achieved $1 billion sales, the fastest organization to reach that landmark at that time. The word Xerox became synonymous with copying: people did not copy documents, they *Xeroxed*.

Xerox wasted no time in globalizing its business idea. It created a joint venture in the UK to form Rank Xerox, which dominated the European market.

Rank Xerox and Fuji Photo Films in Japan created another joint venture, Fuji Xerox, which came to dominate the Asian market. By 1970, Xerox held a 95% market share in the global copier industry.

Then Canon, a Japanese multinational and an industry newcomer in the mid-1970s, created entirely new market segments for copiers not served by Xerox in the USA: small organizations and individuals. In the late 1970s Canon designed a value delivery system offering a $1000 personal copier to target these segments. For almost a decade, Xerox largely ignored this new business idea that Canon had chosen to develop. In fact, in 1978, Fuji Xerox was willing to sell low-end copiers to Xerox to counter-attack Canon in the USA, but Xerox refused the offer and Canon prevailed.

Canon's ability to attain leadership in low-end copiers illustrates another vital issue in any business idea that can be impacted by scenario planning. This is the power of changing the rules of the game by radically redefining the customer base, based on a previously unattended and growing customer value – in this case, personal control in a distributed system.

Two strategies compared: Xerox's big copier business model

Xerox's decision to serve large corporate customers allowed it to build a business model with huge entry barriers. Xerox had more than 500 patents that effectively prohibited new entrants, and with their massive duplicating needs, corporate customers preferred big scale-efficient machines of the type provided by Xerox's technology. Patents effectively prohibited new entrants.

Furthermore, the high cost of salesforces deterred competitors. By focusing on corporate customers, Xerox could build a direct salesforce, since it had a limited number of customers to service. By 1970, Xerox had created an enviable sales-force with technical expertise, long-term customer relationships and deep product knowledge. New entrants wanting to copy its business model would have to replicate their sales network: this was a high fixed-cost activity and thus another major entry barrier.

Finally, the large investment cost of providing a specialized, 24-hour service network acted as an impenetrable barrier. Xerox's customers, primarily Fortune 500 corporations, did not care as much about price as they did about the need for reliability. Because central copy centres typically had one large machine, the entire centre came to a standstill when the machine broke down. It was not enough for Xerox to offer excellent service: it had to guarantee outstanding 24-

hour service. By 1970, Xerox had built a world-class, round-the-clock servicing capability. This proved to be another formidable entry barrier, and this, coupled with the brand name, simply overwhelmed new entrants.

These factors posed significant problems, even for an established office equipment supplier like IBM. Certainly, IBM faced an insurmountable barrier in the form of technology patents. It was a contender to challenge Xerox as it sold computer mainframes to corporate customers through a salesforce and serviced them through an extensive network as early as the 1960s. However, IBM's sales and service staff could not easily be transferred to the copier market without further, significant investments in technology and product training. Because of these factors, Xerox enjoyed a virtual monopoly in the copier industry.

Canon's response: the distributed copier business model

Canon focused first on *overcoming the problem of patents*. It dedicated its research efforts during the 1960s to develop an alternative to Xerox's patented technology. In 1968, it invented the *New Process* (NP) technology, which used plain paper to photocopy but did not violate Xerox's patents. Canon deployed two of its existing competency bases, microelectronics (from its calculator business) and optics and imaging (from its camera business) in developing NP technology. Further, it benefited from a 1975 USA Federal Trade Commission ruling forcing Xerox to licence its dry-toner PPC technology freely to competitors.

The next line of attack was Canon's ability to *redefine the customer base*. In the late 1970s, Canon successfully designed personal copiers at a price significantly below Xerox's big copiers, appealing to small businesses and individuals. Canon's personal copiers, which made 8 to 10 copies per minute, ranged in price from $700 to $1200. In contrast, Xerox's high-speed machines, which made 90 to 120 copies per minute, had a price range of $80 000 to $129 000.

Rethinking distribution was the next area of focus for Canon. Because its target segments involved millions of customers, it could not effectively use the direct salesforce approach. Instead, it chose to distribute its personal copiers through traditional third-party distributors: office product dealers, computer stores and retailers. This distribution approach not only eliminated Canon's need for a huge cash outlay but also allowed it rapid market entry.

Challenging the need for a costly service network was the next hurdle that Canon faced, and its next area of innovation. In fact, they overcame Xerox's formidable advantage in 24-hour servicing in several ways. First, because of the inverse relationship between product reliability and the need for service, it designed its copiers for maximum reliability. Each copier had just eight units that could be assembled on an automated line by robots. Second, it made replacement parts modular so that end-use customers could replace them when they wore out, removing the need for a service network. Copier drum, charging device, toner assembly and cleaner were combined into a single disposable cartridge that the customer could remove and replace after 2000 copies. Third, Canon's design was so simple that traditional office product dealers could be trained to make repairs. Finally, the Canon model enabled people to use other departments' machines when theirs wore down. Unlike with central copying, 24-hour service was not required.

Canon's effect on the copier industry was similar to its earlier, redefining effect on the camera industry. Another key element of Canon's approach was their success in *leveraging their strong brand reputation* for high quality and low cost in the camera industry, benefiting its business when it launched personal copiers.

Sustaining competitive advantage by avoiding flawed, business-as-usual thinking

One of the core values of scenario thinking is its ability to avoid conventional approaches that may be outflanked by a competitor but, instead, invent new business ideas. An important factor here is reaction time and the need to get there before anyone else. This is highlighted by the potential reasons for Xerox's delayed response. There might be several reasons why Xerox did not respond soon enough to Canon's attack with its own version of distributed copying. It might not have perceived Canon as a serious threat because Canon did not initially go head-to-head against Xerox. Perhaps Xerox simply did not expect low-end copiers to become a huge market segment. In fact, during the 1970s Xerox was more worried about IBM and Kodak, which entered the copier industry at the high end by playing by Xerox's rules. Big machines had a high profit margin per unit, whereas personal copiers had a low one. Xerox might have feared the effect of cannibalizing its high-margin business for low-margin copiers. It had invested heavily in a salesforce, which probably would not have welcomed the use of third-party dealers to sell personal copiers that would compete with big

> **Scenario thinking enables businesses to avoid conventional approaches that may be easily predicted and parried by a competitor, allowing new business ideas to be invented instead. Swift reaction times and the ability to get there before anyone else are vital.**

ones. Similarly, Xerox's service network, which operated as a profit centre, had little incentive to support programmes to produce quantum improvements in product reliability. Moreover, under the leasing policy, Xerox had not fully recovered its investment on its installed base, so it was unlikely to want to risk making that base prematurely obsolete by offering personal copiers. Finally, Xerox's customers, heads of copy centres in large corporations, were critical to Xerox's success and so might have had an important influence in its internal decisions. They would naturally resist the introduction of distributed copying for fear of undermining their own position.

Therefore, strong and dominant though they appeared, Xerox had inherent vulnerabilities in its structure and business thinking: an inability to see how potential threats could arise, possibly from a redefining of the industry, highlighted by conventional, business as usual thinking and organisational inertia. This situation might have been exposed through a process that considered radically different future scenarios.

Yahoo! – Competing in Fast-moving Markets

Background[4]

Yahoo!'s meteoric rise to success was matched by an equally spectacular downturn in fortunes. Its rise and fall demonstrates the disastrous consequences that can follow when an organization fails to *plan for changes in markets and customer values*.

When AOL (America OnLine) announced its intended purchase of media giant Time Warner in January 2000, Yahoo! was caught completely unawares. However, Yahoo!'s troubles actually started much earlier, with its failure to *develop and constantly update strategies*, which left it completely unprepared for future changes.

Yahoo!'s main competitor for Internet advertising space, AOL, bought media giant Time Warner, with its vast array of magazines, movie studios and book publications. AOL saw considerable benefits in a tie-up with an old-time media giant, but Yahoo! decided not to follow suit. Its *competitive thinking was flawed* – and this led to disaster.

Three individuals had driven Yahoo's early success and they felt invincible. However, *they did not anticipate* – in this case, they did not anticipate the loss of interest from advertisers due, in part, to the dot-com bubble bursting and, in part, to a growing perceived need from its customers for integrated advertising campaigns – including the Internet, TV, radio and magazines.

Yahoo!'s CEO, Timothy Koogle, president, Jeffrey Mallet and co-founder, Jerry Yang, met to discuss their reaction to the AOL/Time Warner announcement. It is easy to comment with hindsight about the errors in judgement made in this meeting and about how they proceeded to compound these mistakes over the following year. It is also undeniably true *that the organization was impacted by external factors* other than its competitive position in relation to AOL/Time Warner (factors that also affected AOL and others in the industry). However, Yahoo!'s fortunes went from bad to worse, with revenues plummeting 42% in one quarter and market capitalization falling 92%, resulting in redundancies and, over time, in the CEO's departure.

Analysing the Yahoo! example

The story of Yahoo! is a warning for every business, not only start-ups or technology organizations. The source of its problem was its inability to compete and move with the market – or, put another way, its difficulty in planning for the future in a rapidly changing environment. Was there anything that Yahoo! could have done to prevent its problems? It could be argued that if Yahoo! had properly *anticipated and planned for various eventualities,* even ones that seemed unlikely or unthinkable, it would have been better able to weather any storm that tore through their industry. On this basis, we will argue that scenario planning would have highlighted the potential pitfalls of, and solutions to, an over-reliance on advertising revenues. This anticipation could have been achieved in a number of ways.

Clearly understanding internal weaknesses

Yahoo! had a number of internal problems that left it inadequately prepared for the external problems that were about to change its fortunes. Fundamentally, it failed to anticipate the actions of competitors and develop contingency plans for various scenarios, which would have allowed it to respond quickly to competitors.

Ensuring effective leadership

The first internal problem was the leadership of the business. There was a consensus style of management that dulled the decision-making process; a clash of opinions between the CEO and the president allowed the organization to stray off-course, and the lack of a clear and united direction from senior executives left other staff confused and demotivated. In addition, the CEO's distant style of management meant that the organization lacked the strong leadership it required. In visioning the future and getting everyone involved, effective leadership is vitally important.

Building a positive organizational culture

Closely linked with the need for effective leadership is another major area of difficulty: organizational culture. Yahoo! did not invest in the future, preferring instead to live for the moment. Mallet admitted that if a customer was not prepared to enter into an immediate advertising contract with them, then Yahoo! was not interested in spending any time on developing a relationship; it simply moved to the next customer. This policy may have worked in the early, pioneering days of Internet businesses, but was not appropriate as the market became more sophisticated. Yahoo! failed to appreciate the value of building long-term relationships with clients in increasingly customer-focused markets. This requires time, effort and planning – all factors that rely on leadership and a focus on the right priorities. Yahoo! had failed to respond to, let alone plan for, changes in customer needs. When companies were looking for coordinated advertising campaigns, Yahoo!'s limited offerings of banner advertisements looked inferior and poor value.

Keeping close to their customers

Yahoo! lost sight of its customers, and failed to offer a compelling value proposition. If customers could not see the point of advertising online and Yahoo! was not concerned about winning them over, then the business was doomed to failure.

After considerable disagreement at the executive level, the potential purchase of Internet auction company e-Bay was turned down. Yahoo! had rejected the chance to move away from its over-reliance on advertising, which accounted for 90% of their revenues. Almost inevitably, Yahoo!'s fortunes declined as advertising revenue fell with the end of the dot-com honeymoon. In a new, fast-moving market, complacency and an inability to stay close to the market led to a flawed approach. Clearly, the value of scenario thinking in such a situation needs little further explanation.

In contrast, some organizations do manage to change their business idea – Lego, for instance. Here the story unfolds over many years showing that a longer-term, tougher approach to strategic thinking is needed.

Building a Colourful New Future Brick by Brick – the Story of Lego

Background [6]

Lego, a family-owned Danish company, invented the popular moulded plastic building bricks for children's free-form play. This open-ended play system was developed by the founder, Ole Kirk Christiansen, and was extremely successful for many years, but sales levelled out in the late 1980s. Ole Kirk's grandson, Kjeld, took charge of the organisation in the early 1990s and saw the changes that had taken place in customer value. In response, Lego bricks were packaged as themed self-assembly toys (themes including Star Wars and Mindstorms), and this repositioning led to a major increase in sales of Lego products. However, in the highly competitive and fickle world of children's toys, Lego's fortunes and future are far from certain. Profits peaked in 1996 and 1997, and then fell precipitously. In 1998, Lego lost almost $35 million before taxes. In 1999, Lego laid off 1000 people, the first big layoff in company history, but then in 2000, Lego lost $120 million, on sales of about $1.1 billion.

Given the size of these losses, it is unclear whether or not things are improving. The leadership of Lego has to manage a situation that often threatens to pull it in conflicting directions. The organization that Kjeld took over was well managed and poised to expand globally – something that has since been realized. But the organization had also become conservative, so much so that even as it grew, it lost touch with its market. This was in contrast to the radical founding spirit of Kjeld's grandfather, Ole Kirk Christiansen. Lego today is as much the result of Ole Kirk's daring in inventing radical new children's toys, as of his grandson's prudence. Once, for a brief moment, Lego changed the way that children played as well as the way they learned to think. Lego has not been that kind of leader for many years.

> Mature, established organizations in fickle, fashion-conscious industries can be at a disadvantage if they do not leverage their key resources, notably their knowledge, experience and (in Lego's case) their reputation. Again, this is another key aspect of successful business ideas that scenario thinking can inform, facilitate and support.

The challenge at Lego is to try to mix these cultures, and it has a powerful asset: the Lego brand is the seventh most powerful worldwide among families with children, behind only such names as Coca-Cola and Disney. People take Lego seriously, which is a positive start, but that view has also created a burdensome legacy of expectation.

The priorities for development

The Sharpbenders research highlights the fact that, in many businesses, significant structural changes need to take place in order to maintain competitiveness. The value of scenario thinking is that it can highlight *priorities* for development. There are a number of priorities and salutary lessons emerging from Lego's story.

Developing a customer-focused ethos – and letting go of the past

For many years, Lego's attitudes and procedures were slow to change and develop. This was coupled with an over-attachment to traditional core values that were increasingly out of step with customer demands, endangering the whole organization. Lego was a 'nice' organization that greatly valued their products for what they gave children. For an organization that holds its customers in such high regard, it is surprising that they strayed so far off course. One problem for Lego seems to have been that it understood and valued its own image of what was 'best' for children, rather than understanding the realities of what their customers were now looking for from toys. However commendable Lego's sentiment was, it was clearly not enough to ensure continued prosperity: *clinging to past aspirations clouded current business acumen.*

Valuing strategy development and executing the plan

Lego is a highly introverted organization. Even its successful decision to link with Lucasfilm to produce licensed Star Wars toys was nearly suffocated in a protracted and acrimonious decision-making process. Lego clearly needs to learn from its past mistakes: namely, it needs to plan now to better control its future. It must learn to integrate a dynamic strategy-forming process into the organization's culture, if it is to avoid repeating the disastrous results of the past. This will not prove an easy task for Lego, as its existing culture is particularly valued and deeply ingrained. *The challenge is to harness everything that is positive and strong*, of which there is much, and align the whole organization with an effective scenario planning culture.

Sensing and anticipating customer needs

Lego's business history depicts a company that, despite making efforts to identify and prepare for changes in customer needs, found itself displaced by a rapidly changing market. Their limited, protracted and reluctant reactions prevented it from reasserting its dominance in the toy industry, moulding a strong, directed future, or optimizing profitability. The lesson for Lego is to formulate, embrace and implement an improved business idea and ethos for strategic thinking.

Despite changes, Lego is still lagging behind its competitors; customers have moved on and it is questionable whether the current Lego products will offer enough to tempt back significant numbers of customers. When the products are toys for children, it is perhaps easy for passion and sentiment to blur the objective of firmly rooting business models in offering a good value proposition and awareness of competitors. Maximising potential can be a dispassionate, analytical affair, especially when an organization's survival is at stake. Lego's deep respect for and commitment to the importance of children's play is an asset that, *when harnessed*, is an invaluable tool to deliver business success. However, without the guiding hand of forward strategic thinking, it is a poor guarantor of future success.

Making difficult decisions

Tough decisions will no doubt be required in Lego's future, but one thing is certain: tough decisions are often easier to take and more palatable and smoother to implement when they have been anticipated and prepared for well ahead of time. This is never truer than when dealing with what is, in essence, a 'family' organization, where emotional attachments can prove an immovable obstacle to change and a misguided or self-delusional indicator to future success. It may be time for Lego to accept that their 'Lego values' belong to a different age: new values need new approaches and a new business idea.

SUCCESS STORIES

Organizations reviewed in the Sharpbenders research all encountered difficulties but managed to regain control over their situations. As we saw, there is much we can learn from these cases about what matters; which factors make the difference between success and failure. However, this also raises an important question: is it possible to see the potential for trouble in enough time so that it can be avoided altogether? To start answering this, it is helpful to consider two companies that seem to have done things right.

Providing Customer Value – the Rise of Tetra Pak

Background [6]

Tetra Pak, a Swedish multinational corporation and part of the Tetra Laval Group, develops, manufactures and sells systems for processing, packaging and distributing liquid food products. Tetra Pak had only a small share of the paper carton business during the 1970s, yet by 1999 Tetra Pak was producing packaging materials at 57 plants, selling 90 billion containers per year in more than 165 countries, and had captured a 40% share of the European liquid-packaging market. Two brothers, Hans and Gad Rausing, have transformed the organization from a small Swedish milk carton organization into a global liquid-packaging powerhouse.

Tetra Pak succeeded by redefining its industry, effectively changing the concept of customer value in the global liquid-packaging industry. Understanding how this was achieved can help to point the way for other businesses that may wish to consider their own futures.

From traditional to reinvented customer value

Originally, the organization was a niche player focused on one product category: packaging for liquid food items. They did not make other types of cartons, nor did they diversify outside the packaging sector. Growth had to come from global expansion in its product category. Tetra Pak invented a new business idea that altered the traditional model for its industry by offering customers a totally integrated system including filling equipment, packaging materials and distribution equipment (such as conveyors and tray packers). Customer value was transformed from the traditional way, pouring liquids into containers, to Tetra Pak's approach: containers made at the point where beverages are ready to be packed.

Making it happen

The Tetra Pak system delivered two features that were unique in the industry. First, the organization installs their filling equipment in the beverage producers' factories. Second, with Tetra Pak's process, their special vacuum-filling technology keeps air out of the liquids during the filling process, preventing decay caused by light and air in liquid containers. With such an aseptic property, Tetra Pak cartons do not require refrigeration to preserve liquids. Milk has a shelf life of 6 months, juices 12 months. Tetra Pak's business idea has altered the concept of value at every stage of the traditional industry value chain: for container manufacturers, beverage processors, retailers, consumers and finally, and because of these activities, for its own long-term operations.

The benefits of the new system

The Tetra Pak system provides savings in factory space, labour and overhead costs involved in making the containers. It also provides savings in transportation costs, as empty containers do not have to be delivered from container manufacturers to beverage producers. Not only is transportation expensive but also results in breakages during transit. In addition, manufacturers avoid handling and some insurance costs.

For beverage processors, the Tetra Pak approach reduces inventory costs. Cartons are made only when needed, thereby ensuring 'zero' inventories of empty cartons in the pipeline and saving financing costs and storage space. There are lower transport costs: once filled and sealed, the beverages do not require refrigerated trucks for transport to supermarkets, even on long hauls. The Tetra Pak approach ensures an efficient use of space, minimizing storage and transport costs. Whereas bottles and paper cartons cannot easily be stacked on top of each other, the box-shaped Tetra cartons can be stacked up easily and the rectangular, flat structure of Tetra cartons ensures efficient use of space.

Producers also enjoy the benefit of buying complete systems from one supplier – Tetra Pak, with matching equipment at every stage. This provides customers with uninterrupted production. Tetra Pak, in turn, has an experienced and well-trained service force that assures customers fast, efficient repairs and equipment maintenance.

A major value for consumers is the convenience of the Tetra Pak cartons: they are lighter, more versatile, compact, convenient to use, appealing in appearance and competitive in price. In many ways, these customer advantages are the prize: the outcome that must be kept firmly fixed in the mind of the strategist.

The benefits for Tetra Pak's long-term operations

Tetra Pak has found that their system offers clear potential for global expansion in emerging economies like India, China and Brazil. Here, sizable populations living with limited refrigeration facilities are especially well suited to the Tetra Pak system. Without Tetra Pak, these beverage markets would remain largely underdeveloped. Furthermore, Tetra Pak's close relationships with beverage companies have enabled it to dedicate more than 1000 engineers worldwide to focus on customer needs, developing new packaging designs and continuously improving their processing and distribution systems. In this way, Tetra Pak is almost institutionalizing customer-driven innovation, ensuring that future needs are carefully understood and given a focus that might elude many other businesses. This approach can also be self-sustaining largely because of Tetra Pak's secure revenue position. By leasing its filling machines, Tetra Pak offers customers protection from technological obsolescence. Having locked up beverage companies on long-term machine leases, Tetra Pak enters into contracts with customers to supply them with packaging materials at attractive margins. The materials have been custom-designed for Tetra Pak machines, effectively giving the organization a virtual monopoly in providing raw materials to the filling machines. Once familiar with Tetra Pak machines, and having trained employees to operate them, beverage companies have little incentive to switch to other suppliers.

Ideas for reinventing customer value

As the Tetra Pak example illustrates, when an organization redefines its business idea from selling discrete products to selling an integrated system of products and services, customers' dependence on the organization significantly increases. But most customers do not like relying on a single source because the provider has the ability to exploit its resulting bargaining power. From the customer's viewpoint, offering total solutions will be a winning value proposition *only* if three conditions hold.

1. **The solution is best in class** The organization is best in class in every product offered. If not, customer value is reduced because customers can obtain that product from another, superior source.
2. **The solution is seen by customers as being genuinely superior** The integrated solution is genuinely superior to the alternative of customers buying discrete products and services and bundling them on their own. Such superiority can result from one or more of several sources: system design, system assembly and customization of user needs.
3. **The price remains competitive and the gains are shared** The corporation offers the bundle at a price lower than the price customers would pay to assemble the individual products from separate providers. The business should not only demonstrate that the bundle is superior, *but also be willing to share its gains with customers.*

Tetra Pak's success has been the result of paying careful attention to all three of these conditions for providing customer value. Of course, this is no guarantee for the future and, sometimes, things can go wrong. However, the Sharpbenders research findings suggest that with its intense focus on customer value, Tetra Pak is likely to prosper. Even so, with strengths and weaknesses being relative notions, it must find new ways of understanding and anticipating the evolving nature of the customer value landscape.

The same applies to Nokia.

Entering New Markets and Maintaining Growth – Nokia Answers the Call

Background[7]

Nokia has generated impressive growth, driven by innovative mobile phones and some of the industry's lowest production costs. In 1990, the organization sold more than $600 million worth of cellular phones; by 1995, its phone sales exceeded $4 billion, and by 2001 Nokia had become Europe's largest company. Nokia captured the second-largest share of the cellular phone market both around the world and in the USA. In just a decade, Nokia has gone from selling no cellular phones in the USA to controlling nearly 20% of a market estimated to be worth $5 billion.

> The factors behind Nokia's phenomenal growth and its ability to successfuly enter new markets lie in some of the fundamental benefits of scenario planning. These are the importance of scenario thinking in improving reaction times, as well as the impact of scenarios in developing a corporate culture and ethos that promotes thinking through uncertainty, towards achieving a superior business idea.

Reasons for Nokia's growth

In the late 1970s, Nokia was a conglomerate making toilet paper, rubber boots and power cables, mostly for the Finnish market (Finland has a small population of about five million). Nokia's chief executive during part of the 1980s, Kari Kairamo, bought four European colour television manufacturers and a large Swedish computer manufacturer. The acquisitions pushed Nokia's revenues up 56% in 1988 to $4.4 billion. However, while Nokia was a major European player, it was still too small to compete in markets that were increasingly global, and its profits plunged.

The need was clear: Nokia needed to *focus* its business in areas where it would achieve greatest profitability and success. In late 1988, Nokia decided to dispose of its traditional, mature businesses, because it had several other businesses that were suddenly doing very well: telecommunications equipment and cellular telephones. That was where its new focus was directed – and at just the right time.

The next underlying reason for its growth was Nokia's ability to *sense market developments*. The breakthrough came when the telecommunications authorities of Sweden, Denmark, Norway and Finland decided to build the world's first international cellular system. As Sari Baldauf, head of Nokia's cellular systems division, said: 'Some of the big telecommunications companies thought wireless was a pretty small market niche, but we saw it as an opportunity.'

When the Scandinavian system was switched on in 1981, Nokia was there with both equipment and phones. This positioning ensured that Nokia was able to expand with the massive growth in the telecoms industry that took place during the 1980s and 1990s. In the USA, a commercial cellular service began in 1983, and Nokia was again ready to supply phones. However, it faced a major problem: how could a relatively unknown Finnish company break into the US market? The answer lay in *understanding the benefits of strategic partnering*. Kari-Pekka Wilska, head of Nokia's USA operations, recalls, 'We didn't have the money to do it all ourselves.' In order to penetrate the American market, Nokia offered high-quality products and entered into a major alliance with the Tandy Corporation. Nokia produced mobile telephones that were then sold via 6000 Radio Shack outlets in the USA. It was an inspired pairing. Nokia had learned its skills in Scandinavia, where technological innovation was imperative. Tandy brought a new set of priorities. 'For Tandy, the first priority was cost, then it was cost, and then it was cost, and then came something else,' said Pekka Ala-Pietila, president of Nokia's mobile phones division. Nokia learned how to cut manufacturing costs to the bone.

Nokia proved to be a quick organizational learner. For example, from Tandy the business quickly learnt the importance of *high volumes* and *low cost*, two further factors that proved crucial to its growth and success. One of Nokia's strengths was that its new portable phone was designed for production in large volume. Even though cellular systems differ between countries, designing a new phone that is almost identical wherever in the world it is sold is advantageous because when a product is modularized, it can be easily converted or mass-produced. Nokia recognized that it had to produce enormous volume to write off its manufacturing overhead – and this has put them far ahead of other companies.

Nokia's positive story points to factors necessary for growth and sustained profitability. The issue here is that the factors that drive successful strategies can be consciously addressed and developed using scenario planning.

BARRIERS TO STRATEGIC SUCCESS

Lessons Learned

These examples highlight similar points about effectively formulating and executing business strategy. From all of these points, the importance of scenario-based thinking and scenario planning becomes apparent.

Remember the value of anticipation in strategy formulation

Like Tetra Pak, Xerox had a very strong business idea. But in Xerox's case, the very strength and invulnerability of the business idea was its undoing. Xerox was shackled (by its own salesforce and its leasing policy) to its big machines. It could not afford to offer smaller machines to its customer base. It thought that its customers, heads of copying in large corporations, would protect both themselves *and* Xerox and retain centralized copying, since it was in both their customers' and Xerox's interests. Other parties trying the same business idea found that it could not be copied. However, individuals working in those large corporations increasingly wanted the flexible and instant access to copying facilities that Canon technology offered.

Similarly, Motorola was unprepared for Nokia's entry into the US mobile phone market (as we said above, first Nokia made phones for Radio Shack and then sold its phones with a well-known carrier brand stamped on them). Nokia's strategy was to design phones that were user-friendly and modularized – such that even though cellular systems differ from country to country the basic phone was almost identical, no matter where in the world it was sold. Enormous sales volumes of almost identical products allowed Nokia to reduce its manufacturing overheads and unit costs.

Both Xerox and Motorola felt invulnerable, and then the worst happened: a competitor came from nowhere and established a stronghold, based on evolving customer value. They were unable to anticipate what would happen. This was also evident in the case of Yahoo!, as its failure to predict and plan for any market changes left it out of control, reeling on a reactive course rather than pursuing a profitable, proactive route.

Yahoo! highlights how difficult it is for an organization to survive, let alone prosper, when it continually acts in an *ad hoc* manner. Yahoo!'s style could be characterized as permanent troubleshooting; hurtling from crisis to crisis. Situations would present themselves and *then* corporate policy would be discussed and decided. This not only slows reaction time, giving competitors time to dominate the market; it also increases the possibility of making disastrous errors in judgement.

It would be wrong to ascribe Yahoo!'s failures to a few changes in market forces. Rather, its failures can be clearly seen in its inability to plan for possible future events. With the vision and will to implement scenario planning and anticipate developments, its future might have been different.

Challenge current strategies, existing norms and avoid an over-reliance on traditional assumptions

Some organizations, however, are better able than others to see that the future will not be like the past. They understand that the organization's business idea needs to adapt and be kept closely aligned with changes in the world. In the case of Xerox versus Canon, Canon first identified an unmet need, indicating a new market segment and then, having a foothold, it was able to compete for business from Xerox's corporate clients and better meet these clients' changed needs for distributed copying facilities. The simple conclusion: Canon was able to satisfy changes in customer values. Nokia, by contrast, focused on volume production of standardized products, while Motorola seemed unable to appreciate the medium-term significance of Nokia's early adherence to a low-cost production strategy. This proved a winner in the mobile market, with lower cost the overwhelming customer need.

In the case of Yahoo!, the three-person management team seemed to believe that the future would be like the past: markets would remain largely unchanged and their offering of online ads would continue to satisfy customer value. Clearly, this was a failing strategy that, very soon, had to be reversed.

Guard against current success clouding the future

Why did Xerox fail to see how Canon was redefining the copier market? Why were Yahoo!, Lego and Motorola unable to see the impact that new designs, alliances and technology – or simply changing trends – would have on their current success?

The reason is that all these companies, and many, many others, are the prisoners of their own success. Ways of operating became ingrained in companies over the years – this is something for Tetra Pak to think about. Also, dominant management figures can stifle innovation and new thinking within an organization.

A organization's offering must satisfy the moving target of customer value

Tetra Pak seems to have achieved this. In contrast, Xerox, Lego, Yahoo! and a range of other corporations were less able to keep pace with and then satisfy shifting customer values. Business-as-usual thinking, and reliance on previously successful business ideas, can lead to organizational decline, when customers' values change.

Strategy is complex – and it matters

~~It is easy, with hindsight, to see these flaws in thinking for what they are – flawn~~ but a more interesting and relevant question might be, why did the management teams of these large and powerful organizations not see the inevitable sooner? Why were they unable to realign themselves with the changing world? Indeed, were these organizations sensitive to the changes that were taking place? How did the successful businesses manage to vision a profitable future, clearing hurdles and barriers to entry and achieving success?

Creating Value – The Difference Between Success and Failure

Let's try to bring together the various strands of the examples we have considered. What connects all these cases and the Sharpbenders research is the pre-eminent importance for the winning organization of *creating superior customer value*. Winning manifests itself in terms of the surplus created for an organization that can be invested into its future. Tetra Pak created so much value that it could offer a highly attractive deal to its customers while keeping enough for itself to ensure its future. Lego had lost its ability to do so, at least in 2001. Xerox at one time generated so much value that its future seemed assured forever, but then value moved somewhere else, where Canon had a better fit. So, value is the crucial starting point. But where does value come from? And since it is continually evolving, how can it be identified, in the present and in the future?

It is useful at this stage to look at economics, where it is argued that value is always associated with scarcity. There is little or no value in providing something that is in plentiful supply from other sources. The best you can hope to achieve is to recover your costs without achieving much of a surplus. After all, customers do not have to come to you, and with many alternative competing suppliers, any possible surplus will quickly be competed away by existing players or new-comers. This does not happen in an area of scarcity, where there are no alternative suppliers. Here, the customer will judge the value of the service not by what other suppliers have to offer, but by the additional costs they incur if the service is not provided at all. To the extent that these extra costs of doing something else are in excess of the cost of providing the service, a surplus is created that can be shared between the supplier and the buyer.

Value is Created in a Domain of Scarcity

At one time, cheap photocopiers were scarce, and Xerox could respond to this. Then Canon managed to push costs down in a field where personal control became an overriding value. At one time, the need for banner advertisements on websites seemed inexhaustible. After the dot-com collapse, the need moved to more integrated approaches. Sell-by dates is a severe bottleneck for the beverage industry, so overcoming this by inventing new packaging techniques creates huge potential customer value.

Organizations that want to connect or reconnect with customer value have to explore this scarcity landscape, now and in the future. They have to ask them-selves: where are the current bottlenecks in the economic and social system, and where are they likely to evolve towards? In our finite world, there will always be bottlenecks, but they won't remain in the same place. Current areas of scarcity will become abundant tomorrow, and the bottleneck areas will have moved else-where.

Strategy requires that we map out this future scarcity landscape, and scenario planning is an invaluable tool for achieving this. The examples show clearly that organizations have difficulties dealing with this make-or-break question. Also, the Sharpbenders research shows that few organizations seem to have this essential exploration of the business environment on their conscious agenda. There seem to be powerful barriers stopping people from doing the obvious.

SUMMARY: UNDERSTANDING THE BARRIERS TO SCENARIO PLANNING

Scenario exploration of the business environment is a scarce resource. This makes using scenarios a powerful business idea, but the bottleneck is not on the supply side. Scenario methods are neither difficult nor new – in Chapter 5 we will show that scenarios have been around for hundreds of years. There is enough help available. The reason why people stop short of using the obvious tools for the development of future strategy is not in their availability, but in the *thinking flaws* that stop them from engaging in this exploratory activity.

We have argued that the future of organizational success lies in understanding the future of scarcity; understanding where the bottlenecks lie. In the case of scenario planning, this means understanding the thinking flaws that act as barriers to entry in this domain. We should now consider these thinking flaws in further detail. We have identified thinking flaws at three levels in society: individual, organizational, and the level of communities and cultures. Examples of these barriers at work can be clearly seen in our case studies. In the case of Lego, decisions remain highly personal affairs in this family-owned organization. We can see how, after an initial period of innovation, the decision-makers get stuck in a trial and error approach that has its roots strongly in a *business-as-usual* way of thinking. Much the same situation existed at Yahoo!, where decisions were personally determined, and the few individuals at the top clearly had a problem with stepping out of the limited thinking box that they had built for themselves. Xerox is a case of organizational thinking flaws. The organization had been so successful that a form of group-think had entered the internal strategic conversation. Living in this environment, it had become extremely difficult to even raise the possibility that its business strategy was wrong. We would argue that the Xerox case is also a good example of the effect of culture on thinking. Xerox thinking was strongly based on an American corporate 'world-as-a-machine' view, where emphasis lies on making the machine ever more efficient. The more organic Japanese assumptions about the world would more easily bring into focus the value that individuals put on the perception of being in control and getting immediate results.

Our next job is to understand the barriers to scenario thinking, and the underlying flaws causing them. Chapters 2, 3 and 4 will deal with these important issues. In Chapter 2, we consider personal thinking flaws that can stand in the way of sound and vigilant decision-making by individuals. In Chapter 3, we consider flaws in thinking that are caused by interpersonal dynamics in organizations. Even if it was possible to overcome personal thinking flaws, we would still need to pay serious attention to how things may go wrong in this interpersonal domain. Moving up one further step in the system of human interaction in Chapter 4, we will consider the limitations that communities and societies impose on thinking, giving rise to what is known as the 'culture' of the group. Throughout, we will consider how scenario thinking can be helpful in overcoming these flaws.

How Managers Think about the Future

CHAPTER 2

Understanding the *psychological* context in which managers approach the future and make decisions is key to improving strategic thinking. In this chapter, look at the prevalence of routines and biases in management thinking – and the strength of scenario planning as a means of overcoming these flaws.

Overview

How do managers think about the future? Do they approach each major decision in a new and innovative way? Or do they fall into routines and habits – with little thought, such that business-as-usual is the default strategy for the future? In Chapter 1, we described case examples of the pitfalls of business-as-usual thinking. In this chapter, we focus on its causes.

This chapter will demonstrate and explain:

- **The prevalence of routines in management thinking.** These lead to strategic inertia that distorts an ability to develop successful and adaptive strategies.
- **The prevalence of biases in thinking.** Typically, the human mind is biased in many different ways. For example, how an issue or situation is framed or described determines our thinking about the future. We seek evidence to support the continuation of the currently-favoured

---

CONTINUED ... Overview

strategy. We are overconfident in our judgements and predictions –
and we don't learn from experience.

- **The nature of decision avoidance.** Stress reduction underpins the
  psychology of 'coping' with difficult strategic dilemmas, and this leads
  to decision avoidance. Escalation of commitment, bolstering, procrastination and 'buck passing' are all aspects of decision avoidance.
  Understanding the causes of inappropriate escalation in commitment
  to existing strategy, even when it is failing, is an important first step to
  facing up to difficult strategic dilemmas

- **The strength of scenario planning as a practical tool for decision-
  makers.** Scenario planning is uniquely positioned to help decision-
  makers overcome the problems of strategic inertia – the feeling that 'If
  it ain't broke don't fix it' – by providing a comprehensive means of
  overcoming biases and flaws in strategic thinking.

UNDERSTANDING MANAGEMENT THINKING

When managers are faced with a deteriorating business environment, their
cognitive habits can underpin the organization's failure to change from a
business-as-usual strategy. This then leads to a failure to design and pursue
successful strategies. The inability to realign an organization's strategy can be
clearly seen in managers' over-reliance on recipes that are applied habitually,
within a singular frame of reference. This situation, which we call *strategic inertia*,
effects decision-making and is caused by many thinking flaws that bedevil the
decision-making task.

Clearly, decisions with poor outcomes can often be traced back to the way
those decisions were made: the alternatives were not clearly defined; the right
information was not collected; the costs and benefits were not accurately weighed.
But, sometimes the fault lies not in the decision making process, but in the mind
of the decision-maker – the way that the human brain works can sabotage the
choices we make.

For example, when strategy starts to fail, individual managers tend to escalate
commitment in order to try to achieve a successful outcome. Such escalation is

often irrational. This bolstering of failing strategy is one of many ways in which managers avoid difficult, stressful, decision dilemmas. We'll discuss these processes further later in the chapter.

Routines in Management Thinking

In assessing how managers cope with the future, it is useful to review the findings of psychological experiments conducted 50 years ago[8]. Lessons learnt in the laboratory can be applied to help us understand the complexities of management thinking about the nature of the future.

One series of studies involved a number of opaque water jugs of various sizes, which could either be empty, full or partly full. The participants could not gauge the amount of water contained in each jug, as the jugs were opaque. The participants were presented with three jugs containing varying, but specific, quantities of water, and their task was to achieve the 'goal state' from the initial state by a series of pourings. In the table below, the figure in brackets for each jug is the capacity of that jug, and the second table represents its current contents in litres.

	Jug 1 (8-litre capacity)	Jug 2 (5-litre capacity)	Jug 3 (3-litre capacity)
Initial state	(8) 8	(5) 0	(3) 0
Intermediate states	(8) 3	(5) 5	(3) 0
	(8) 3	(5) 2	(3) 3
	(8) 6	(5) 2	(3) 0
Goal state	(8) 6	(5) 0	(3) 2

To achieve the goal state:

1. Use jug 1 to fill jug 2.
2. Then, use jug 2 to fill jug 3.
3. Next, pour the contents of jug 3 into jug 1.
4. Finally, pour the contents of jug 2 into jug 3.

As you will see, *the goal state can only be achieved by a particular sequence of pourings.* The experimenters gave respondents a large number of similar problems – where the goal state could only be achieved by a repetitive sequence of pourings. Finally, respondents were presented with the following water jug problem and nearly all the respondents achieved the goal state by way of the three intermediate states shown below.

	Jug 1 (8-litre capacity)	Jug 2 (5-litre capacity)	Jug 3 (3-litre capacity)
Initial state	(8) 8	(5) 0	(3) 1
Intermediate states	(8) 3	(5) 5	(3) 1
	(8) 3	(5) 3	(3) 3
	(8) 6	(5) 2	(3) 0
Goal state	(8) 6	(5) 0	(3) 3

Note that there is a more efficient way to achieve the goal state – by simply filling jug 3 from jug 1. When shown the 'easy' solution, respondents expressed surprise and shock that their thought patterns had followed a routine which seemed to have become so obvious to them that it made them totally overlook the (much easier) direct solution. This thought pattern has been termed 'mechanization of thought' or 'recipe following'. In strategic decision-making, such thought processes have been termed *managerial recipes*. These recipes (or success formulas) can become deeply ingrained in organizations – particularly ones that have been successful over a number of years.

Over-reliance on Routines: Success Formulas and Managerial Thinking

Consider Foster Brothers – a casual menswear retailer – who owned shops on most major high streets in the UK in the 1970s. One year, sales began to decline, and the organization responded by reapplying the traditional success formula of cost-effective procurement of finished goods, sourcing cheaper supplies of menswear made to Foster Brothers' own designs. Over the next few years, this recipe was repeatedly reapplied and the well-made items of menswear were retailed at very competitive prices in the shops. Foster Brothers maintained its margins on the basis of its excellent procurement process.

However, this success was to prove temporary. Shortly afterwards, Foster Brothers went out of business. The reasons for this failure can be traced back to the inertia evident in its strategic thinking. Men in the UK had become fashion-conscious and preferred to shop at Next, Gap and other emerging menswear retailers which were more in tune with men's newly acquired consciousness and style. In short, Foster Brothers' success formula – cost-effective procurement of finished goods from around the globe – was no longer in alignment with customer values. An aspect of the business environment had changed in a way that Foster Brothers seemed unable to appreciate.

As seen in Chapter 1 with Xerox, Yahoo!, Lego and others, many organizations follow managerial recipes in a similar way as Foster Brothers did, allowing recipes to become routines that are guides to thinking and acting. As writers on strategic management have argued: to survive, an organization's strategic decision-making must retain or improve its alignment with the external world. In other words, recipes should not be routinely followed and should be changed altogether when inappropriate. However, strategic inertia – defined as the degree of commitment to current strategy – grows over time, as current ways of operating become increasingly embedded in an organization. Commitment to the status quo will tend to escalate in a smooth, undisturbed fashion, with incremental adjustments or improvements to current strategy over time. Nevertheless, since no strategic choice is perfect, 'organizational stress' will develop, as the alignment between strategy and environment is perceived, belatedly, to have deteriorated. Managers pay little conscious attention to strategic choice, as long as organizational performance is perceived to be satisfactory – that is, when stress is low.

Identifying *why* some organizations are able to make step-changes to realign strategy when faced with a changed environment, while others are not, highlights the need to make fundamental changes in mental attitudes. This is in order to ensure continued prosperity during times of change. Inappropriate mental models:

- prevent managers from sensing problems;
- delay changes in strategy; and
- lead to action that is ineffective in a new business environment.

For example, Porac et al.[9] studied competitive models of senior managers in the Scottish knitwear industry. Although Scottish knitwear producers account for less than 5% of world production, when managers were asked to define their competitors, they identified Scottish organizations as their main competitors. Hodgkinson[10] found that UK residential estate agents' mental representations of competition remained stable, *despite* a significant downturn in the market over the 12–18-month period of his study.

Clearly, outdated mental models that underpin organizational weaknesses, such as recipe following, may remain untouched if companies enjoy profitability. Conversely, in companies that survive or flourish in environments that then become inhospitable, a change in their managers' mental models is apparent. In an empirical study, Barr *et al.*[11] analysed the content of letters to shareholders published by two railway companies over a 25-year period. It was evident that the surviving organization had created new strategies to more closely match a changing environment, while the failing organization had not made fundamental changes to its strategy until it was near bankruptcy. At that point, a discontinuous change in strategy occurred. Such changes are commonly prompted by a newly-appointed CEO who holds a different mental model – as the Yahoo! and Lego cases in Chapter 1 demonstrated.

BIASES IN THINKING

The Relevance of Framing Flaws

The roles that people occupy influence the way that problems are seen, or framed. For example, when profits fell in one cosmetic products organization in the early 1980s, key managers were asked to investigate and report on the causes. The marketing managers identified a lack of advertising and promotional support as the key problem; manufacturing and distribution managers blamed the marketing group for inaccurate sales forecasting and lack of customer knowledge, while the finance department blamed budget overruns by all departments. Finally, the legal department believed that a lack of new franchising and licensing agreements meant that the organization lacked new products.

Poor framing may lead managers to solve the *wrong problem*, because they have created a framework for a decision with little thought. The best options may be overlooked. Well-rehearsed and familiar ways of making decisions will be dominant and difficult to change – as the case of Foster Brothers illustrates. In large and successful organizations, current ways of doing business will become more deeply embedded as the years pass.

> **Changes in customer preferences mean that past demand is not predictive of future demand.**

Consider the majority of companies within the UK and USA automotive industries in the late 1970s. The focus was on manufacturing long production runs with minimum redesigns. By contrast, other countries' manufacturing frames were more customer-oriented. Here, responsiveness to changes in customer demand was the focus. In the UK and the USA, the high level of commitment to a previously successful production-oriented strategy meant that management was slow to adapt. This mattered greatly in a world where volatility in customer preferences meant past demand was no longer predictive of the future. As we saw in Chapter 1, attention must be paid to the changing needs of customers.

An organization may decline or go out of business if its managers fail to change their business frame to ensure it is in tune with changes in the world. Many examples illustrate this point. In the late 1970s, a watch manufacturer found itself ill-matched to new watch technology. In earlier times, manufacturers of bowler hats, solid rubber car tyres, valve radios and valve televisions found themselves in similar predica-ments, as advancing technology changed customer demands. Each of these manufacturers would have

> **Valued competencies become irrelevant, with the advent of changing** *technology* **or developing** *fashions.*

had developed capabilities or competencies, perhaps unique ones, in their manu-facturing or development processes. The problem is, of course, that valued competencies become irrelevant with the advent of changing *technology* or developing *fashions*. The key to success is not to be tied too closely to current ways of doing business. These success formulas and tried-and-trusted approaches should be open to challenge, debate and dissent.

As we have seen, managers habitually follow recipes for success and see emerging issues through single frames of reference – often built up through the habitual application of a success formula. But, sometimes, success formulas *are* seen by managers to be failing. As the next case example – the launch of New Coke – shows, recognition that a strategy is failing is not enough to guarantee a successful change of strategic direction.

How a Failed Product Launch Actually Boosted Sales: the Sparkle of New Coke[12]

The origins of New Coke began with the advent of the 'Pepsi Challenge' in 1975. In city after city, Pepsi claimed to be winning head-to-head taste tests: Coca-Cola officials rushed to conduct their own tests. The results came as a sharp dis-appointment: Coca-Cola could not prove its superiority. The numbers were kept under wraps, but word swept quickly through the ranks of the Coca-Cola family that the product had a taste problem.

While presenting a public façade of bravado, executives in the Coca-Cola tower grew increasingly concerned. They could ill afford to ignore Pepsi's gains, no matter how difficult it might be to pinpoint their causes. Coke's market share had been shrinking for decades, from 60% just after World War II to less than 24% by 1983.

The main reason for Coke's decline was *segmentation*: the proliferation of diet drinks, citrus flavours, caffeine-free colas and other new beverages that had flooded the soft-drink market, luring consumers away from sugar colas like Coke and Pepsi. The Coca-Cola organization was marketing many of these new products, of course, and profiting from the trend. Even so, the taste problem was a major issue for a core product, and it needed to be resolved.

Time for a change

The head of Coca-Cola USA, Brian Dyson, became almost evangelical on the taste problem. Testing had persuaded him that consumers' tastes had changed over the years, and he believed they had begun to prefer Pepsi's sweeter, smoother flavour. His deepest concern was that Pepsi might overtake Coke while he was in charge. 'I'm not going to sit on my ass and watch that,' he told an interviewer. In *The New York Times* in 1984, Dyson issued a prescient warning: 'There is a danger when a company is doing as well as we are. And that is to think that we can do no wrong. I keep telling the organization, we can do wrong and we can do wrong big.'

In the closing months of 1984, surveys showed Coke's lead in the cola market narrowing until Pepsi trailed by fewer than three points, the closest margin ever. Those numbers, along with the results of the taste test, finally convinced the chairman and CEO of Coca-Cola to take action. During the holiday season at the end of December, they met with Dyson and Ike Herbert, the director of corporate marketing, and resolved to proceed with the reformulation.

Herbert went to New York for a secret meeting with the top executives of McCann Erickson – the organization's advertising agency. In a secluded office named 'the bunker', the men from Atlanta divulged the news of their decision and assigned John Bergin, McCann's president, to start work on a campaign to launch New Coke. The target date was April 1985, just four months away. If any word of Project Kansas leaked prematurely, Herbert said, levelling a direct threat, the agency would be fired. Meanwhile, back home, Dyson widened the membership in the project to include Coca-Cola's top marketing and public relations (PR) officials, who were given the monumental (and confidential) task of coordinating New Coke's debut.

One other consideration remained, and that was the issue of what, if anything, to tell Robert Woodruff, the aging patriarch of Coca-Cola and the most devout defender of the secret formula. Roberto Goizueta, one of Coca-Cola's most popular chairmen, always maintained that he flew to Woodruff's estate in Ichauway to explain the decision, receiving his blessing for the new formula – an account that provoked scepticism both at the time and afterwards. In an interview, Goizueta recalled that he had been briefing Woodruff for several years on Coca-Cola's shrinking market share and poor performance in taste tests with Pepsi.

The customer decides

Long before they had ever tasted a sip, millions of Americans decided they hated New Coke. All across the country, and especially in the South, people responded to the change in formula as if the organization had killed off a beloved member of the family! The surge of emotion over old Coke defied all reason. Hundreds and then thousands of angry callers began inundating the organization at Atlanta. Remarkably, many of them were not Coca-Cola drinkers at all; they were simply American citizens, upset and feeling a profound sense of loss.

On 11 July 1985, Roberto Goizueta and other senior executives returned to the stage, this time without fanfare, in the auditorium of the Coca-Cola USA building in Atlanta, where Goizueta announced the return of Coke Classic. The news had been leaked the previous day, when Peter Jennings of ABC News interrupted the soap opera *General Hospital* to break the story on national television. Headlines filled the front pages of newspapers across the country the following morning heralding what insiders called 'The Second Coming'.

That day the organization's hotline recorded 18 000 calls and, for the first time in over two months, they came from people who had kind words to say. 'You would have thought,' Ike Herbert later commented, 'we had invented a cure for cancer.' Outside Goizueta's office a small plane circled, trailing a banner that read: 'Thank you, Roberto.'

Coca-Cola Classic proved phenomenally popular. Against all expectations, Classic immediately began outselling New Coke, and much to everyone's surprise it kept rising, overtaking Pepsi early in 1986. Straining to explain the craze over Coke Classic, senior executives at Coca-Cola told *The Wall Street Journal*, 'It's kind of like the fellow who's been married to the same woman for 35 years and really didn't pay much attention to her until somebody started to flirt with her.' It was a good analogy, yet it glossed over the absolute bewilderment that everyone in Coca-Cola felt about the outcome. No one could explain the renewed appeal of the old formula. New Coke was supposed to be the top cola, with Classic satisfying the demands of the traditionalists. Instead, New Coke virtually disappeared (rapidly shrinking to a 3% market share), while Classic began selling better than the original.

The lessons

The executives at Coca-Cola introduced New Coke after it outscored both Pepsi and the original Coke in taste tests. However, the launch of New Coke contained an *untested assumption*: that flavour mattered more than the image of Classic Coke. The information gathered served only to confirm the decision that the launch of New Coke should proceed. But this confidence, as we have seen, turned out to have been misplaced. Although the situation was eventually resolved in Coca-Cola's favour, this does not preclude the possibility that the resolution could have been disastrous. The lesson to be drawn from the Coca-Cola's predicament is that companies' strategic decision-making may rely too heavily on a natural tendency to seek confirming evidence.

Confirmation Bias

Typically, we seek confirming evidence to support continuation of the current, favoured, strategy. The following examples illustrate this.

The waiter's dilemma

Imagine that you are a waiter in a busy restaurant and, because you cannot give good service to all the people who sit at the tables that you serve, you use your judgement to identify those people who will leave good tips or poor tips. You have developed this ability well, and most of the people whom you predict will tip generously do. Also, most of those that you predict will not tip do not. Are your judgemental predictions accurate?

It would seem that they are. However, note that the waiter will give good service to those he thinks will tip well and will ignore those he thinks will not tip. If the quality of service, in itself, has an effect on whether or not a customer tips, then the waiter's actions will, by themselves, determine the tipping outcome.

There is a strong element of a self-fulfilling prophecy here. The only true way that the waiter can test out the quality of his judgement is to give *poor* service to good tip prospects and *excellent* service to poor tip prospects. Clearly, his original judgements could be less valid than he assumes, as he has not accurately tested them.

A mathematical puzzle[13]

In another demonstration of confirmation bias, a class is told that we have a rule in mind that classifies sets of three integers – which we call triples. The class is given an example of a triple that has been produced by our rule: 2, 4, 6. Members of the class attempt to discover the rule by suggesting other triples to test. We say whether they conform to the rule or not. Participants are told not to call out what they think the rule is until they are certain that they have deduced it. Our rule is simply 'any ascending sequence', but most participants think that the rule is more complex – for example, 'ascending in equal intervals', suggesting triples such as 4, 8, 12 or 20, 40, 60. Eventually, they announce their rule and are convinced of its correctness. In other words, people tend to think only of positive tests of their view of the rule that can never be falsified: a bias toward confirmation, rather than disconfirmation, of our decision. This result suggests that, without prompting, we are unlikely, as waiters, to give service to those predicted to be poor tippers or, as interviewers, to hire those we view as poor prospects.

The recruitment dilemma

The decision to hire new employees is analogous to the waiter's situation. Most of us feel that we are able to interview fairly, and we feel comfortable with our hiring decisions – confident that we can identify appropriate employees. But we seldom hear what happened to the candidates that we declined. Unless we gain accurate feedback on the interviewees that we turned down, we do not know if our decisions were sound. It follows that the only true test of our interviewing capabilities is to hire those that we feel we should reject. But few of us would willingly put our judgement to such rigorous tests!

Hindsight Bias

As strategic decision-makers, we are likely to seek confirming evidence that our favoured strategy is still working well and that it is aligned with the business environment. Inevitably, we do not place ourselves in situations where we can test the quality of our judgement. We only seek information that will confirm the quality of our predictions. For example, we tend to read adverts about the car that we have just purchased rather than those describing the virtues of the other cars. This may seem relatively harmless; unfortunately, the picture is bleaker. In one famous study[14] in the early 1970s, MBA students were asked to predict possible outcomes of President Nixon's forthcoming trip to China. Would a named treaty be signed? Would the President visit a named city? Many questions of this sort were posed. The students wrote down their predictions, putting a confidence figure next to each prediction. Two weeks then elapsed and the students returned to the MBA classroom. Unexpectedly, the same students were asked to recall their confidence estimates of each prediction. Given that the events had been reported widely in the press, students knew which of their predictions had, or had not happened.

The findings were instructive. If an event had occurred, the students tended to recollect that they had predicted it with a high degree of confidence. If a named event had not occurred, the students either claimed that they had not predicted it, or that they had placed a low degree of confidence on the poor prediction. In short, the students evidenced what has been termed the 'I-knew-it-all-along' effect or 'hindsight bias'. In general, then, it would seem that we don't learn from experience because we believe that experience has little to teach us: our recollections of our judgemental predictions confirm these to have been accurate! We believe that our judgements, predictions and choices are well made, but this confidence may be misplaced.

The Problem of Overconfidence

The following excerpt clearly illustrates overconfidence in our ability to make good judgements. The journalist was analysing the reasons for the USA's lack of preparedness for the 1990 Iraqi invasion of Kuwait.

> *In the days leading up to the invasion, the intelligence agencies sent President Bush a list of predictions. The list was arranged in order of probability. 'None had as their first choice the prediction that Saddam Hussein would attack,' says one intelligence operative who saw the reports. Prediction No. 1 was that Saddam was bluffing. Prediction No. 2 was that he might seize part of the Rumaila oilfield that straddles Iraq and Kuwait, and possibly Warba and Bubiyan islands, two mudflats blocking Iraq's access to the Persian Gulf. It was assumed that he would pull back from Kuwait once the islands were secured.*

'The line we kept hearing around here was that he has just massed there along the Kuwait border to drive up the price of oil,' recalls one senior Pentagon officer. 'If people were saying he is for real and he is going to invade, it was not briefed to us as definite.'
Newsweek, 28 January 1991. Reproduced by permission of *Newsweek*.

One recent study asked individuals to rate themselves as car drivers on a scale from 'well below average' to 'well above average'. Most ticked a box indicating above average – but by definition, we can't all be above average! In another study, budding entrepreneurs were interviewed about their chances of business success. Their estimates were unrelated to objective predictors such as post-school education, prior supervisory experience or initial capital. Moreover, more than 80% described their chances of success as 70% or better – while the true five-year survival rate for new businesses is only 33%.

THE LIMITATIONS OF JUDGEMENTAL FORECASTING

We have a strong tendency to see an individual forecasting problem as a unique one-off event, rather than as instances of a broader class of events. We tend to pay particular attention to the special features of the single event we are called upon to forecast, rather than attempting to consider either our past success at predicting similar events, or base rate occurrences for such similar events. To see this, consider a gambler betting on the spin of a roulette wheel. If the roulette wheel has produced an outcome of red for the last ten spins then the gambler may feel that her confidence for black on the next spin should be higher than that for red. However, ask the same gambler the relative proportions of red to black on spins of the wheel and she may well answer '50-50'.

Since the roulette ball has no memory, it follows that the relative frequency assessment is a more accurate one. But often, of course, the key events that managers most want to be able to predict cannot be evaluated in terms of relative frequency – such as Saddam Hussein's intentions, discussed above.

In conclusion, individuals follow cognitive habits, seeing challenging situations through a singular frame of reference that makes assumptions about the nature of problems or opportunities that arise. Additionally, we feel that our judgement is good. Furthermore, this perception is reinforced by both the confirmation bias and the hindsight bias that underpin an inappropriate confidence in our judgement. Such overconfidence will lead to inappropriate 'best guess' thinking about the future – as illustrated in the USA's unpreparedness for Saddam Hussein's invasion of Kuwait.

DECISION AVOIDANCE

Escalation of Commitment

It is common that when decisions start to go wrong, or strategy begins to fail, the decision-maker commits further resources to reverse the situation. At Coca-Cola, the heated disputes and work that had gone into the creation and launch of New Coke was hard for their executives to write off. The relaunch of old-formula Coke only came after intense efforts to make New Coke a success had failed. This effort persisted in the face of ridicule – executives were characterized in the media as vandals who wanted to deface a national treasure. Indeed, Roger Enrico, Pepsi's president, held a press conference to ask if his rival planned to start a 'Cola-of-the-month Club', querying if the nation's grocery shelves would have enough space for New Coke, Coke Classic, new Diet Coke, old Diet Coke, new caffeine-free Coke, old caffeine-free Coke . . . The basis of such inappropriate escalation of commitment in the face of compelling evidence to 'call it quits' has, once again, been demonstrated in the psychologist's laboratory.

The high responsibility condition

Typically, the experiment runs as follows: individual respondents are asked to allocate research and development funds to one of two operating divisions of an organization. The organization and the decision context are described in detail and the respondent is then told that, after a year, the investment had either proved successful or unsuccessful, and that they now faced a second decision concerning a second allocation of funds. This first group was known as the 'high responsibility' condition, as they have a personal commitment to the original decisions taken. Individuals in a second group were told that another financial officer of the organization had made the earlier decision and that it had been either successful or unsuccessful. They were then asked to consider making a second allocation of funds to the division. This second group was labelled the 'low responsibility' condition, as they had no personal commitment to the original decisions. The results proved illuminating:

- When the outcome of the earlier decision proved to be an unsuccessful investment, the high responsibility respondents allocated *significantly more funds* to the original division than the low-responsibility ones.

- By contrast, the allocation decisions made by both groups of respondents were roughly the same, if the earlier decision had produced a successful outcome.

Common factors leading to inappropriate escalation of commitment

As W.C. Fields once said: 'If at first you don't succeed, try, try, again. Then quit. No use being a damn fool about it.'

What are the common elements of decisions that result in inappropriate escalation of commitment? First, there is a decision to make, resulting from a previously unsuccessful decision. Second, there is the degree of personal responsibility for the important prior decision. In such situations, before committing funds to the second of what may be a series of linked decisions, the following results are often observed.

- Managers pay more attention to information that confirms the validity of their earlier decision – as the confirmation bias discussed earlier demonstrated.
- Since the second decision is made in a situation that is negatively framed, individuals will tend to select risk-seeking options that, potentially, can 'recover' what has become an adverse situation.
- A blame culture within an organization will either magnify the likelihood that failure will be concealed, or it will ensure that additional effort is made in an attempt to turn the situation around.

Solutions – evaluate decision processes

How can an organization halt such a non-rational escalation of commitment? The key is for organizations to evaluate managers based on good decision *processes* rather than good outcomes. Good decisions carry the risk of poor outcomes. Managers should be allowed to reverse decisions if they begin to fail. Yet, reversing a decision is not always easy. Three examples show the strength of irrational escalation of commitment.

Taurus

In the 1990s, the London Stock Exchange's biggest ever computer project, Taurus, was halted. Millions of pounds had been spent on a project test that was conceived in the early 1980s, as an automated settlement process between stockbrokers. It was a central computer to maintain all records of shareholdings and share transactions. Overall, £75 million was spent on software and hardware with no payoff. In the end, a consultancy organization, Andersen Consulting, revealed that there was no overall architecture for the Taurus System. So, in 1993 the City was left with the same problem it faced in the early 1980s: how to build a modern stock market settlement system.

Barings Bank

In the mid-1990s, Nick Leeson lost Barings Bank over £800 million in his futures market derivatives trading. He attempted to recoup his losses by doubling, then redoubling, his stake. He covered up his mounting losses in a secret account for three years.

The Millennium Dome

In early 2000, the UK government's investment in the Millennium Dome came under increasing scrutiny by the news media, public and politicians:

> According to Peter Mandelson, Prescott had been asked for his opinions at the end of a 1997 Cabinet committee meeting called to decide whether to go ahead with the Dome. Without blinking, he had said the Government had to proceed. Otherwise, they would be accused of losing their nerve. Having welcomed the imprimatur of his deputy, Blair promptly disappeared to keep an urgent church appointment, leaving Prescott to chair the Cabinet. *Independent*, 28 May 2000

A MORI poll in January 2000 found that 36% of respondents thought that the Dome should never have been built; on 21 September 2000, Cabinet member Claire Short declared the Dome a disaster that should never have been built. The Dome project had swallowed £628 million and was subsidizing the dwindling number of visitors at £148 a visitor during 2000. As *The Economist* observed on 9 September 2000, 'Each new dollop of public money has hitherto been announced with an assurance that this will positively, definitely, be the last time the Dome has to be bailed out.' There had been a £60 million grant in February and £29 million in May, a £43 million advance on the sale of the site in August and then a further £47 million to keep it open until the end of 2000. The Dome was intended as the natural focus for celebrating the millennium.

In many situations, individuals who hold themselves responsible for a poor initial decision throw good money after bad, consistently failing to recognize that the time and expenses already invested are lost costs. The decision-maker, in the face of negative feedback about the consequences of his earlier decision, feels the need to affirm the wisdom of it by further commitment of resources in an attempt to 'justify' the initial decision or provide further opportunities for it to be proven correct. Negative feedback is rationalized by treating the information as ephemeral rather than as indicating key points about the quality of the prior decision.

> Groups or individuals that make the initial decision tend to escalate their commitment to the decision despite negative feedback, whereas those that inherit decisions are less likely to do so.

Staw and Ross[15] showed that the tendency of high-responsibility individuals to escalate commitment was particularly pronounced when there was some way to develop an explanation for the initial failure, such that the failure was viewed as unpredictable and unrelated to the decision-maker's action (for example, the economy suffered a severe setback). Bazerman *et al.*[16] showed that groups who made an initial collective decision that proved unsuccessful then allocated significantly more funds to escalating their commitment to the decision than did groups who inherited the initial decision. Clearly, the social processes causing escalation of commitment will tend to magnify adherence toward a current, but failing, strategy.

Bolstering, Procrastination and Buck-Passing

When the risks involved in continuing to follow a particular course of action are, perhaps belatedly, seen to be high, and the risks of changing to an alternative are also seen to be high, then the psychological stress of dealing with the decision dilemma rises. Intense conflicts, Janis and Mann[17] argue, are likely to arise whenever a person has to make an important decision. Such conflicts become acute as the decision-maker becomes aware of the risk of suffering serious losses from whatever course of action is selected; for example, continuing with business-as-usual or changing strategy.

Decisional conflicts refer to simultaneous opposing tendencies within the individual, to accept or reject a given course of action. The most prominent symptoms of such conflicts are hesitation, vacillation, feelings of uncertainty and signs of acute emotional stress whenever the decision comes within the focus of attention.

The conflict theory of decision-making describes a number of basic ways in which decision-makers cope with the threats or opportunities that are often part of crucial decisions. Often, decision-makers defensively avoid the stress of difficult decision dilemmas by adopting coping patterns in their decision behaviour. There are three major coping patterns. *Procrastination* entails delaying the decision, for example waiting for a long time before thinking about the dilemma. *Shifting responsibility* (or buck passing) entails passing the ultimate responsibility for the decision to other individuals or groups. *Bolstering* involves uncritically boosting the advantages of the 'least worst' option of those options that are available – often the status quo or business-as-usual option. Escalation of commitment is characteristic of bolstering. All three coping patterns lower the stress inherent in facing a difficult decision.

Regardless of which of these three defensive avoidance coping patterns are adopted, either singly or in combination, there are two common outcomes – incomplete search for, and evaluation of, incoming information that would aid choice, and lack of contingency planning in the event that the course of action followed begins to fail badly.

Example of a Management Team Facing a Decision Dilemma

In one study we were involved with recently, we interviewed nine individuals on the senior management team of a major corporation who were facing just such a crucial decision dilemma[18]. The current strategic direction was failing, and all alternative strategies were fraught with risk. Essentially, the organization had strong core competencies that underpinned its older business idea, but this idea was failing in a changing world. Quotations from our complete interview data – collected from the top management team – were categorized under Janis and Mann's headings.

The following quotations illustrate that the risks were perceived to be serious if the organization didn't change its current failing strategy:

> *The business needs more income streams . . . therefore, diversification is crucial now to build significant other income streams . . . (Participant 1)*

> *A key danger is that there is too much emphasis on our core business activity . . . New technology could result in the death of [Beta Co's main offering] by 2005, 2010, 2015. Who knows when? We need to move to new areas that will result in new revenue streams . . . The failure of [Beta Co] to develop alternative revenue streams would be another bad scenario (participant 2)*

If we go on as we are, in ten years from now we won't be here . . . (Participant 3)

There is a perception round here that [Beta Co] has very much got all its eggs together in one basket. If one of [Beta Co's major customers] pulled out . . . At a personal level, I am very much concerned that we have job security . . . (Participant 5)

And the risks are also seen to be serious if the organization did change its strategy:

We are a group of talented amateurs rather than experienced in areas of potential diversification . . . (Participant 4)

[Beta's latest experimental venture] has been a protracted and salutary experience. There are very few short-term gains to be made . . . (Participant 6)

We are naive on the business side [Beta Co's latest experimental venture] is necessary for our future, but we have had a slightly unrealistic view of how easy or difficult it would be to break into an existing market in which potential customers have settled relationships and [Beta Co] has no track record . . . (Participant 7)

The senior management team was also attempting to shift responsibility for its adherence to the current failing strategy to the top-level board of directors, i.e. 'passing the buck':

One main board director is on the record as having said that [Beta Co] should make no attempt to adapt to changing market conditions . . . (Participant 1)

The board faces a key decision, not us. They need to take a keen interest in terms of what shape [Beta Co] should take in the future . . . (Participant 3)

We have to try and resolve the diversification issue one way or the other, but I am not sure that this is a decision we can take . . . (Participant 7)

There was also evidence of delay and procrastination:

The failure to diversify would probably mean the business would still be OK in 10 years from now, but after 15 years it would be starting to decline . . . (Participant 1)

There is still mileage in [Beta Co's main offering] for the next 10 years . . . (Participant 5)

Things will be slower than most people think... We are 20 years away from complete change, i.e. our business will still be serviceable in 20 years' time . . . (Participant 6)

There is no real rush to adapt . . . Five to 10 years away there will still be a healthy market for [Beta Co's main offering] . . . (Participant 7)

Finally, there was evidence of bolstering the current failing strategy:

> *The slow pace of change in our industry is of benefit to us . . . if [Beta Co] becomes the only [provider of its current main offering] there will be less pressure on us to develop other products . . . [Beta Co's] current performance and historical record are its key strengths . . . (Participant 2)*

> *One of the problems we face in respect of new products is customer inertia . . . Customers are generally conservative because they don't want the hassle of changing [suppliers]. These same forces are potentially prolonging the life of [Beta Co's current main offering] . . . (Participant 2)*

> *Ultimately, I was brought in [to Beta Co] to play a key role in enabling the organization to diversify and/or add to its core business – though diversification may not be needed if [Beta Co] becomes [the major player within the market of its current main offering] within the next two to three years . . . (Participant 2)*

In short, the current risky strategy was failing, alternative strategies were perceived to be risky, and buck passing, procrastination and bolstering were apparent. But what of information search and contingency planning? The following quotations illustrate deficiencies and limitations in these dimensions of strategic thinking. As illustrations of limited information search, consider:

> *I believe you can always buy the skills you need. You may have to pay a bit more or wait a bit . . . (Participant 1)*

> *We don't know enough about the real strategic aims of [Beta Co's main customers] . . . (Participant 4)*

> *We lack understanding of real customer requirements . . . We know even less about potential customers . . . (Participant 4)*

> *There is a learning process we need to go through, but I am sure we can do it and beat the competition . . . (Participant 5)*

As examples of poor contingency planning, consider:

> *Currently the business is cash rich but not investing . . . (Participant 1)*

> *Another key requirement is for investment in R&D to secure the organization's future through the creation of new revenue streams, but how should this be done? (Participant 2)*

> *I guess we ought to be doing other things to protect ourselves . . . (Participant 5)*

We lack the ability to talk to the right people in [key alternative sectors]. Are we heavyweight enough? . . . Our main sources on the [xxxx] side tend to be conferences, suppliers or reading the press . . . (Participant 7)

How do we diversify and into what? (Participant 9)

Thinking Flaws: A Synthesis

The issues discussed in this chapter raise two, critically important questions. How can the biasing elements of the results from psychological studies be attenuated, and how can multiple perspectives on a decision problem be facilitated? Several decision researchers have spoken out on these issues but the prescriptions have often been general calls to 'be alert', rather than clear guidance for overcoming bias. For example, it has been recommended that in situations that could lead to escalation, the decision-makers should set limits on their involvement and commitment in advance, and remind themselves of the costs involved.

Irving Janis recommends that the leader should: withhold her ideas at first; encourage new ideas and criticisms; make sure that the group listens to minority views; and use processes designed to delay consensus.

Russo and Schoemaker[19], in discussing decision framing, argue that one should challenge the actions that are normally taken on an issue, and seek a devil's advocate viewpoint – welcome diverse opinions and be creative. One tool that they recommend to achieve 'frame awareness' is their frame analysis worksheet. Essentially, this asks decision-makers to state the following:

- What aspects of the situation are left out of consideration?
- What does the frame emphasize?
- In what ways do other people in the industry think about this question differently from the way you do?

The extent to which such advice aids the decision-maker to challenge a current view has not yet been investigated.

Figure 2.1 presents our view of a systemic relationship between the findings of this chapter[20]. In this diagram, we attempt to integrate the results of psychological research with current knowledge of inertia in strategic decision-making. In the diagram, it is shown that:

- The resting state of the system is that of a low perceived level of environmental threat, leading to a low stress level, which leads to strategic inertia.

Unconflicted adherence to a business-as-usual strategy characterizes this resting state.

- Nevertheless, the environment is monitored for environmental threats, but this monitoring is attenuated due to confirmation bias and overconfidence. If the environmental threat is sufficiently severe, it *is* perceived as threatening unconflicted adherence to the current strategy, then the stress level rises and, soon afterwards, coping patterns such as bolstering, procrastination and buck passing are evidenced.

- Bolstering, characterized by escalation of commitment to the current strategy, can lead to a feeling of perceived organizational invulnerability to events in the business environment. Such coping patterns lower the perceived level of environmental threat, which results in a lowered stress level and, hence, to strategic inertia.

In short, all roads lead to inertia in strategic thinking. The underlying business problem that gives rise to the initial feeling of threat is often not addressed in managerial thinking – since psychological coping patterns act, subconsciously, to reduce this threat. Over time, in the real world – rather than in the mind of the manager – the gap between the organization's strategic positioning and the actual business environment may widen. Only when the gap is too big to be dealt with by coping patterns will stark reality be faced. At this point, it may be too

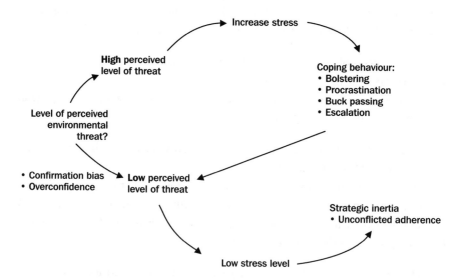

Figure 2.1   The relationship between the business environment and the strategic process

late for the organization to take action to become more closely aligned to the changed business environment.

OVERCOMING STRATEGIC INERTIA: THE POTENTIAL BENEFITS OF SCENARIO PLANNING

The practice of scenario planning is a means of overcoming strategic inertia, since it implicitly accepts that managers' best guesses about the course of future events, and confidence in the appropriateness of current strategy, may be mistaken. Essentially, scenario planning interventions within organizations support the construction of multiple frames of future states of the external world, only some of which may

> **Early recognition of, and reaction to, emerging events promotes a strong organizational response.**

be well aligned with current strategy. Scenario planning can facilitate 'vigilance' in strategic thinking – in that alternative futures are thought through, and strategic options can be subsequently evaluated against these futures. The process of scenario planning enhances the evaluation and integration of information, and promotes contingency planning for unfolding of both favourable and unfavourable futures. Procrastination, shifting responsibility, and bolstering commitment to failing strategies, are thus attenuated by the scenario planning process – as we shall see in later chapters. How do scenarios achieve this?

A Scenario is not a Forecast of the Future

Multiple scenarios are pen-pictures of a range of *plausible* futures. Each individual scenario has an infinitesimal probability of actual occurrence but the *range* of a *set* of individual scenarios can be constructed in such a way as to *bound* the uncertainties that are seen to be inherent in the future – like the boundaries of a multidimensional space. Multiple scenarios provide alternative frames on the nature of the future.

Scenarios Focus on Key Uncertainties *and* Certainties About the Future

This information can then be used to construct pen-pictures, in an information-rich way, in order to provide vivid descriptions of future worlds. It is worth comparing and contrasting scenario planning, as described here, with planning methods that require judgemental forecasts and confidence assessments. The judgemental process that produces such numbers is often not verbalized or recorded. Inherent in these planning methods is the assumption that it is useful and possible to attempt to predict the future, whereas scenario planning assumes that the best that can be done is to identify critical future uncertainties and plan for the range of futures that could, plausibly, unfold. Essentially, scenarios highlight the reasoning underlying judgements about the future, and give explicit attention to sources of uncertainty, *without* trying to turn an uncertainty into an (overconfident) probability.

A major focus is *how* the future can evolve, from today's point-in-time to the future that has unfolded by the horizon year of the scenario – say 10 years hence. The *process* of scenario planning thinks through the relationship between:

- the critical *uncertainties* (as they resolve themselves);
- important predetermined *trends* (such as demographics), and
- the behaviour of actors who have a stake in the particular future (who tend to act to preserve and enhance their own interests).

The result is that the pen-pictures produced are, in fact, seen as plausible to those who have constructed the scenarios.

Scenarios Help Identify Information to Anticipate How the Future Will Unfold

Alternative world views can be communicated easily in an organization via the medium of scenario 'stories'. Additionally, once a story has been read, and the reasoning underlying its unfolding understood, a future has been 'rehearsed'. Thus, once the early events in a scenario occur, the decision-maker will be able to anticipate how the future might unfold. These 'trigger events' will be seen as *information* among the stream of *data* that impacts upon the decision-maker.

Early contingency action. Just as the purchaser of a new car becomes aware of and sensitive to the variety of models of that make on the road, the scenario thinker becomes sensitive to a scenario starting to unfold and becoming reality. Such sensitivity can lead to early contingency action towards an unfavourable future.

Early recognition of opportunities. New business opportunities can be quickly grasped as soon as favourable scenarios begin to unfold. Such early recognition and reaction to an emerging future is seen, by some practitioners, as more useful than the creation of robust strategic options.

Typical Outcomes of the Scenario Planning Process

Typical outcomes of the scenario process include:

- Confirmation that the overall strategy of an organization is sound, or that new, underpinning strengths need to be added to create more *robustness*. (Robustness implies that a strategy performs well in each scenario.)
- Confirmation that lower-level business choices are sound, or that new, alternative options are more robust.
- Recognition that none of the business options are robust and, therefore, contingency planning against unfavourable futures is necessary.
- Sensitivity to the 'early warning' elements that are precursors of desirable and unfavourable futures.

SUMMARY: OVERCOMING THINKING FLAWS WITH SCENARIO PLANNING

The process of scenario planning provides conditions under which the appropriateness of the development of a particularly strategy, or a particular *class* of closely related strategies, can be falsified. Additionally, the expression of dissenting opinion about what the future holds is facilitated. Single best guesses about the evolving state of the external environment are thus attenuated, and the degree of alignment between strategy and the range of plausible futures is the focus of attention.

Summary Checklist – the Limits to Managerial Thinking

Issue	Key points
1. **To what extent does your strategic thinking rely on routines or previously successful formulas? Are you able to think 'outside the box'?**	Thinking limitations can result in managerial 'blind spots' that lock management into an obsolete world view, causing strategic inertia. In such circumstances, the organization will gradually become misaligned with the environment and stakeholders, such as customers – as illustrated by the launch of New Coke.

Issue	Key points
2. Are you keeping in touch with market developments and the needs and expectations of your customers? Are you prepared to challenge inappropriate confidence in existing orthodoxy?	We have seen – in the cases of Xerox, Motorola, Yahoo!, Lego and Foster Brothers – how strategic inertia in the face of a changing environment is characteristic of companies. Fashion and technology can significantly and swiftly change markets – strategic thinking must take account of this tendency, and anticipate change and discontinuity.
3. Are you prepared to accept that a strategy is failing, or are escalation, procrastination or bolstering more characteristic of your reactions to a strategy that is beginning to show signs of failure?	By focusing strategic energies on assessing multiple futures, companies are better placed to gain considerable advantage by the early recognition of and reaction to a changing business environment. In an increasingly volatile world, companies ready for the unforeseen will outmanoeuvre their competitors.

Scenario planning contains components to promote alternative views about the nature of the future and also challenges potentially inappropriate confidence – both in a single 'best-guess' future and also in a single, tried-and-trusted strategy. However, in terms of Figure 2.1, interventions with scenario planning may be seen by managers to be unnecessary. This is because the increased stress of a misfit between strategy and environment may either have not been experienced because of the dominance of outdated mental models, or have been reduced to tolerable levels by psychological coping mechanisms.

In Figure 2.1, the most appropriate point for a scenario planning intervention in an organization is, theoretically, *after* there is recognition that the environmental threat to current strategy is high, but *before* the psychological processes inherent in coping behaviour are engaged. As yet, however, little is known about whether or not there is a time delay (and if so, how long) between management's recognition of a serious environmental threat to current strategy and the engagement of coping patterns. Janis and Mann's model infers that the engagement and deployment of coping patterns are automatic and subconscious – such that individual managers will not recognize their deployment. It follows that strategic inertia in the face of environmental threat may be widespread, and that specific recognition of the value of scenario planning to an increasing perceived threat and to facilitate strategic change may be lost.

In the next chapter, we will demonstrate how management teams, rather than individuals, can also become locked into pathological routines, which often spiral downwards until complete failure is inevitable. We will show how to address the causes of such 'process loss' within organizational dynamics and see that scenario planning also has components to promote process gain in organizational thinking.

How Organizations Think About the Future

CHAPTER 3

Whereas Chapter 2 focused on how people think about the future individually, we now turn to the ways that people act collectively in organizations. In this chapter, we outline how internal systemic forces in organizations act autonomously, 'locking in' the collective mindset, and discuss what can be done to change this situation and prepare for the future. An individual's insights cannot change a locked-in organization – this can only be addressed by *process gain*.

Overview

This is the second of three chapters focusing on 'decision flaws'. Whereas Chapter 2 reviewed flaws in personal thinking, and Chapter 4 will examine thinking flaws in communities due to tacit cultural assumptions, this chapter describes decision and action flaws due to *organizational dynamics*. In this chapter, we explain how:

- **Organizational thinking is often flawed** and, in particular, how systemic loops, if left to their own devices, will drive the organization into pathological states of either group-think or fragmentation.
- **Organizational identity**, based on stories about the past, determines how organizations lock in on frames for observations and decisions. No organization can make a complete break with the past, and it is impossible to decide anything except on the basis of what has been learned already.

CONTINUED... Overview

- Organizational intervention is needed, as there are decision and action flaws that cannot be addressed by rational reasoning and persuasion alone. Locked-in organizations cannot hear good advice from individuals who understand the problems. Individuals, being rational about things, cannot deal on their own with organizational flaws.
- **Observations point towards the need for good process to over come these problems.** This phenomenon of *process gain* underlies the advantages of the scenario planning approach.

FLAWS IN ORGANIZATIONAL THINKING

In Chapter 2, we explained how individuals make decisions using flawed thinking. Individual managers follow cognitive habits in their thought processes and behaviour – a situation known as *recipe following*. Our description of the waiter's dilemma illustrates the power of a bias towards confirmation in our thought processes. The waiter did not test the adequacy of his ability to identify the good tippers. He could only have done this by giving good service to those he thought would not leave a tip. So, if left alone, the waiter would unknowingly have misplaced confidence in his judgement. However, if someone had explained to the waiter the flaw in his thinking he could appreciate that his judgement may be flawed and would, perhaps, decide to test this possibility by giving good service to those he thought *unlikely* to leave a tip.

Other flaws in decision making are, perhaps, less amenable to such thought-led analysis. Consider our model of the relationship between the business environment and the strategic process, illustrated in Figure 2.1. Here, strategic inertia, shown by unconflicted adherence to a potentially failing strategy, is a product of hot cognitive processes. These processes reduce the stress of decision dilemmas and act subconsciously to establish mental equilibrium in the face of threats to the organization. Such hot processes are *not* amenable to change as a result of insightful advice or introspective thought.

In this chapter, we turn to the organizational context within which managers work. Do organizational structures and characteristics have an effect, positive or negative, on the prevalence of individual thinking flaws? Would a thoughtful manager's attempts to be more vigilant in his decision-making be helped or hindered by the organizational context?

Communication Difficulties

A well-known story that addresses this issue is the *Abilene paradox*[21]. Here, the author, Jerry Harvey, sketches out a scene in a house on a Sunday afternoon in Coleman, Texas. In the scene, the ambient temperature is hot, at 104°, and the wind is blowing fine-grained topsoil. However, the Sunday afternoon is tolerable with a cooling fan, cold lemonade and a game of dominoes to play. Dominoes is a slow, non-physical, unhurried game.

Suddenly, Jerry's father-in-law says, 'Let's drive to Abilene and have dinner at the cafeteria.' Jerry thinks, 'Why go to Abilene? Fifty-three miles in a dust storm and with this heat, in a non-air-conditioned Buick.' But his wife says, 'Sounds like a great idea, let's do it. How about you, Jerry?' Jerry replies, 'Sounds good to me, I just hope your mother-in-law wants to go too.' 'Of course I want to go,' she says. 'I haven't been to Abilene in a long time.'

So, the family went to Abilene in the heat, dust and a fine layer of perspiration, where they eat a terrible meal. On completing the long round trip, each of the family argues that they would not have gone if the others had not wanted to go. Even the father-in-law claims, 'I never wanted to go. I just thought you might be bored. I would have preferred to play dominoes, but you visit so seldom that I wanted to make sure you enjoyed the time with us.'

Jerry Harvey argues that the Abilene paradox is similar to many organizational paradoxes: choices are validated even though all the individuals concerned have reservations – they just aren't voiced. Individuals avoid conflict because conflict carries risk. In organizational life, confronting the issues and the individuals who hold opinions that you disagree with, carries the risk of loss of face or even one's job. So, if someone senior to you in the organization suggests that a 'trip to Abilene' is the favoured choice, then you are likely to vote for the choice. Interestingly, the senior's suggestion of the trip may not be his own preference, believing, perhaps wrongly, that it is a choice that you would favour if you were asked, and were assertive enough. The key issue is the lack of honesty in communicating thoughts and feelings.

The issues that face an organization are usually more serious. Choice of strategic direction is one such area of contention. What happens when individuals do begin to voice opposition? The behavioural processes invoked have been termed *group-think*.

Group-think in Organizations

The tendency of management teams to concur is an illustration of group-think. People with homogenous backgrounds often constitute management teams: for example, university degree holders, middle-class people and nationals of the country where the organization is based. Also, many will have families, mortgages and career paths, so they may be sensitive to the fact that to speak out may put one's job at risk. In high-consequence situations, such as major investment decisions, or discussions of strategic direction, the likelihood of dissenting voices being raised after the most senior person has stated their opinion is low. The likelihood of continuing dissent (at least overtly) is even lower. Irving Janis has remarked:

> *In my earlier research with ordinary citizens, I had been impressed by the effects – both unfavourable and favourable – of the social pressures that develop in cohesive groups . . . . Members tend to evolve informal objectives to reserve friendly intergroup relations, and this becomes part of the hidden agenda at meetings . . . Ordinary citizens become more concerned with retaining the approval of fellow members of their work group than with coming up with good solutions to the task in hand* [22].

Essentially, group-think is the suppression by the group (or management team) of ideas that are critical of the direction in which the group is moving. It is reflected in a tendency to concur with the position and views that are perceived as favoured by the group. Such cohesive groups tend to develop rationalizations for the invulnerability of the group's decision or strategy, and inhibit the expression of critical ideas by dissenting members of the management team. These pitfalls are likely to result in an incomplete survey of alternative courses of action or choices, resulting in a failure to examine the risks of preferred decisions.

One recent study, by Esser and Lindoerfer[23], analysed the decision to launch the space shuttle Challenger on 28 January 1986. The tragic outcome of that flight, the death of all seven crew members within minutes of launch, focused attention on the process leading to the decision to launch. The transcripts of the Presidential Commission report on the disaster highlighted positive and negative instances of the examples; causes and consequences of group-think. During the 24 hours before launch, the ratio of positive to negative interactions had increased significantly. Level III NASA management faced increasing difficulties in maintaining their flight schedule, and this was expressed as direct pressure on the dissenters who wanted to delay the flight (the engineers), and *mindguarding*.

Mindguarding refers to the removal of doubts and uncertainties in communications to others. In this instance, Level III NASA management told the engineers that they would report their concerns to Level II NASA management, but they failed to do so adequately.

Group-think results in a failure to thoroughly examine the risks of the preferred strategy and, consequently, a failure to work out contingency plans if the preferred course of action fails. High levels of both group cohesiveness and external threats are characteristic of group-think. In the case of the Challenger launch decision, a non-launch would have threatened public support for what had been promoted as a standard, almost routine operation.

Clearly, the processes underpinning the Abilene paradox and the results of group-think will tend to result in a self-selected group of individuals who will concur with one another. This concurrence could be shown in their commitment to a choice of strategic direction. In the case of Abilene, the concurrence will be unsubstantiated, while with the Challenger example, the concurrence will be real, but potentially flawed. In both cases, the behavioural consequences will be similar – a convergence of vocalized opinion.

As we outlined in Chapter 2, inappropriate escalation of commitment is likely to be a behavioural tendency if the chosen strategy begins to fail. This tendency, compounded by psychological coping mechanisms that reduce the stress of a failing strategy, will result in flawed, non-vigilant, thinking. Clearly, *social* processes in organizational life will tend to magnify individual managers' tendencies towards strategic inertia and business-as-usual framing, by providing a group-based commitment to a potentially failing course of action.

Fragmentation in Organizations

On the other hand, individuals and groups sometimes do manifest their dissent from an emerging consensus among others at the same or higher level of the organization. However, this emerging dissent is likely to be suppressed, with opinions present in the background – in informal exchanges rather than in formal meetings. Jerry Harvey lists the characteristics of conflict, and its subdued expression, within an organizational context where a dominant grouping's viewpoint is in the foreground (see box)[24]. As we saw in Chapter 1, this dominant viewpoint is characteristic of business-as-usual, within a previously successful mental model, or recipe, for success.

The expression/suppression of organizational conflict

- Organization members feel frustrated, impotent and unhappy when trying to deal with conflict. Many are looking for ways to escape. They may avoid meetings at which the conflict is discussed, they may be looking for other jobs, or they may spend as much time away from the office as possible by taking unnecessary trips, holidays or sick leave.

- Organization members place much of the blame for the dilemma on the boss or other groups. In backroom conversations among friends, the boss is termed incompetent, ineffective, out of touch, or a candidate for early retirement. To his face, nothing is said, or at best, only oblique references are made concerning his role in the organization's problems. If the boss isn't blamed, some other group, division or unit is seen as the cause of the trouble: 'We would do fine if it were not for the damn fools in Division X.'

- Small sub-groups of trusted friends and associates meet informally over coffee, lunch and so on to discuss organizational problems. There is significant agreement among the members of these sub-groups as to the cause of the troubles and the solutions that would be effective in solving them. Such conversations are frequently punctuated with statements beginning with, 'We should do . . .'

- In meetings where those same people meet with members from other sub-groups to discuss the problem, they soften their positions, state them in ambiguous language, or even reverse them to suit the positions apparently taken by others.

- After such meetings, members complain to trusted associates that they really didn't say what they wanted to say, but also provide a list of convincing reasons why the comments, suggestions and reactions they wanted to make would have been impossible. Trusted associates commiserate and say the same was true for them.

- Attempts to solve the problem do not seem to work. In fact, such attempts seem to add to the problem or make it worse.

- Outside the organization, individuals seem to get along better, be happier and operate more effectively than they do within it.

This unresolved, underground conflict is likely to lead to fragmentation within the organization. Fragmentation will be magnified if one group's views on an issue, or series of issues, holds the dominant position – perhaps the proponents of the dominant viewpoint hold senior positions high in the organizational hierarchy. In such circumstances, the other groups are more likely to focus on their own self-interests rather than showing support for the ideas held by the dominant group. At this point, the confirmation bias described in Chapter 2 ensures that the separate and differentiated groupings of opinions remain unchanged. In short, the enemy is seen to be firmly *within* the organization.

In extreme situations, the basis of the conflict cannot be discussed. Things can even become so difficult that this fact (that the basis of the conflict cannot be discussed) itself becomes taboo and beyond discussion[25]. Formal meetings between the warring factions are, themselves, non-controversial. By contrast, the opposing factions focus (in private meetings) on each other, as the organization sinks into decline.

LIMITATIONS IMPOSED BY IDENTITY

A third source of organizational thinking flaws results from identity assumptions that steer action. The relationship between external events observed by the organization, and the same organization's actions, is not one-to-one. An important intermediating mechanism in the process, leading from events to perception to action, is the organization's *identity*.

Balancing Change and Constancy

The external world is large, with far more signals than one can ever pay attention to. If an organization attempted to evaluate them all, it would be permanently in calculating mode and no decisions would ever be taken. Organizations solve this problem by using an effective shortcut, or filtering mechanism, that separates events that can be ignored from those that may be of interest. We call this the 'for us/not for us' filter. It is related to how members of the organization see their joint identity.

Every organization has stories about its history that people tell each other. Experience gained over time is expressed in accounts of what worked and what didn't when producing and marketing a product. These gradually provide a shared metaphorical meaning to the organization, on which people decide their roles. As we saw in Chapter 2, the stories gain status in the decision-making process in the form of 'recipes' which are shared and which steer action in the company (this is also evident, to a lesser extent, in a whole industry). The stories are of interest to everyone in the organization, as they are used to organize observations and to gain some degree of cognitive control over what is happening. If situations cannot be understood in this way then control is lost, and the organization ignores the signals. Hence, the total set of stories and recipes constitutes the 'for us/not for us' filter.

For example, a typical car-making culture will lead employees in automotive manufacturing to ignore news from the dairy industry. There are no stories to relate to; it is not for us. The effect of this is that events in the dairy industry do not reach consciousness in the car-making organization.

This is the organizational equivalent of personal 'frames of reference'. For example, scenario planners are often surprised to find how much coverage news-papers give to an issue they are currently working on. This emphasizes how much information escapes our attention, as our personal 'for us/not for us' filter makes us overlook information that does not seem relevant. Consider this story: a child is blowing up a balloon. At 23 breaths, the balloon keeps getting bigger and prettier. A pessimist warns that it is going to pop. The child does not listen and the warning does not penetrate. Its mental story is about making the balloon bigger, not about quitting. With its twenty-fourth breath, the pessimist was proven wrong: the balloon is prettier than ever. Again, with breath 25, the balloon is even prettier! At breath 26 the balloon pops. The child cries. It has lost control over the situation.

Similarly, in the organizational domain, a strong identity may serve an organization well, as long as it fits the underlying economic conditions. It simplifies decision-making, reduces the cost of search, and provides a feeling of control, which in turn reinforces the organization's identity. However, periods of stability are interspersed with bursts of change in the environment that invalidate the old recipes. An organization not used to looking over a broader terrain will experience loss of control: the balloon will burst. It will also lose its ability to find a way to regaining control. Most examples of organizational failure are concerned with organizations that were confirmed in their business-as-usual identity to a degree that made them ignore early signals of change. The 'pessimist' was not heard. But changes have an uncanny ability to happen rapidly, and to overwhelm organizations before readjustment is possible.

Organizational identity can frustrate and block necessary change. Organizational self-esteem requires that people defend the organization's identity. Acting inconsistently with one's own life story denies one's identity. However severe the situation, there is no motivation for taking actions that will threaten the accepted organizational identity. The dilemma is that we know what we are killing off, but are highly uncertain about what we are creating in its place. Potential winners are uncertain of their gains, while potential losers are certain of their losses. The latter will prevail. Options that are inconsistent with identity feel like a cure that is worse than the disease – they will not be acted upon. In such cases, people use many tactics to divert attention (as we saw in Chapter 2). Managers resist attacks on the identity of their organizations. An idea for an innovation that has no basis in the understood history of the company is seen as an attack, and will be strongly resisted (such as the launch of New Coke).

However, innovation and change are possible. We see it all around us. When change is perceived as consistent with the companies' historical identity, we see companies genuinely reinventing themselves – mostly triggered by economic pressure in times of adversity. This is apparent in large and small companies alike. IBM is a remarkable example of a large organization managing successful strategic change, by finding a strategy that, while fundamentally changing its business, could be seen to continue fundamental IBM values and strengths.

Our research has consistently showed that the issue of whether a change in strategy leads the organization into unknown territory is a subjective judgement, made by the people who share in the strategic conversation. This can be changed. The key is to maintain consistency between the change option and the identity. Although, theoretically, this might be achieved by discovering 'just the right plan', in most cases the fit is created by reinterpreting history and identity, in order to create consistency with the change plan, where it was not perceived to exist before. The principle involved is redefining the aspirations of the organization at a higher, superordinate level, which can act as an umbrella under which both the new and the old can be consistently connected.

Overcoming the Limits of Organizational Identity: the Example of IBM

IBM provides a good example. Traditionally, the company identified itself with its product – the mainframe computer. Anything that was not consistent with that was considered a sideline. This concept of its identity caused IBM to leave the future profit potential in distributed computing to other companies, like Microsoft and Intel; something they have undoubtedly regretted ever since. When distributed computing started to grow, and the mainframe market peaked and then started to decline, the company saw its results suddenly fall away. The solution was not immediately obvious. CEO Akers encouraged people in the company to experiment, but the solution to the problem did not emerge from this 'free for all' approach. This took a strategic decision to redefine the goal system of the company at a higher level, from supplying mainframe computers to supplying computing solutions. This was a typical *upframing* exercise. Asking why supplying mainframe computers had seemed

> **Change requires constancy. You cannot construct a building without a firm foundation. This foundation is the organization's *identity*, and much organizational failure can be traced back to an inability to reinterpret it in the context of a new business environment.**

such a good idea led to the articulation of the superordinate goal of, 'We were providing customers with effective computing solutions.'

The key point here is that solution-provision brings consultancy services under the umbrella of the company's identity as a mainstream activity, while under the 'mainframe computer supplier' identity, consultancy was only a subordinate service provision, and could not be perceived as the basis of saving the company, as it eventually proved to be. IBM had, over the years, built up consultancy strengths, but in a subordinate role, as support of its mainframe business, not as a business in its own right. The redefinition of its core business towards solutions allowed consultancy to be promoted from a sideline to a mainstream contributor to IBM's activities. This reconfiguration allowed the organization to exploit others strengths, such as brand and reputation for reliability, into a new business arena that met the needs in a market where customers were keen to find help they could trust. This new combination proved to be the answer, turning the organization into the powerful and successful player it is today.

ORGANIZATIONAL LOCK-IN

Understanding Organizational Lock-in

The reason why it is so difficult to deal with organizational flaws is the phenomenon of *lock-in*. Lock-in is a feature of systems that feed back on to themselves. Both individuals and organizations can be subject to lock-in. The waiter's behaviour described in Chapter 2 is an example of individual lock-in. The waiter's belief in his ability to identify good tippers is a typical example of a system feeding back on to itself. His theory-of-action leads him to do things that produce an experience that then reinforces this theory-of-action. The waiter cannot escape its flawed conclusions. Significantly, there is a huge difference between this problem occurring at the individual or the organizational level. It is easy to explain the problem to the waiter and help him to change. Assuming he is a rational individual, he will get the point and change his approach. Since the feedback loop lives in one individual mind, the person can break the loop and get out of the locked-in position.

Organizational lock-in is considerably more difficult to deal with. Group-think is clearly the result of a feedback loop. With the conversation in the group addressing a diminishing slice of reality, mental models become impoverished and, gradually, people only see what happens in the small slice. Consequently, the conversation becomes more and more focused. This also leads to lock-in, but the difference between this and the waiter's situation is that no single individual has the power to step out of it. Even if they potentially understand the problem, they cannot escape, as they are forced to spend all of their time in the narrowly-based conversation. They become victims of circumstances.

The Consequences of Organizational Feedback Loops and Lock-in

Organizational lock-in leads to people doing things they wouldn't want to do if they had all the information, and looked at the situation objectively. In an organization, an individual, however rational, does not have the power to change the loop on her own, even if she could be persuaded; there are so many others in the group who always pull them back. The people travelling to Abilene all understood the nonsense of what they were doing, but they could not stop themselves, they were locked-in.

The feedback loops that we are dealing with here can (potentially) move in two directions. The group can spiral into group-think, or away from it into fragmentation, due to the dynamics of the same organizational feedback system. Once the group is moving towards group-think, it is reducing its focus and conversation to encompass a diminishing part of reality and, consequently, mental models become depleted. Soon, people only see what happens in the small territory of their attention, which leads to a more and more focused conversation. One individual in the group cannot change the situation.

The same loop can work in the opposite direction. If people start drifting apart in their thinking they will have fewer meaningful conversations, which makes them all focus increasingly on their own interests, not on group interests. As a result, they have fewer joint experiences and their thinking drifts further apart. This is also a lock-in situation, in that one member in the group, even if she understands the situation, cannot change it on her own. In its pathological form, organizational fragmentation is extremely dangerous as it leads to organizational paralysis – an inability to take action. It will become apparent that there is no critical mass of support for any idea or proposal. Even top management cannot make things happen. People do the minimum that they can get away with, and it is only a matter of time before the organization unravels altogether.

Morgan[26] suggests that in most normal situations this locked-in thinking gradually assumes a shared metaphoric model for the organization, such as a machine, an organism, a prison, a war zone or a brain. This encourages people to define and understand their role in that context which, in turn, further locks the situation. Brains are better at learning than machines, and if you have decided you are a nerve wire in such a system, it makes sense to put energy into passing on signals you have received, internally or externally. Alternatively, machines are more efficient. Once you have decided that you are a cog in the wheel, there is no motivation to try to make an unsolicited contribution to the group. You just try to do your own little thing as accurately as possible. That is what makes the machine go round.

Such models, once entrenched, are extremely difficult to dislodge.

BEHAVIOURAL FLAWS

Learning and Action

The systems described lead to flawed behaviour in the organization as a whole. One example is the *execution* problem, when a sound strategic change that was generally agreed on is impossible to realize in practice due to difficult-to-understand organizational barriers. An established way of doing things seems locked in and most rational and powerful strategies do not seem to matter. Mintzberg[27] makes a distinction between 'intended' and 'emergent' strategies, and he makes the point that almost everything that happens on the ground seems emergent rather than intended.

Single-loop learning

In general, organizations locked into the machine metaphor show an emergent behaviour that can be described as *single-loop learning*. An analogy is that of a thermostat that scans and monitors its environment for changes in temperature. As the ambient temperature lowers, then the thermostat fires the boiler to increase heat. Once a required level of heat is achieved, the thermostat shuts down the boiler. Recall our example of Foster Brothers' menswear, and its dominant but outlived procurement strategy, discussed in Chapter 1. In the business-as-usual world view, the 'machine' carefully follows a recipe and small adjustments are made in response to perceived changes in the business environment to adhere to the predetermined blueprint. Just as the thermostat is incapable of insightful learning, so is the organization. Budgets are a manifestation of such single-loop learning, here, expenditure, sales and profits are monitored to ensure that the organization's activities follow a narrow path and are contained within pre-determined parameters.

Double-loop learning

By contrast, with *double-loop learning* the control system is intelligent and is able to question whether or not operating norms are appropriate. This happens in the 'brain'-type organization. Budgets are changed to allow for unexpected opportunities – for example, the granting of a new export licence may mean that new production equipment is bought that was not part of a previously set budget. With double-loop learning, operating procedures are changed in response to emerging situations. But all in this world is not perfect either. The brain organization tends to be more chaotic and much less efficient than the machine. If the organization is of some size, fragmentation always looms around the corner, with its resulting strategic paralysis.

The circumstances will determine which metaphor will survive. In a fast-changing environment – such as the dot-com boom of the late 1990s – 'machines' had a problem competing. In a more traditional industrial environment, however, efficiency is a winning streak.

An Organizational Dilemma

This situation poses a fundamental dilemma. On the one hand, we like the strength that comes with the efficiency of a solid 'machine' model, with single-loop control. However, we also want the organization to adapt quickly and smoothly to external change, and this comes with the double-loop learning of the 'brain' model. This is the paradox. Group action requires a degree of consensus, or at least accommodation, of different views, before action can result. The more that the members of a group agree with each other, aligning their individual mental models, the stronger their joint action will be. The experience that results from joint action causes the group to learn about the outside world together, on the basis of which new decisions can be made and new actions taken that lead to further learning – and so the process continues. However, consensus focuses on, and reinforces, the business-as-usual mental model. The tunnel vision that comes with business-as-usual makes it difficult or impossible for the organization to perceive signals of unexpected change from unexpected quarters. Without such signals, swift and effective adaptation in the double-loop learning mode is impossible.

A balance therefore needs to be found between these two desirable, but mutually contradictory, goals. There is strong evidence that this does not happen naturally. Systems theory will predict that a system with such a strong, positive feedback loop (as explained above) is unstable, and will, if left to its own devices, develop a locked-in position. This will be at one of the two pathological extremes: group-think, with its tiny organizational radar screen, or fragmentation, with its resulting paralysis. The situation requires active management to keep the system at a healthy mid-point.

Management and Action

Even if all these problems can be overcome, and a reasonable balance can be found between exploration and exploitation of the organization, there still is no guarantee that conclusions, however valid, will be translated into action. Pettigrew and Whipp[28] argue that awareness of an environmental imperative is not enough to make an organization take action: other conditions need to be in place. The absence of any of these can effectively kill off the change project.

On the basis of extensive research, Pettigrew and Whipp suggest that there is an observable difference in the way that successful organizations manage change, compared to their worse-performing counterparts. They also see a pattern emerging in the actions taken by the higher-performing organizations. There seems to be five key, inter-related activities and conditions that contribute to successful management of change.

1. **Environmental assessment of the need for change**, providing the business logic for the change project. Without a critical mass of understanding in the organization of *why* change is necessary, it is unlikely to occur.
2. **Leading change**, with champions emerging at critical times to drive forward the project. Change projects tend to be pushed back in management's attention by the pressures of the day-to-day. Unless a champion is available to put the project back on to the agenda it may well be scuppered for ever.
3. **Linking strategic and operational change**, including the ability to manage the change project over time. A weakness in many change projects is the failure by management to express the project in sufficiently concrete and detailed terms to make people in the organization aware of what is required from them, as individuals, in its execution.
4. **Linking the management and development of the total skill base of the organization with the change process.** Change is created by people. Not only does the project need to be expressed in sufficiently concrete terms to allow people to play their role, but they must also be empowered for this. This has organizational implications, including training of individuals and groups, information flows and so on.
5. **Creating management coherence on the change project.** If there is one reason why change projects fail it is mixed signals from the top of the organization. It is fundamental that management has one coherent view concerning the project.

So far, in this chapter, we have discussed the first and the last of these factors, and the conditions under which change and adaptation do not happen. These are the areas in which scenario planning has the biggest impact. It is important to remember, however, that effective leadership, project management and motivational management are also essential conditions, without which all organizational effort will come to nothing.

An exercise

As we have seen in this chapter, overt questioning of larger-scale strategic direction, where conflict is likely to be engendered, is the exception rather than the rule. This may be due to group-think or fragmentation in an organization. The realities of organizational life do not encourage the dissenting manager to speak out and question the prevailing wisdom. This phenomenon is systemic, meaning it is unintentional. However, the dire consequences are very real, as we saw in Chapter 1. The need for such questioning is clear in all organizations, 'machines' and 'brains' alike, and is illustrated by many case histories of organizational failure.

We recommend that you consider situations in your own organization when, even at the highest levels, individual insights seem to evaporate as soon as people are back in their day-to-day work situations. In evaluating them, would you describe the problem as group-think or fragmentation?

OVERCOMING THE PATHOLOGIES OF ORGANIZATIONAL LIFE

What, then, can be done to encourage the debate and questioning of prevailing world views within the organization? How can group-think tendencies, or fragmentation, in the management team and the organization at large be alleviated? There is clearly a leadership need here. The solution lies with the leader of the organization. Common sense argues that, to overcome group-think, the leader should:

- withhold his own ideas at first,
- encourage new ideas and criticisms;
- make sure that the group listens to minority views;
- use processes designed to prevent the management team from forming an early consensus.

But how do you achieve this? Individuals in the organization, including senior managers, will seldom have the power to move the existing orthodoxy on their own. The underlying assumptions and metaphorical models exercise too much power over people's minds.

Using Organizational Processes

The most powerful instrument that leaders have is intervening to make process changes. The phenomenon of process gain is real and significant, in that organizational change can be created on the basis of process change, but this is not an overnight exercise. Process gain requires persistence and consistency over an extended period.

Michael[29] has thought about *how* a leader can change the basic assumptions that stand in the way of open communication in organizations. He suggests that the main responsibility of senior management should be to create an environment in which people feel able and committed to participate in the learning process. In this type of culture, scenario thinking and strategic conversations will thrive. As a result, people will pull together and accommodate each others' needs and wishes; the corporate needs will surface and be acknowledged. In short, the whole organization will pull together to form a genuine learning organization.

The Benefits of Scenario Planning Interventions

Scenario planning contains key components to overcome the pathology of organizational life, and to promote effective exchange of opinions and beliefs among a management team. The construction of multiple futures is a basis for airing differing opinions about the nature of the future, and provides a forum for the debate, questioning and synthesis of complementary, contrasting and conflicting viewpoints. Those enmeshed in particular fragments of the organization are provided with a process that can achieve a synthesis of viewpoints which is likely to unite previously opposed factions.

The scenario process combines space for differentiation of views with integration of views towards a synthesis through the strategic conversation implicit in it. In this way it assists management in steering the organization away from the excesses of group-think on the one hand, and fragmentation on the other, towards a more balanced position in between, where not only strategic thinking takes place, but the future is reconciled with the past, so that action results in experience-based organizational learning.

> **Scenario planning by itself cannot overcome organizational flaws, and other essential ingredients include motivational leadership and process management. However, scenarios can be extremely helpful. If the intent is there, together with persistence and consistency, significant progress can be made.**

SUMMARY: HOW ORGANIZATIONS THINK ABOUT THE FUTURE

This chapter has explained how organizational thinking is flawed and how organizational identity, based on stories about the past, determines how observations and decisions are framed by organizations. As a result, organizations are effectively locked in to a view of their own identity and the past, rather than developing a more dynamic, realistic assessment of the future. The limitations of thinking in organizations result in the business idea (see Chapter 1) – the reason for success – being eroded and left without replacement. As we discussed in Chapter 1, internal factors can easily and frequently combine with external situations to erode the business idea. These limitations include the limited rationality within which decisions are taken: learned routines of behaviour and thinking that lock people in to a single view of the world, known as inertia. The social dynamics within an organization can create extremes of behaviour, from *fragmentation* to excessive integration of views or *group-think*.

- *Fragmentation* exhibits no consistent or coherent view of the purpose of the organization.

- *Group-think* manifests a shared mental model that is so strong, often delusional, that it leaves little scope to challenge the existing view.

Much of this behaviour is guided by tacit knowledge within a group of managers, and affects the way that the organization manages its environment and the future. Rather than developing proactive responses to environmental change, these limitations result in managerial blind spots and inertia, locking management in to an obsolete world view. Eventually, the organization will face strategic drift, gradually, if imperceptibly, moving away from a fit with their environment and customers. The occurrence of organizational systemic lock-in is a powerful force that can limit an organization's ability to learn and adapt to environmental change. The forces for organizational systemic lock-in act as filters that restrict or prevent signals for change from entering into managerial discussions or wider strategic conversations. Significantly, the scenario process can help organizations overcome these limitations, introducing novelty and encouraging thinking beyond a single view of the world.

> Developing and analysing multiple futures promotes a responsive and effective strategy, delivering control in an uncertain and rapidly changing environment.

Managers may not realize that their organization is suffering from such a phenomenon. It may be that a manager feels uncertain about the future, or an intuitive need for management development. Regardless of the catalyst, scenario thinking is a powerful mechanism for learning and change in organizations. In reality, locked-in organizations cannot be changed simply by good advice from individual leaders who may see the situation and understand the problems. The solution is effective organizational intervention, as there are decision and action flaws that cannot be addressed by rational reasoning and persuasion alone. The advantage of the scenario planning approach is that it points towards a solution to these issues, providing the opportunity for process gain.

In this chapter, we have focused on flaws affecting strategic decision-making and management actions due to organizational dynamics. In Chapter 4, we will examine thinking flaws in communities, due to tacit cultural assumptions.

The Impact of Culture and Cultural Assumptions on Strategy

CHAPTER 4

One challenge encountered by managers is to ensure that the costly errors of traditional strategies are avoided. *Cultural insensitivities* and *inappropriate assumptions* can be potential pitfalls: understanding subtle, complex and often unpredictable cultural values needs a skilful approach. In this chapter, we will explore how scenario thinking is the most effective way apply to understand cultural diversity, and look at its impact on organizational activity and strategy.

Overview

This chapter will review the types of problems that arise due to conflicting organizational cultures and look at what can be done, using a scenario-based approach, to resolve them. Examining the issue of culture at a macro-level, where differences are perceived across national cultures, as well as at the micro-, organizational level, highlights how conflicting cultures cause obstacles for strategy development. Using case studies, this chapter will explore:

- **Cultural diversity in its political, cultural and organizational forms.** Developing long-term, sustainable business relationships depends on an ability to understand the values and beliefs that underpin cultural differences.

CONTINUED ... Overview

- The cultural impact on organizations of globalization and localization. Differences in culture will inevitably impact organizational success. Ignoring local differences has proven to be a costly mistake for many organizations.
- **Conflicting cultures between professional groups.** Professional groups develop different values during education and professional development, and this frames their thinking and approach. Groups are further divided by language: jargon excludes other groups, while shared words may possess different meanings, leading to confusion.
- Models for cultural analysis. Developing appropriate models, using multiple perspectives, enables organizations to move beyond cultural preconceptions. Cultural differences are not clear-cut; many influences are evident. It is important to address these issues using methods that, in challenging our own preconceptions, can move towards a better understanding of others. This will help to avoid the costly trial-and-error learning that erodes the profitability of many companies.
- **The application of scenario thinking, enabling the exploration of different potential cultural responses.** Scenario thinking is best suited to deal with the complexity of cultural influences. The unpredictability of conflicting cultures necessitates a strategic approach which assumes that outcomes cannot be guaranteed. By assessing cultural responses in a non-threatening, rehearsed and controlled way, outcomes of possible future histories can be fully anticipated and preparations made.

UNDERSTANDING THE IMPACT OF CULTURAL ISSUES

Culture can be defined as 'The total set of socially determined tacit assumptions that the group shares about how the world works but does not articulate to each other'[30].

Managing the culture of an organization so that, for example, it is constantly looking to improve, possesses a positive, blame-free atmosphere, or values continuous improvement and organizational learning, is often difficult to achieve. This is because of the *tacit* nature of culture: the fact that it conceals its presence and significance, and is so intangible as to defy obvious management techniques. However, significant problems can arise within organizations, caused by conflicting cultures creating blockages at the organizational and professional level. In Chapter 3, we explored the problems arising from locked-in organizational issues, such as fragmentation. An appreciation of how cultural factors affect the outcomes of such developments is essential if their potential to seriously damage the organization is to be avoided.

The Significance to Strategy of Globalization and Cultural Issues

The emergence of the new 'global culture' and of the 'shrinking world' has received a mixed response. Some view the move towards greater globalization as positive, while others see the spread of global products and values as a negative influence. Globalization could be regarded as inevitable. However, the increasing fragmentation observed today in the world, with the resurgence of interest in local cultures, products, history and heritage, would seem to mitigate this argument. Furthermore, anti-capitalists are opposed to *any* increase in globalization.

This may seem a rather abstract and irrelevant commentary for a strategy book focusing on the value of scenarios. However, possessing a mechanism through which organizations can assess the outcomes of conflicting views will help them to identify signals, appropriate responses and steer policy to gain competitive advantage. Knowing which belief or direction will prevail cannot always be predicted – indeed, different ideas can exist simultaneously, and it is important to understand the balance that exists between them. Being able to recognize changes is not as simple as waiting for events to be reported. More importantly, the challenge facing management is being prepared for any eventuality in cultural convergence or conflict. If policy is being formed for the first time in response to an event, the organization may have lost a valuable source of competitive advantage to those who anticipated the event. They are in a weakened position, which their competitors can exploit.

> **Possessing the ability to assess the outcomes of conflicting views will help managers to identify signals and appropriate responses to situations – and steer a course through a constantly shifting business environment.**

The reality is that are multiple cultures co-exist, with some degrees of overlap and convergence, but some conflict and divergence. However, any coalitions and alignments of cultures are not static; they are constantly changing and being redefined. Arguably, the situation today is less predictable and more rapidly and easily changed than at previous times. In the aftermath of the terrorist attacks on the World Trade Center and the Pentagon on 11 September 2001, there has been a redefinition at a global level of the terms 'friend' and 'foe'. Some of these realignments of relationships may be indicative of longer-term trends, while some represent short-term and pragmatic expediency.

It is relevant to question the longevity and nature of any 'new' world order. Moreover, scenarios are not concerned with the rights or wrongs of any predictions. They are primarily concerned with ensuring organizational robustness if such changes were to occur. Changes in attitudes are not unique; they cannot be predicted in advance with absolute confidence, and they are certainly not permanent.

This chapter will illustrate the issues that affect culture, where differences distinguish, and often separate, groups. We will then outline models that will enable management to understand the significance of differences across and between cultures, as they affect organizational performance.

From Mickey Mouse to The Lion King: the Tale of Disney in France

Background[31]

The Walt Disney Organization has enjoyed considerable success through its theme parks. The concept of the original park in California presented 'an idealized vision of America spiced with reassuring glimpses of exotic cultures all calculated to promote heart-warming feelings about living together as one happy family'[32]. The success of the original concept was repeated in the 1970s with the development of Disney World in Florida; in the 1980s, the formula was successfully transferred to Japan. In the late 1980s, Disney executives turned their attention to Europe. Basing their decision on demographic factors and subsidies, Paris was chosen as the location for the next theme park. There was considerable competition from 200 other locations around the world, all offering a variety of pleas and cash inducements in support of their bids. The French government offered $1 billion in various incentives, in the expectation that 30 000 jobs would be created. For Disney, there was the attraction of a potential market of 17 million customers within two hours' driving time, and another 310 million only a short flight away. Both parties entered into negotiations with heightened expectations and optimism. However, culture clashes rapidly developed, creating an acrimonious tone for negotiations. Disney executives became frustrated by what they saw as the slow pace of talks.

A difficult start

French intellectuals voiced their disgust at the construction of 'a cultural Chernobyl' in a city with a history of sophisticated culture. The French Minister of Culture announced he would boycott the opening of this 'unwelcome symbol of American clichés and consumer society'. Despite these negative comments, the summer of 1992 saw the opening of the £5 billion EuroDisney complex. Soon, the entrances were blockaded by French farmers, not in specific protest at Disney, but in response to a US government call for cuts in subsidy levels to French agriculture. This globally televised protest focused attention on what Hill terms[33] 'the loveless marriage of Disney and Paris'. In addition to these external factors, there were a number of internal issues that highlighted Disney's lack of cultural awareness in the design and operation of the park.

Customers

Disney's policy of not serving alcohol caused astonishment in a culture where wine with lunch and dinner is commonplace. Also, relying on intelligence that 'Europeans do not take breakfast', they provided for a small number of continental breakfasts; they were unprepared for an influx of several thousand customers wanting to be served bacon and eggs in a 350-seat restaurant.

Staff

In addition to the problems faced with customers, Disney also faced problems with staff. In trying to promote the same teamwork model that they used in the USA and Japan, the organization ran into opposition to what was viewed as its 'brainwashing' approach. Nearly 1000 new employees, 10% of the total workforce, left during the first nine weeks. As one disgruntled ex-employee noted, 'I don't think that they realize what Europeans are like . . . that we ask questions and don't all think the same way'[34].

A different customer base

Disney was also unprepared for different customer attitudes. While these cultural differences were inconvenient, the major problem that reduced revenues was that Europeans viewed theme parks differently. In the USA, Disney was accustomed to visitors spending extended vacations in their luxury hotels. Conversely,

Europeans regarded a theme park as a day trip or, at best, a short break. From the outset, Disney attracted almost nine million visitors a year; however, the luxury hotels remained at half capacity, representing a huge loss on investment. To compound the problem, less than 40% of the visitors were French; many customers were Americans living in or visiting Europe, or were Japanese tourists on European tours. Neither group chose to stay in the hotels for extended periods during their vacations.

A new strategy

By the end of 1994, EuroDisney had lost $2 billion and Disney executives decided that a change of approach was necessary. Several significant changes were made:

- The park was renamed Disneyland Paris to strengthen its identity.
- Provision of food was changed. It was discovered that, while customers sought French-style food, they wanted American-style self-service.
- An initial redesign of fashion goods was based upon a change from the American product to a more understated French style, and a further redesign followed later to restore a more definite Disney image.
- Finally, prices were cut across the board, both for admissions to the park and for the hotels.

As a result, the number of visitors rose from a low of 8.8 million in 1994 to 11.7 million in 1996.

The lessons learned

The early story of Disneyland Paris appears to indicate a failure of the Disney organization to align its new European operation with the cultural needs and expectations of the European market. However, after consideration of the situation, it is questionable how far Disney could have predicted the effects of cultural differences with complete accuracy. This does not imply that, given this inaccuracy, organizations should not attempt to make predictions: quite the contrary. Rather, by exploring possible futures and how different cultures will impact the different scenarios, organizations are better prepared for a multitude of outcomes, regardless of their inability to predict exactly which outcomes will occur.

> **To develop long-term, sustainable business relationships, it is essential to understand the values and beliefs that underpin different cultural factors.**

For example, it was unlikely that Disney could have predicted that customers would demand a combination of French-style food and American-style service. Perhaps it was naive to assume that the norm in the USA would be successful in Europe. Alternatively, assuming that Disney could have found one 'correct' approach to cultural understanding to act as a basis for design may be more naive. Realistically, the dynamics of conflicting cultures would suggest that only a *series of possibilities* could be discovered. Each should be considered equally valid, necessitating further investigation, testing and analysis. This is both the essence of scenario planning and its strength.

The case of EuroDisney highlights a number of obvious culture clashes: from simple matters like drinks preferences to more complex issues such as employee expectations of management. There is a clear attempt to transpose the tried and tested formula from one culture into another, with the consequent rejection by the recipient culture. There is no evidence of an emerging 'global village' in which the all-pervading products of global brands are universally accepted. Neither do we see outright rejection and retrenchment into separate worlds. What is noticeable is the gradual blend of these two aspects: acceptance of goods and services that appear to be universal, alongside pragmatic modification and adaptation by the provider in order to align with the specific needs and demands of the customer. While these issues are raised at an international level, in this chapter we focus on how they are relevant at the micro-level of an organization.

> Understanding a series of *possibilities* can prepare for a new initiative where the outcome is vital, yet uncertain. The benefit is not in guessing the right one: the real benefit lies in analysing options and testing assumptions. This leads to the development of an informed view – and this approach is at the heart of scenario planning.

We are usually aware of cultural differences at the macro-, national level and the surface level, regarding language, religion and social structure. However, we often remain unclear of the fundamental values and beliefs underpinning the thoughts and actions of others. At worst, we ignore the surface-level manifestations of culture by expecting others to conform to our own standards of language, religious belief and social interaction. At best, we may attempt to understand or conform to these surface manifestations, learning the language of others or attempting to fit in with behavioural norms. Unfortunately, without

> The dynamics of conflicting cultures result in a series of possible outcomes, all requiring assessment. Each possibility must be considered equally valid, necessitating further investigation.

engaging with the *fundamental* values and beliefs that underpin all these issues, we risk failing to establish the types of understanding that will lead to the development and support of sustainable, long-term business relationships.

DEFINING CULTURE FOR PRAGMATIC PURPOSES

Geert Hofstede defines culture as 'the collective programming of the mind, which distinguishes the members of one group or category of people from another'[35]. Hofstede extends this core definition to cover 'national culture', as the programming induced 'by growing up in a particular country'. These definitions of culture are based upon the recognition of differences. As we have seen with Disney, the lack of appreciation of differences caused many problems. It could be argued that the development of cultural awareness would eliminate problems. However, concentrating on differences in intercultural working can also cause many problems – both across different national cultures at the level of international business, and across different social and disciplinary cultures at the local or organizational level. This leaves management with a seemingly insurmountable task.

Recognizing Differences in Others

There are a variety of problems that exist in the intercultural business environment. There are obvious problems related to differences in language, religion, beliefs and values that are easily recognized, allowing us the opportunity to address them or ignore them. The growth of business globalization and the universal recognition of brands and products means that similarities in appearance can often obscure the different fundamental values and beliefs of others. For example, conducting meetings with counterparts who wear the same clothes, use the same laptops and arrive in similar cars can mislead us into thinking that they share the same value systems. In today's business environment, organizations cannot afford to judge others either by appearance or by our own standards in business.

At a basic level, we often regard the differences between countries as the starting point for addressing cultural aspects. However, as Hofstede[36] points out, nations are relatively recent human inventions, introduced on a global scale only in the last century. Many nation states that exist today are largely based upon the colonialism of those powerful nations that carved up the world map. For this reason, national boundaries can often bear little or no resemblance to the social groups that the population identifies with – groupings that are more entrenched. The conflict that erupted following the break-up of the artificially created state of Yugoslavia demonstrates the explosive potential of concentrating on cultural differences.

Even where we acknowledge differences and resolve to address them, we may fall into the trap of making unsophisticated generalizations about other cultures. Typically, we start our assessment without appreciating that it is influenced by our own *collective programming*. The open-minded and enlightened Western business person may feel the need to become acquainted with the culture of the 'Far East' in the hope that a greater understanding of this culture will be conducive to a better business relationship. However, it is important to recognize that, as *The Financial Times*[37] pointed out in 1995, there is no single culture in Asia, and that:

there is much diversity to south east Asia than might first appear in most simple terms

Moreover, even if they learn that the cultural differences are more complicated than simply looking at one national stereotype, they are likely to remain ignorant of the many cultural influences that differentiate themselves from others – geographically, socially and intellectually.

The Value of Scenarios in Assessing the Impact of Cultural Factors

While, as individuals, we may make generalizations about cultures – for example, how Western cultures are rational and scientifically oriented, while African cultures are subjective and person-oriented – we often fail to see the subtle differences that exist within these generalizations. Clearly, our assumptions have the potential to influence our findings, therefore, questioning these starting assumptions will help us to arrive at more refined conclusions.

Managers need to review in some detail the following aspects of cultural awareness:

- how we recognize differences between cultures;
- how we determine which elements of products, services and processes are transferable across cultures and which are not;
- how we manage relationships, particularly with customers, across cultural boundaries.

The scenario process is best placed to identify the range of possible and plausible cultural interactions and to assess their impact on decision-making and analysis.

Scenarios allow us to:

- surface different understandings of our situation from multiple cultural perspectives;
- investigate the interactions among driving forces;
- test out different plausible and possible outcomes – depending on the different ways in which various stakeholders and their own cultural programming and preferences will play out.

Within the context of the scenario planning process and its implementation, there are further factors that must be considered. Alongside an appreciation of cultural impact in an external context, it is essential to surface the problems in an internal context:

- What are the national, organizational or professional beliefs and values of different individuals and groups within the scenario team?
- What are the power dynamics of, for example, senior and junior members in teams working within different cultural settings?
- What are the differences in interpretation, intent and meaning across group members?

NATIONAL CULTURAL DIFFERENCES AND THE ROLE OF SCENARIO THINKING

Global Organizations and Local Service Offerings: IKEA Shelve Their Universal Approach

Background

Since its establishment in Sweden in the 1940s, IKEA has grown into a global organization selling typically Swedish products. The organization sees itself as existing in – and as part of – the national cultures of countries as diverse as Russia and Kuwait, Canada and Malaysia. Specific national websites demonstrate the individuality of the dispersed business units, yet the organization emphasizes that 'it is no accident that the IKEA logo is blue and yellow. These are the colours of the Swedish flag'[38]. The products are intrinsically Swedish, yet are tailored to the markets in which they are delivered. They are both generic and particular.

Building upon its success in its home market, IKEA expanded rapidly across Europe during the 1970s and 1980s. It sold the same products in the same way, and broke some key principles of retailing. Some of these rules are now broken universally, such as telling the customer that 'we flatpack our products because it is easier and cheaper for *us* to transport and store them' – seemingly ignoring the rule of 'putting the customer first'.

The American problem

When IKEA expanded into North American markets in the 1980s, it discovered that there was no single formula that would sell universal products across the global marketplace. In contrast to its experiences in Europe, the organization's new stores in North America did not become rapidly profitable. IKEA learned the hard way that the emergence of global markets and the acceptance of ideas and concepts across cultures does not lead to the delivery of universal solutions. In North America, IKEA realised that it had to blend its traditional Swedish design and low-cost offerings with context-specific responses to customer needs and wishes. For example, IKEA changed its offerings to include chests of drawers with deeper drawers in the US market, in order to accommodate more knitwear. Further, to better suit customer preferences, king- and queen-sized beds were offered, being dimensioned in inches rather than centimetres. By 1997, nearly half of IKEA's offerings in the US market were sourced locally, and nearly one-third of its total product offerings were designed exclusively for the US market. Similarly, in recently opened branches in Russia, the products shown on the website vary from those shown for other European countries.

The lessons learned

IKEA's approach clearly demonstrates that:

- the growth of business across cultures cannot be based on universal solutions;
- despite becoming more international and eclectic in our tastes, we can still be very particular and localized in those tastes.

IKEA is not unique in applying this mix of generalization and localization to its products and services. As the giants of the motor industry seek more generalizations of products (such as engines, transmissions and floorpans) across models, brands and countries, they also recognize the need for diversity to suit local tastes. In developing the Focus as an international car model, Ford has addressed the failings of its earlier attempts to offer the Escort as a

> **A successful global strategy must offer context-specific responses to local customer preferences.**

universal product. The model may be the same, but the product has differences – such as trim and suspension settings – to suit both different tastes across markets and different pragmatic needs, based upon environmental conditions. Similarly, MTV has moved from being a universal provider of 24-hour music on television to exploiting differences in local markets. In Europe, MTV now provides different language stations; this not only allows it to meet local demands, but also allows it to tap into local advertising markets and to generate additional revenues locally.

At a time of business globalization and the apparent convergence of cultures at the surface level – with universal brands such as Sony, McDonald's, IKEA and CNN – successful strategies also allow for increased variety and differentiation. Successful global companies operate with generic competencies and brands, but offer bespoke solutions within particular contexts. This is in order to align with local needs and demands that are largely driven by cultural differences. To successfully deliver such solutions, organizations need to engage with the members of a particular community or society; by understanding tastes and standards of expectation and acceptability, the needs and desires of its members can be determined. This requires an understanding of the criteria that will underpin proactive design of acceptable products, rather than receiving negative reactions to unacceptable offerings. At a basic level, this understanding can avoid the mistake of trying to sell hamburgers in Islamic countries, where the consumption of ham is forbidden under Islamic law. At a deeper level, it facilitates more productive relationships, based on mutual understanding and respect. This does not require convergence towards a set of shared values and an expectation of similarity, but rather an overt acceptance of divergence and a willingness to 'agree to differ' in a state of 'creative conflict'.

The key questions for managers are:

- How can I understand the values that are held by others?
- How can I understand the values I hold?
- How do we then share understanding of these values, building a successful working relationship?

How Can We Explore Differences in National Cultures?

In considering cultural differences across nations, it is important to remember that nations are artificial entities, constructed by some societies and imposed upon others. Those who constructed them are more likely to recognize the boundaries as meaningful, while those that have the boundaries imposed on them are less likely to regard them as such. As we consider those generalizations that are used to distinguish cultures – to recognize the distinctions of a nation's values and norms – we must also recognize the internal variations that distinguish groups and individuals within nations. To complicate the situation, we must also consider the effects of increasing migration across nations and continents.

In exploring the differences in values that would affect behaviour within organizations, Hofstede conducted extensive research into the cross-cultural aspects of IBM across 72 countries, involving 116 000 questionnaires in 20 languages. Hofstede proposed a number of categories that could be used to illustrate differences in values across nations, and these will be discussed in the following sections.

Power distance
This is a measure of the interpersonal power or influence between two individuals, as perceived by the less powerful. This dimension focuses on attitudes in society to inequality in power and influence, and whether this is accepted and allowed to grow, or downplayed. High power distance is characterized by hierarchy, while low power distance is more egalitarian and delayered.

Uncertainty avoidance
This is the degree to which individuals feel uncomfortable with uncertainty. In high uncertainty-avoidance cultures, individuals place great store on job security and continuity, regard for rules and regulation, and the minimization of uncertainty and ambiguity. In low uncertainty-avoidance cultures, there is a greater readiness to take risks and a lower emotional resistance to change.

Individualism and collectivism
This is whether the individual within the group context is concerned primarily with self-orientation and self-sufficiency, or if individuals subordinate personal interest to the greater good of the group. In individualistic cultures, there are looser social ties between individuals, whereas collectivist cultures show more regard for the extended family and the duty of every member to look after the interests of the group, rather than his own interests.

Masculinity and femininity

This is whether the society places emphasis on the acquisition of material posses-sions and on individual achievement, or emphasizes the quality of life and interdependence. In masculine cultures, the male role is sharply differentiated from the female role, with the cultural 'ideals' based upon male characteristics of achievement and the effective exercise of power. Feminine cultures show less differentiation between roles; both genders work in the same jobs and are less competitive and aggressive.

Hofstede identified major differences in values and attitudes across nation-alities. He found countries with high power distance, such as India and the Philippines, in which management styles are autocratic and based upon the legitimacy of position. In low power distance countries, such as the UK and Australia, management styles were more dependent upon interpersonal bargain-ing, with less concern for hierarchy. He identified countries with low uncertainty avoidance, such as Denmark and Sweden, where members of society are socialized into accepting and coping with uncertainty and ambiguity. In other societies, such as France and Greece, there is stronger uncertainty avoidance, with greater nervousness and emotionality around future uncertainty. Within Anglo-Saxon countries, such as Canada and New Zealand, he found strong individualism, whereas most Asian countries, including Korea and Indonesia, show high collectivist tendencies. Finally, he differentiated countries with very high masculinity indices, such as Japan and Venezuela, from those with very high femininity indices; for example, Denmark and the Netherlands.

Hofstede's work gives us a general framework for looking at differences across cultures, identifying what drives others to think and act in the way that they do. For example, it enables us to engage with the question of why a Japanese business person would seek to reduce the degree of uncertainty within any negotiation; have regard for the formal role and status of individuals and their achievement; and be concerned with the collective of the organization. In contrast, a Swedish negotiator would express lower regard for status and hierarchy; show greater concern for individual emotional well-being; and be more comfortable with uncertainty about the future.

There are some obvious criticisms of this research. It only studied one organization within one industry, where the organization's values could have been superimposed. Also, Hofstede himself would have been influenced by his own European cultural preprogramming, with European and American values potentially steering the investigation. It is certainly questionable whether a group of European and American researchers, investigating their own values within an organization that espoused many of these values, could produce anything other than stereotypical judgements on the values of others. Notwithstanding these criticisms, Hofstede's work provides some clear models for helping us to engage with differences of values and beliefs across groups – whether at the national or organizational level. General conceptualizations of differences in cultures can be used to provide a basis for investigating the conflicts and differences managers face when dealing with individuals – whether or not we agree that these fit within a general framework that defines national characteristics.

DIFFERENCES IN ORGANIZATIONAL CULTURES

A Clash of Personality: The Merger of Daimler-Benz and Chrysler[39]

Background

In May 1998, the announcement of the impending merger between two of the world's major automotive manufacturers, the USA Chrysler Corporation and Germany's Daimler-Benz, elicited mixed reactions. For some commentators, the two companies would 'complement each other in terms of product range and international coverage'[40]. Some saw the merger as logical, enabling luxury attributes to be extended to other models[41]. However, the major test of the merger would be how the two organizations would deal with issues of culture difference: blending the cautious culture of the German firm with the 'swashbuckling' style of its American partner[42]. Problems were expected to arise from stereotypical differences between national cultures – Germans were reputed to be disciplined, punctual and industrious, while Americans were reputed to be more informal and action-oriented. Interestingly, one commentator[43] suggested that these stereotypes were unreliable. He recounted his personal experience of German disorder, lateness, casual approach and extended holidays, suggesting that 'Germans and Americans are very much alike . . . and (would) get along just fine'. Since Daimler-Benz already operated its own plant in the USA, some felt that 'national differences or communication problems (were) less likely to cause corporate conflict than car-making cultures'[44]. In fact, it was the difference between *organizational* cultures that was to prove problematic.

The organizational cultures

Initial senior-level meetings in December 1998 had shown some signs of conflict in the formal sessions, but both groups were brought together in social activities. Within a year of the merger, however, the situation had deteriorated. It appeared that Daimler was firmly in control of Chrysler, with former Daimler-Benz chief Jurgen E. Schrempp at the helm. There was open conflict between members of the two organizations, owing to cultural differences. For example:

- While Daimler board members had executive assistants who prepared briefing papers on key issues, Chrysler members had no designated assistants, preferring to talk directly to engineers and designers.
- The Daimler approach to decision ratification involved working through the bureaucratic process until top management gave a decision that was then cast in stone. The Chrysler approach was to allow middle management to make decisions on their own initiative, often without prior executive approval.
- The Daimler approach to work involved long hours on a regular basis, whereas Chrysler management tended to work long hours only when necessary. At one point, a Chrysler executive snapped to a Daimler executive, 'You might work late, but you don't work smart'.

A major source of conflict came with Schrempp's decision to take over the ailing Nissan Motor Company, to give the group access to the Asian market. Nissan was Japan's second largest car-maker and its price was very low. Schrempp had invested considerable time and energy on the deal with the president of Nissan. The DaimlerChrysler board failed to support the deal, and Schrempp had to accept that the negotiations had been a waste of time and would not proceed. Renault bought a share of Nissan and effectively took control, while DaimlerChrysler settled for buying into the smaller Mitsubishi organization. Over the following months, the organization's share price fell as American investors withdrew, and a number of key players from the Chrysler side left – including Schrempp's co-chairman Robert Eaton, who had led Chrysler into the merger only two years earlier.

The lessons learned

In the case of DaimlerChrysler, we can see value differences between two sets of board members moving into open conflict. At first, it may appear that the problems arose because of the different national cultures of the management teams: German formality and discipline clashing with American informality and low bureaucracy. However, the proposed Nissan deal contradicts this view: the Daimler management wanted to take the risk, whereas the American management was more sceptical and risk-averse. Here, the behaviour of the individuals and groups from the two organizations ran counter to Hofstede's national culture analysis. Throughout, it was the American management that showed greater emotional resistance to change. Clearly, in understanding organizations at the local level, we need to look beyond the generalizations of the macro-level.

DaimlerChrysler experienced clashes between board members, resulting from fundamental differences in some of the values set out above. The Daimler members appeared to adopt an approach to management that was paternalistic and authoritarian, while Chrysler members were more participative and involving. Daimler culture appeared to be more rule-oriented, while Chrysler culture was more adaptive and pragmatic. Communication in Daimler appeared to be more fragmented and hierarchically structured, while Chrysler communication was more connected and supportive of sharing across fields of interest. While the merger was initiated on the basis of compatibility of markets and products, there was an apparent failure to address the incompatibility of organizational cultures, with detrimental consequences.

> It is impossible to change behaviours and actions without first understanding the underlying reasons for current behaviour and action.

Organizational Culture and the External Environment

The organization/environment relationship needs further examination. Schein argues that: 'The more turbulent the environment, the more important it will be for leaders to argue for and show that some level of control over the environment is desirable and possible'[45]. However, it is arguable that few organizations enjoy sufficient critical mass to enable a high degree of control over their external environment. Further, no organization can possibly control its entire external environment. While we may be able to exert influence over many issues, we cannot guarantee predetermined and calculable outcomes.

Given this inevitability, organizations must first seek sufficient insight into the nature of their external environment, to enable them to exercise control and devise appropriate responses to external driving forces. If management is aware of the key drivers of their business in the external environment, and are prepared for any reasonable possibility that can be foreseen, then they can seek to influence the areas over which they have some control. More importantly, by being proactively prepared and able to respond immediately to change, they will give the illusion of having control over those areas that are beyond their influence.

DIFFERENCES IN PROFESSIONAL CULTURES WITHIN ORGANIZATIONS

The Call of the Wild: How Varying Interpretations of Management Intent Divided Senior Executives in an ITC Business

Background [46]

An information and telecommunications (ITC) organization that we shall refer to as Tamara was created by a former public sector utility in the 1990s, to move into the emerging ITC sector. The organization initially grew by acquiring small, entrepreneurial businesses with a diverse range of service and product offerings, but with a common theme of being in the ITC sector. The organization was characterized by its mixture of senior management. Some came from the parent public utility, having backgrounds in and a current focus on science and engineering values. They talked in terms of rationality, safety, rigour, cumulative knowledge and tight cost control. Others came from the acquired businesses, with a focus on new product development and entrepreneurial exploitation of opportunity. They talked in terms of innovation, short-term products, speed to market and value added.

The professional identity

Under the leadership of a new CEO, the organization sought to leverage future expansion from internal competencies, rather than by further acquisition. A new management regime was introduced, and was announced to all senior management. The intention was to promote internal entrepreneurial development through cross-business unit working on new product and service offerings, using multi-disciplinary teams within a management development programme. In order to foster and support individual and group-driven responses, the CEO told the assembled managers, 'Don't come to me for permission, come to me for forgiveness.' This statement was intended to indicate freedom of action. However, it proved problematic to both groups of senior managers.

- The group characterized by 'engineering values' interpreted this as indicating disregard for due process in the development of new products. They were already concerned that cutting timescales and levels of control was leading to duplication of effort and shortcuts in development. Risk elimination, trial and testing, and proper systems of monitoring and control were essential and were being ignored.

- To the entrepreneurs, however, it was indicative of a disregard for the need to support proactive and innovative action. The risk of making mistakes in order to be first to market was being stifled through the threat of reprisal for commercial failure.

As part of the restructuring, to support cross-business unit working, the CEO also announced that the organization would be reorganized under a single profit and loss (P&L) account.

- For the engineering values group, this represented the familiar and acceptable methods of the public utility, and this change was viewed as rectification of an earlier incorrect management decision based upon bad judgement.
- To the entrepreneurs, this change indicated that all expenditure would be tightly controlled, suggesting authoritarianism and loss of control.

While the intent of the CEO and top management was to pull together the diverse group of senior managers and to leverage growth from creatively combining their varied skills and competencies, the basic value differences of the two groups of engineers and entrepreneurs proved to be a major impediment to this. During the implementation of the management development programme, the engineering values group consistently judged the entrepreneurs according to their own value set, as 'fly-by-night' risk-takers who threatened their very existence. In a similar vein, the entrepreneurs judged the engineers as change-averse, threatening the need to innovate and produce new product ideas. These differences pervaded the relationships within teams from the outset, and had to be addressed before development of the new product and service projects.

Tamara is typical of many contemporary companies, being multidisciplinary and in a state of constant and rapid change. Its organizational culture was clearly fragmented. There are no universally accepted values for companies to depend upon. Differences in values are rooted in people's previous experiences, not in national terms but to some extent in organizational terms, and more specifically in *professional* terms. The engineers made judgements based upon a set of values programmed into them during their education and throughout their professional development. These were not explicitly espoused at any point in the development of the business or during the initial implementation of the management development programme; rather, they were used as a basis for negative reaction to proposals.

The lessons learned

While it may be relatively easy to appreciate differences in culture across nations and to engage with differences of language and beliefs, it is much more difficult to engage with differences of *professional culture*. It is apparent that different professional or disciplinary programming leads to the development of different value systems. People who study accountancy tend to assess organizational problems from a financial and numeric point of view, while those who study human resource management (HRM) make judgements from the point of view of individuals and interpersonal relations. The different groups frame their thinking according to their respective value systems, constructing arguments using their own disciplinary language. While the words of these languages may be shared, the meanings attached to them will be dependent upon their disciplinary context-specific usage. The end result is confusion and frustration: those who speak 'accountancy'[47] will not be able to understand or be understood by those who speak 'HRM'[48], without developing the skill of translation. To compound the problem, groups may deliberately use their own language in order to exclude others from their conversations and their business proposals.

MOVING BEYOND CULTURAL PRECONCEPTIONS AND STEREOTYPES

Understanding Cultures Across Boundaries

The cases examined above demonstrated cultural conflict at various levels. In the case of Disney, the initial observation suggested a simple conflict between American and French cultures. However, after considering the organizational culture, the situation was seen to be more subtle and complex. Moreover, access to further detail would highlight the additional conflicts within sub-cultures of particular groups and individuals. The end-result of the organization's product and service development was not specifically American or French. Neither was it generically Disney. As IKEA did, Disney developed context-specific solutions, based upon generic concepts. Both organizations brought together their own home country's culture, values and beliefs, but they also incorporated the results of investigating and understanding their host countries. The wasted opportunity, in both examples, is that the successful route was only discovered after a period of relative failure and costly reactive learning in response to customer dissatisfaction.

For Tamara, cultural conflict was apparent at a more local level, and in a more subtle way. Conflict arose due to the application of different values – values that are acquired during education or learned through involvement in a particular business approach. Although English was a shared language, the different meanings professions attach to identical words caused confusion, while specific jargon can exclude other groups.

Language, Meaning and Overcoming Ambiguity

Through decades of exposure to cross-cultural communication in popular media, most of us have become culturally programmed to recognize differences in spelling (programme/program), pronunciation (tom-ah-toe/tom-ay-toe) and meaning (pants = underpants/trousers) at a basic level across languages that are, basically, identical. Recognition at this basic level should be sufficient to forewarn us of the minefield that lies ahead in terms of differences of expression, meaning, body language and other factors when we enter into cross-cultural business. But we often fail to recognize that, while we are sure of the meaning that we attach to our words and our expressions, others may read them very differently, even where we communicate in the same language. While we cannot expect to become able to communicate in all other languages, either verbally or non-verbally, we can endeavour to become culturally attuned to cope with differences. We can look out for, make explicit and grapple with variations of meaning and value, in order that ambiguity and difference become explicit, and do not remain unstated as barriers to shared understanding.

Increasing Diversity in a World of Similarity

In the past, migration often separated cultures. The world today, however, is becoming more integrative, with blurring of cultures and increased cross-cultural interaction. The recent increasing migration of groups, whether seeking political asylum or improved economic opportunity, will inevitably lead to shifting and unpredictable cultural influences. They bring with them their language, religion, social structure and their fundamental beliefs and values. Recent years have also witnessed the spread of products and services that are universally recognized, yet frequently subject to subtle redesign and modification to suit local tastes. With increasing cultural complexity in nations and societies, the question facing management is: how far does this process of context-specific design have to be taken?

The Starting Point for Cultural Appraisal

In judging others, the starting point must always be where we ourselves stand. Our own cultural programming derives from our national, social, family and professional contexts. These undeniably vary over time, yet we often fail to accept that time is relative between individuals, and that others are situated at different points. The British may deplore other nations allowing children to work in factories, yet it is not long ago that the British sent children up chimneys to sweep them or down coal mines to access the narrowest passages. Of course, this does not imply that child labour is correct; rather, that we need to understand the cultural context in which this is acceptable, arising from the cultural norms, values and beliefs of those directly involved. We make judgements about others on the basis of where we are looking *from*, rather than where we are looking *at*. In a complex and ambiguous world, it is impossible to categorize actions into hard and fast terms of 'right' and 'wrong'. It is easy to make judgements based on a simplistic analysis of culture constructed from our own standpoint.

Developing Multiple Perspectives

In order to be successful in an increasingly globalized, yet also a highly localized world, we need to develop tools and techniques for understanding the cultural programming of others, as this constitutes the starting point for conducting business. This is not just a matter of etiquette and diplomacy, but an essential requirement for being successful. It has often been claimed that Westerners fail to make efforts to understand Asian cultures, while Asians become adept at comprehending Western cultures, to their business advantage[49]. This understanding is based not just upon mastering language, but on understanding non-verbal communications and behavioural norms. It goes beyond copying the different ways of doing things to developing an understanding of why these things are done. Once such skills are mastered, they can become tools for the manipulation of business situations. For example, one Chinese writer[50] recommended that Chinese negotiators resort to delaying tactics when dealing with Americans, since such delays will often frustrate and fluster Americans and encourage them to pay more in order to close the deal more rapidly.

To be successful in the complex and uncertain world of business, managers must develop skills in looking at the business landscape from the viewpoint of other cultures and through the multiple lenses that are used by sub-cultural groups.

THE APPLICATION OF SCENARIO THINKING TO CULTURAL UNDERSTANDING

Applying the Defining Factors of Organizational Culture to your Organization

Edgar Schein[51] set out a series of factors that define the nature of organizational culture, in particular those criteria indicative of a learning organization.

Issue	Key points
1. **The organization-environment relationship** Does the organization consider itself in control of its own destiny or is it controlled by external factors?	The learning organization considers itself more in control of its own future.
2. **The nature of human activity** Are members reactive and fatalistic about their own power over their future, or are they proactive, seeking to design it?	Again, the learning organization is characterized by proactive development.
3. **The nature of reality and truth** Are there formal rules about what is acceptable and true, or is truth dependent upon what is pragmatic and workable?	Learning is not grounded in formal and immutable regulation, but in adaptability to suit what is found to be workable and successful.
4. **The nature of human nature** Are humans perceived to be immutably lazy and evil, or basically good and capable of change?	Little learning is likely where organizational members are considered lazy. Learning requires that all actors in the organization are valued for their contribution and it requires a belief that behaviour can be changed.
5. **The nature of human relations** Is there an emphasis on the group or on the individual, and is the nature of control paternalistic and authoritarian or individual and participative?	Participative and active involvement, allowing individuality to be expressed, fosters learning.

Issue	Key points
6. **The nature of time** Is the orientation to the past or to the future, and is it to the short- or long-term?	Learning organizations are classified as being focused on the near and medium future, rather than on the present and on history.
7. **Information and communication** Are systems of communication fully connected or fragmented?	Fragmentation leads to ineffective learning, since there is limited capability for sharing experiences across fields, projects, etc.
8. **Sub-cultural uniformity or diversity** Are there high levels of uniformity or diversity across sub-cultures?	Diversity of sub-cultures enables multiple perspectives to be taken in considering any problem or situation, and allows multiple options for action to be explored.
9. **Task versus relationship orientation** Are individuals primarily concerned with the task at hand or with necessary relationships with others?	A learning organization is one that is concerned both with the task and with the nature of the relationships necessary for successful completion.
10. **Linear versus system field logic** Is thinking concentrated on linear patterns along a single continuum, or is it systemic and concerned with multiple linkages?	As with communication, multiple linkages, enabling transfer of ideas up, down and across the organization, are more supportive of learning than simple linear thinking.

Along with Hofstede's cultural dimensions, Schein's factors enable us to critically engage with the organizations that we do business with, enabling us to look beyond the obvious. Rather than taking actions and words at face value, and simply wondering why we cannot get through to a group of people, or why a negotiation process is not working, we can appreciate the underlying beliefs and values that underpin their thinking and action. This insight is invaluable. For example, when dealing with an organization that has a culture which sees itself vulnerable to external factors, in which management is fatalistic and regards workers as lazy and in need of authoritarian control, it would be pointless to initiate a project requiring innovation, risk-taking and teamworking!

Developing a Scenario Culture

If we are to develop a broad-ranging view of any and every business problem that will enable us to view it from multiple perspectives, we must first of all seek to 'unculturize' ourselves. We must critically engage with our own cultural programming in order to surface and make explicit our own tacit understandings and our own cultural insensitivities at the most basic level. We must consider why, for example, ethnic minorities in the UK might be upset by the suggestion that they should engage more fully with British culture and adopt English as their first language. Have the British abroad been accustomed to integrating fully with other cultures and adopting the customs and languages of their 'hosts'? Or have they lived in the same type of ex-patriate enclaves with the same type of 'home culture abroad' approach that they currently challenge in those coming to their homeland? In engaging with our own programming, we must consider how even the simplest of terms, such as 'the Far East', are grounded in and framed by cultural assumptions – far from what and east of where? In order to understand why other cultural groups hold the beliefs and values they do, and why they act in the way they do, we should first question how we would, or do, act and behave in similar circumstances, and why.

Beyond problems of cultural programming and conflict at a nationality level, we have highlighted problems at the level of professional groupings. As we have outlined, these problems can be more difficult to identify. If we seek 'expert' opinion on a subject or a problem from one domain, without being 100% clear that the problem exists only and completely within that domain, then we open ourselves up to a myopic perspective. Approaches to problem analysis that seek to clarify the expert perspective on a problem without broadening the range of expertise will fail to uncover alternative perspectives. For example, the 'bootstrapping' approach to problem analysis, which uses expert systems to make expert opinion 'more expert', simply gives us a better and more accurate view through one particular lens. We would argue that most, if not all, management problems are multicultural, and require multiple professional, if not national, cultural inputs for analysis and resolution. So, we argue for multicultural teams of 'problem-seekers', who can open up divergent conversation around the emergent managerial and organizational issues. We advocate widening the organizational perspective by going beyond the organizational boundaries, bringing in expertise and viewpoints through 'remarkable people', who will challenge the prevailing cultural perspectives, and bring alternative interpretations of situations to the consciousness of the managerial team.

> **'Remarkable people' are observers who understand how the world works. They help scenario teams to think 'out of the box'. Their role is explored fully in Chapter 6.**

In advocating a multiple perspective view on any problem and an awareness of the understanding of others, we do not argue for adoption of the values and beliefs that attach to these understandings. Neither do we argue that in any situation any one view is right or wrong in absolute terms; in fact, we argue that there is no absolute right and wrong in most social and managerial problems. However, if we are to truly understand and engage with others in relative terms, we must first understand ourselves in order to make critical comparison. So, a scenario culture is developed from the basic premise that we start by asking not what are we looking *at*, but where are we looking *from*.

Key Questions

In assessing the relevance and specific importance of cultural issues to your organization, it is helpful to review your own experiences. The following questions may stimulate self-awareness and reflection.

- To what extent have you or your organization been culturally sensitive to the different needs, demands and values of other groups and individuals?
- Have you sought to modify your own thinking and action in order to accommodate differences across cultures?
- Have you successfully worked in or with other cultures, whether at a macro- or micro-level, and been able to successfully deal with cross-cultural conflict?
- If so, can you identify what has enabled success, and if not, can you engage with the reasons for failure?

In this chapter, we have explored cultural theory at various levels, and have illustrated the consequences of failing to appreciate diversity at these different levels. While some of the organizations learned through trial and error, such a costly and laborious process is inefficient. Also, it is questionable whether organizations can learn from their failures to recognize cultural differences. Consider two important questions:

- In a world of constant and ever-increasing change, is it sufficient to learn reactively, or is it necessary to learn proactively?
- In a world of both cultural congruence (through global products) and simultaneously increasing cultural diversity (through the resurgence of interest in the local), is there the capability to transfer solutions from one context to another without question and without fine-tuning to suit local tastes and needs?

The answer to both of these questions is an emphatic *no*. Scenario thinking is the most effective model to apply to explore cultural diversity and its impact on organizational activity and strategy.

Any organization seeking to expand its operations into a new cultural context, whether at the macro- or micro-level, can explore the general environment, but they must also explore those drivers for change that may bring about deviation from the norm. Will the ever-expanding penetration of universal brands and products continue, or will local tastes and preferences dominate? Identifying key indicators will highlight the likely outcome, improving the success of strategic developments.

Finally, cultural diversity and differences of meaning and interpretation must be explicitly surfaced and considered in any scenario project. While recognizing the surface-level differences of nationality and language, and exploring under-lying differences of meaning, values and beliefs, we frequently fail to recognize differences in values and beliefs expressed through different meanings attached to words in the same language. As we have seen, we often fail to understand the differences in culture and beliefs of those who speak 'accountancy', 'human resource management', 'ICT' or 'engineering', particularly where the words they use also appear in our own professional language.

It is, perhaps, finally worth considering that the full value of scenario thinking can be best realized when it becomes part of the organizational culture. One of the inherent strengths of scenarios is that they work across boundaries and cultures. In the next chapter, we will see how this approach has grown and developed, and how many of the enduring scenario techniques that are proven to succeed when dealing with cultural issues first emerged.

In Chapters 2, 3 and 4 we have seen how the effectiveness of organizations is limited by thinking and decision-making flaws at the level of individuals, organizations and cultures. We have seen in each case that scenarios promise a way to overcome at least a part of such blockages, tipping the balance towards organizational success. In the next chapter, we will show how scenario thinking is not a new idea, but has a long history as a way of assisting decision-makers in fast-changing environments.

Shaping The Future: The Emergence of Modern Scenario Techniques

CHAPTER 5

Scenario thinking is a dynamic approach leading to adaptive organizational learning. Its full value is experienced only when it has become a firm component of organizational thinking; part of its culture. These are not new insights, but principles that practitioners have discovered over many years of scenario work. In this chapter, we will look at the *origins of scenario thinking*, exploring what has driven the scenario approach and why it has become one of the most compelling approaches to business management.

Overview

Scenario thinking has an established and successful heritage, with deep roots in the development of decision-making. Making the unthinkable a part of current thinking has shaped policy. It has enabled people, organizations and countries to better control their situations and cope with changing conditions. History drives home one point in particular: people are natural scenario planners; it is how we make sense of the world and how we decide upon which course of action to take in everyday life. In an institutional context, identifying and harnessing the intricacies of causality, as we do as individual thinkers, is the true intellectual measure of potential.

CONTINUED ... **Overview**

In this chapter we will:

- **Explain why scenario planning is an enduring, human phenom-enon,** exploring the widespread nature of scenario planning, how it developed and 'proved' itself, as well as seeing how it is extensively woven into conscious and subconscious decision-making.
- **Highlight the proven benefits of scenario thinking** by reviewing its development since World War II, showing the many facets and factors that drove its development and emergence into an increasingly popular and effective business tool.

SCENARIO PLANNING: THE HUMAN DIMENSION

Having discussed the flaws in thinking that underpin poor decision-making at individual, organizational and community levels, we now turn to look at what can be done about it. It is the contention of this book that scenario methods are some of the most powerful tools available to address this need. To realize this potential, we have to relate scenario planning to organizational success and failure, and show how scenarios help in thinking processes as well as in related action and behaviour. This is a situation of *scenarios leading to organizational learning*, combining thinking with action. In the following chapters, we will argue this point on first principles and empirical evidence. In this chapter, we will review the history of scenario planning, demonstrating how people have over many years experienced the beneficial effects of the scenario approach. This history demonstrates how people have perceived scenarios as grounded in ordinary human thought. The following short story illustrates the views that have drawn people to scenario thinking from the beginning.

Bringing the Future into the Present: The Story of Margareta Lonnberg

Margareta Lonnberg is responsible for management training in a large Finnish multinational company. She has long championed scenario planning, ensuring managers are thoroughly briefed on its relevance and importance. When queried about why scenario planning has been such a cornerstone of her management training, she gave the following anecdote.

Weekend retreats on one of the many islands near Helsinki are popular. Close proximity to Helsinki commands a much higher price and most ordinary folk build their retreat further afield where property is more reasonably priced. People know, close in is only for the very rich, and they don't even think about it. That was the situation with us until my children started to grow up. They became obsessed with how a property close by would be preferable and kept introducing the subject round the dinner table. Gradually this conversation influenced the way we all thought; it was no longer something completely out of our sight; rather, our thinking was guided to dream of options and solutions. For instance, when I went to a party, I would find myself asking people about weekend houses and properties for sale. Early on I didn't succeed. This was not easy. But the 'strategic conversation' at home kept me interested and made me persevere. People started to know about my hobby and invited me to other parties. Eventually I found a man who was willing to sell but the price was prohibitive; I had no money at all to invest. But the family mind had been conditioned. And we did not rest until we had come up with an option. Under the

a cheaper area. We went for it and now we have our dream summerhouse. In short, we had become skilful scenario planners, noticing many things that would otherwise have passed us by. Although many may regard the outcome simply as luck, I feel that the conscious drive to keep the idea in our mental space made it more likely to become a reality. This 'scenario thinking' attuned and prepared our thinking to make us observe opportunities that would previously have eluded us. I agree with Louis Pasteur's well-known dictum: 'Luck favours the prepared mind'.

Individuals cope with the problems of thinking flaws quite naturally by thinking in terms of scenarios. Also, in business scenarios, thinking prepares the mind and makes people see opportunities that they may otherwise miss. Margareta believed that, if she could turn people in her company into institutional scenario thinkers, it would open up new opportunities that would fundamentally change the fate of the company.

Memories of the Future: Scenarios Filter What We Perceive

David Ingvar, a leading Swedish psychologist, would see the fantasies Margareta Lonnberg's family indulged in as *memories of the future*: stories about possible futures that then became stored in their collective memory, not as historical events, but as reference points for possible developments[52].

In a series of famous experiments, he showed the overriding importance these memories of the future have on what we perceive, or do not perceive, in the world around us. Of the signals that we receive, only a very small percentage become part of our conscious perception. This can happen only if there is a context available in our mind through which the signals can be understood. Ingvar showed how this happens. In going through life, we build up a store of memories of the future. Whenever an event penetrates into our subconscious awareness, our mind will test what it could mean for us by exploring multiple possible pathways into the future. Later, with these new memories of the future in place, we encounter other events. If one of these relates to one of the stored memories of the future, it becomes a meaningful perception. This then leads to further scenario spinning in our mind, new memories of the future, and a continually evolving attention span.

Ingvar showed how the situation can become locked in on a narrow attention span, with a poor arsenal of memories of the future leading to a narrow range of perceptions, in turn reinforcing the narrow attention span. Fanaticism is a manifestation of this locking-in loop. For example, he showed how drug addicts could become mentally trapped in an exclusive focus on their next fix, with a resulting inability to perceive anything outside the desire for their next fix, adding to the problems of rehabilitation. His suggestion was to try to enrich the arsenal of memories of the future by helping people to engage in scenario spinning over a wider area. This would broaden their attention span, moving away from the compulsive focus that makes them incapable of receiving other signals.

What Margareta tries to do in the institutional context of her company is something conceptually similar. She is concerned that becoming too focused on one business-as-usual scenario, and not having exercised other possible futures, the company will become a poor observer of the environment, and slow to respond to the 'dots on the horizon' that could be early signals of change and opportunity.

Scenarios: A Cornerstone of Human Thought

It is common to dismiss new business tools and techniques as fads or fashions – a common reaction to terms such as 'balanced scorecard', 'business process re-engineering' and other management inventions. It is important to realize that scenario planning is not an ephemeral idea that will have come and gone in a few years' time. Its long history

> All thinking is essentially a form of scenario thinking. The human mind reacts naturally to uncertainty by exploring it through a series of scenarios of what could happen.

shows that something more robust is involved here. We suggest that one reason for this is the way scenarios fit with and represent an integral part of how we function, through our intellectual machinery of perception, action and learning.

Humanity has always been spinning scenarios of the future, and conditioning our attention span is directly related to it. Ingvar argues that scenario thinking underpins all our thinking. The human mind reacts naturally to uncertainty by exploring it through a series of 'stories' – scenarios – of what *could* happen. For example, people faced with considerable uncertainty around important decisions will naturally explore and develop alternative scenarios for the future in their mind.

Planning or simply postulating about the future is a distinguishing feature of humans. Scenario thinking has always been a tool for indirectly examining society and its institutions. This has often taken the form of treatises on utopias or flawed societies, and can be traced back to the writings of early philosophers such as Plato and Seneca.

SCENARIO THINKING AND WAR GAMES

Uncertainty and Crisis

Certainly, Ingvar's observations apply to individual psychology. However, it is important to assess whether this fundamental mechanism is also at work at the institutional level. As a strategic planning tool, scenario techniques are rooted in the military, where strategists have employed scenarios throughout history. Military organizations face considerable uncertainty in areas where decisions have to be taken fast and where the consequences are critical. They have used scenario planning, in an organizational context, in the form of what are known as 'war game' simulations. History has taught war leaders that preparation is crucial for success; war games improve the level of preparedness.

War is a crisis situation. It is useful to distinguish a crisis from a disaster. In a crisis, you retain a degree of control and, therefore, you are able to prepare. Even so, there is significant uncertainty involved in crisis management. A crisis involves a series of events of diffuse origin. It will not be immediately clear who needs to take what action – in fact, there will be multiple actors around the situation with their own different perspectives and interests. Crisis situations tend to be too complex to allow one to aim for 'the one best answer'. Instead, in a war game, people play the roles of the various actors involved in the real situation to explore the logical developments of various scenarios, helping them to assess the validity and impact of different decisions.

War Game Preparations

It is helpful to break down the task of dealing with the crisis into a number of key steps. In the case of military war games, the first step would be to identify the important parameters in the war: 'What are the key variables that success or failure depend on?' Some of these variables would be under the players' control, while some would be external, imposed on everyone as exogenous variables (such as the weather).

The preparatory work can be approached in three stages.

1. **The simulation model is prepared.** The basic rules and interdependencies of the interaction have to be specified in a simulation model that will determine and indicate to the players the consequences of their decisions, and show exogenous variables during the game.
2. **The initial situation has to be described.** In order to start the game, it is necessary to show how historical events have led to the conditions when the game starts.
3. **The way that the game will develop needs to be decided in advance.** The way the exogenous parameters develop during the simulation, alone and in interaction with each other, has to be decided in advance. (These are the scenarios.)

When the three preparatory stages are in place, the game can commence. On the basis of where they find themselves, players will start making decisions, and the reactions of the opposition, all mediated through the simulation model, will inform them of the consequences of those decisions. Following on from this, further decisions are taken, and so on, until the preset end of the game is reached.

It is essential to follow the game with an effective and analytical debriefing. After a game is concluded, the logic, as it presented itself to the various warring parties, needs to be ascertained and understood. This is crucial preparation for the real thing, as it provides insight into how real-world situations may be interpreted by the enemy. Clearly, it is important to carry out more than one round of the game, as we will want to explore the effect of different starting conditions and different scenarios of the external environment. Through repetition, we can learn the importance of particular elements of the situation – for example, numbers of weapons and type of equipment, or external circumstances, such as the weather. Military leaders, facing enormous uncertainty, will tend to be risk-averse, leaving options open, deciding only what needs to be decided – often choosing the robust option that will stand up under a range of circumstances. Making multiple runs in the war game allows them to develop a feel for the relative robustness of different scenarios.

A Natural Scenario Planner: Field Marshal Lord Alanbrooke

Despite their long history in the military, the first documented outlines of what today might be regarded as scenarios do not appear until the nineteenth century in the writings of von Clausewitz and von Moltke, two Prussian military strategists who are also credited with having first formulated the principles of strategic planning.

General Alan Brooke (who later became Field Marshal Lord Alanbrooke) has been described as a natural scenario planner. He is, perhaps, not as well known as other field commanders of World War II. However, many people agree that he, in his position as the Chief of the Imperial General Staff commanding all British and Empire forces, was the mastermind behind the allied forces defeating Nazi Germany.

Alanbrooke's approach started from a number of basic principles of warfare that he considered self-evident, such as 'fight the enemy where he is weak, not where he is strong'; 'avoid experiments; only engage if you are confident you can win' and 'always consider the whole system you are confronting'. He would not take a decision unless it was necessary. Instead, he tried to get into the minds of the enemy to understand what actions they might be expected to take. He preferred to keep a number of detailed scenarios to hand that he used to sharpen his thinking. He had a team of planners to work out these scenarios, which included a careful assessment of all resources required in various configurations. Generally, his approach was directed towards developing policy, rather than setting specific targets. In this way, he ensured that his team would remain open to new information.

His American colleagues found his methods difficult to understand. They wanted to decide on long-term goals, and preferred sufficient detail to enable immediate planning and preparation. A clear example of this was the invasion of France. In 1943, the Americans wanted to set a date for the invasion; they saw keeping their military options open as

> Alanbrooke understood that the scenario approach was not a way of predicting the future. Rather, it was a learning device aimed at becoming more skilful in dealing with uncertainty. This was vitally important, given the inherent uncertainty in the decisions he faced.

wavering. Alanbrooke remained steadfast, determined to explore the situation fully. He avoided the illusion of consensus until he finally felt that they all understood the fundamental weaknesses of the enemy. It was only then that he decided on the appropriate strategy and action.

Crisis Management Training

Scenario simulation has found an ongoing application in the area of crisis management. A crisis in this connection is a serious disruption of the basic structures, or an impairment of the basic values and standards, of a social system. Many organizations endeavour to make preparations and put plans in place *before* a crisis occurs. These plans need to include policy decisions to be taken in various scenarios.

It is not surprising that crisis management experts emulate war-gaming methods. Preparing for a situation in which decisions are made in an arena involving many participants, under phenomenal time pressures and where nobody quite understands what is happening, is not an exercise in strategic planning. Rather, it has to be approached via a scenario-based method. The purpose is to create an exercise system that uses simulation games to boost both the mental flexibility of the participants and the quality of their perception and decision-making processes. It is by engaging in multiple exercises that scenario-based crisis management preparation has its greatest impact.

THE ERA OF POSSIBILITY: THE MAKEABLE* POST-WAR WORLD

The Age of Forecasting and Systems Engineering

In the immediate years following World War II, the first need was for recovery and reconstruction, not only from war damage, but also from the ravages of the economic depression of the 1930s. The world entered a period of significant and steady growth that lasted until the 1970s. The period witnessed rapid and radical changes, such as the development of computers and the new sciences of operations

---

* The word 'makeable' is used to describe attitudes in the post-war world, where a positive spirit believed that most problems could be solved with central planning, control and the application of technology. This was later to give way to the realization of complexity, making planning and control inadequate for the scope, depth and speed of change – and a different, scenario-based approach was needed.

research (OR) and systems engineering. Economics had become a quantitative discipline, providing a new holistic approach to understanding performance. Other sciences progressed by leaps and bounds. Technology had made rapid progress during and after the war and was still racing ahead. World War II had been replaced by the Cold War, providing the motivation to develop technology to stay ahead of the enemy.

With so much capability, a new optimism and a new sense of control penetrated society. It was felt that the new econometric models provided the opportunity to regulate, or even eliminate, the business cycle and economic recession, using Keynesian methods. Statistical forecasts could indicate the action(s) to take to reverse any problems. Operations research (OR) encouraged many to believe that, through modelling, society could be designed for the benefit of all. There would be progress everywhere. The time was approaching when poverty and disease would be overcome. We would even control people's irrational behaviour to protect modern democratic society. Crucially, the new digital computer allowed us to address problems of a complexity that had been beyond our capability to handle before. We could now look forward to a time when we would predict, model, simulate, optimize and control everything in society. This was only the start; but technological capability was developing fast. This was the new *makeable* world. Central planning seemed the obvious way forward, either based on ideology (such as socialism in Northern and Eastern Europe) or technocracy (as in France or the USA). Every problem could eventually be solved. Utopia again seemed to be just around the corner.

Of course, everyone knew that the future was uncertain, but if this was interpreted statistically, one could even quantify the uncertainty by establishing probability levels for different possible outcomes. In this way, uncertainty did not have to stand in the way of optimization. Modern-day scenario techniques emerged in the post-war period. The 1950s witnessed the rise of two geographical centres in the development of the scenario method – the USA and France. Both were working firmly in the 'predict and control' frame of mind, and scenarios were highly quantified affairs, largely used as statistical instruments.

The US Perspective

After World War II, the US Department of Defense had to decide which projects should be funded for the development of new weapons systems. The task was a difficult one, given the increasing complexity of systems, resulting from scientific advances made during the war years. The decision-making task was complicated by the uncertainty surrounding the issue. For example, the result of the development of new weapons systems, which required long lead-times, was itself uncertain. The future political environment was shrouded in uncertainty: not knowing the conditions under which these systems would eventually operate left the development of weapons systems precariously positioned. Also, their effectiveness was not quantifiable, as this depended on technological developments taking place in other countries.

The Rand Corporation: the Emergence of Scenario Techniques

The decision-making needs in this situation gave rise to two specific needs:

- the need for a *methodology* to obtain the reliable consensus of a large and diverse group of experts;
- the need to develop *simulation models* of future environments that allowed policy alternatives, and their consequences, to be investigated.

The need to elicit and synthesize expert opinion inspired the development of the Delphi technique. The need for simulation models led to the development of an approach known as 'systems analysis', from which emerged the explicit use of scenario techniques. Both these techniques were developed in the 1950s by the Rand Corporation – an acronym from Research and Development. This was a research group that evolved out of a joint project between the US Air Force and the Douglas Aircraft Company in 1946 and which, up until the 1960s, was engaged almost exclusively in defence management studies for the US Air Force.

The platform for the emergence of scenario techniques at the Rand Corporation relied on a combination of the following three factors: first, the development of computers provided the capability for simulated solutions for otherwise intractable problems; second, game theory provided the theoretical structure for the investigation of social interaction; and third, the development of sophisticated war game simulations for the US military.

Using this platform, Herman Kahn, an authority on civil defence and strategic planning at the Rand Corporation in the 1950s, began developing scenarios for the US Air Defense System Missile Command, a large-scale early warning system.

Due to the specialized and highly classified nature of this work, the content and methodology of this pioneering scenario work were not widely publicized until 1960, when Kahn published *On Thermonuclear War*[53].

The Impact of Herman Kahn and the Hudson Institute

In 1961, Herman Kahn left the Rand Corporation and established the Hudson Institute, where he began to apply his scenario methodology to social forecasting and public policy. He subsequently published numerous futuristic scenario-based studies, the most controversial of which was the book *The Year 2000: A Framework for Speculation*, which he wrote with Wiener and published in 1967[54]. This book came to be regarded as a landmark in the field of scenario planning. Its introduction of new methodology to thinking has meant that Kahn is often referred to as the father of modern-day scenario planning. His book was seminal because it provided one of the earliest definitions of 'scenarios', introducing the word into the planning literature. It demonstrated the use of scenarios as a methodological tool for policy planning and decision-making in complex and uncertain environments. As a result, Kahn's work strongly influenced the subsequent development and diffusion of scenario techniques as planning tools in the USA, by providing a methodological foundation for similar future studies. Finally, Kahn generated much controversy, leading to numerous counter-studies (notably *Limits to Growth*) some proving just as controversial, heightening the focus on scenarios and scenario techniques.

The story about how the word 'scenario' was introduced in this type of work is enlightening. His work on the subject of thermonuclear war meant that Kahn was thinking about extreme futures, describing scenes with casualties running into hundreds of millions. During a presentation, part of the audience expressed concern, questioning his judgement. Kahn impressed on them that they should not confuse these 'stories' with forecasts – they had no predictive value. 'They are only scenarios, intended to be used as thinking tools, nothing more,' he said. In a 'predict and control' world, Kahn surprised his audience with this idea of drawing pictures of the future without pronouncing on their probability. The word scenario was intended to indicate that one was doing something different from predict and control – that is, thinking. Kahn was ahead of his time.

> Scenarios liberated planning from the traditional 'predict and control' approach. They are not accurate forecasts; they are, as Kahn said, thinking tools.

Soon after Kahn's departure from the Rand Corporation two other Rand alumnae, Helmer and Gordon, also left and founded the Institute of the Future. Encouraged by the publicity and controversy caused by Kahn's books, Helmer and Gordon – (along with several individuals at the Stanford Research Institute Futures Group and the California Institute of Technology) began to experiment with scenarios as a planning tool. Most of these pioneers were initially concerned with scenarios as a tool for public policy planning.

The French Perspective

In Europe, the French are reputed to have been the first to have systematically studied and investigated the 'scientific and political foundations of the future' using scenario techniques. At the same time that Kahn was developing scenarios for the military in the 1950s, Gaston Berger, a French philosopher, founded the *Centre d'Etudes Prospectives* where he developed a scenario-based approach to long-term planning. He named it prospective thinking, or 'la prospective'. This approach reportedly emerged as a direct consequence of the repeated failure of 'classical' forecasting attempts, a serious problem in a country that had invested so much in the concept of central planning.

Berger was concerned with the long-term political and social future of France. The underlying philosophical premise of his work was that the future is not part of a 'predetermined temporal continuity', but something that is to be created and which can be 'consciously modelled to be humanly beneficial'. The primary objective of the Centre was to formulate an acceptable scenario-based methodology for developing alternative, positive images of the future. These 'normative scenarios' were to enter the political arena to serve as a guiding vision to policy makers and the nation, providing a basis for action. Although Berger died in 1960, the Centre d'Etudes Prospectives flourished, and by the mid-1960s it had begun to apply the 'la prospective' methodology to a range of public issues (including education, the environment, urbanization and regional planning).

The pioneering work of Berger was continued by Pierre Masse, Bertrand de Jouvenel and, more recently, by Michel Godet. As the director of National Economic Planning in France in the 1960s, Masse introduced the use of the prospective scenario approach in the development of the Fourth French National Plan (1960–1965). Subsequent national economic plans have continued to use prospective scenario techniques. Meanwhile, de Jouvenel – the founder of the

Futuribles Group (Association Internationale de Futuribles) which was a catalyst in the development of the international futures movement – joined the Centre d'Etudes Prospectives in 1966.

De Jouvenel postulated that it was the particular view of the future held by small, but dominant, political groups within a nation which determined how the future of that nation unfolded. This could be avoided, he argued, by encouraging futurists to act as catalysts in articulating idealistic images of what the future could be like; images that could serve as blueprints for a nation. The thrust of de Jouvenel's work was in using scenarios to construct positive images of the future, 'scientific utopias', and then in specifying how they could be realized to improve society. In the mid-1970s, Godet, the head of the Department of Future Studies at the SEMA Group, began to develop scenarios for several French national institutions such as EDF and Elf. Although firmly rooted in the 'prospective' methodology developed by Berger, Godet developed his own probabilistic approach to scenario development, including several computer-based tools (MICMAC and SMIC) to compute cross-impacts.

As in the USA, the pioneering scenario work in France was almost exclusively associated with public policy and planning. However, two features of the French approach to scenarios differentiate it from that in the USA. First, whereas the early scenario work in the USA tended to be of a global nature, scenario development in France was more narrowly focused on the socio-political foundations of the future of France. Although there has since been a diffusion of scenarios into the business community, scenario planning in France continues to have an important role in public sector planning. Second, the French approach has a strong bias towards normative scenarios that are not so much descriptions of alternative futures as descriptions of ideal states towards which society can aspire.

CHALLENGING ESTABLISHED THINKING: THE DEVELOPMENT OF SCENARIOS IN THE 1970s

The Club of Rome

The Club of Rome is a group of private individuals from across the world, concerned with the increasing threat of interdependent problems faced by mankind. In 1972, they shook the world with the publication of their first report, *Limits to Growth, a Reprint for the Club of Rome Project on the Predicament of Mankind*[55]. This reported on a study, commissioned by the Club of Rome and researched by the systems dynamics group at the Massachusetts Institute of Technology (MIT) in Cambridge. MIT was asked to study the effect of five macro-developments, namely accelerating industrialization, rapid population growth, widespread malnutrition, depletion of limited natural resources, and environmental deterioration. This was an attempt to apply scientific methods, systems analysis and computer power to improve the mental models used to take decisions in these important areas. MIT tackled the problem by developing its first 'world model', in which variables could be studied in an integrated way to conclude long-term effects.

The conclusions were dramatic. It was suggested that the limits to growth in the world could be reached within 100 years, with cataclysmic effects on population and industrial capacity. However, equilibrium could also be reached, provided that far-reaching policies were implemented for the developing world and the use of natural resources.

In fact, the conclusions did not follow inevitably from the report, which was couched in sound scenario terms. The model was used to simulate the developments under a number of scenarios – certainly, some outcomes proved bleak, but not all. This was the first time that such issues had been discussed logically by reference to an underlying systems model. The report had a major impact, stimulating many people to look behind the rhetoric to understand why we were suddenly facing such major dangers. A lively discussion ensued, echoed in the popular press. For example, another American university reported in *The Economist* that applying the economic equations of the MIT model to data from the beginning of this century could produce a scenario in which the world was overwhelmed in 1970 – which obviously had not happened. The discussion became so lively that many tried to reproduce the results for themselves. Claims and counter-claims were parried, while newspapers kept the ideas in the public arena.

Undoubtedly, the lively discussion was partly due to the overwhelming 'predict and control' mentality that still pervaded thinking in 1972. Many people did not read the report as it was intended, as a set of possible scenarios, but instead saw it as the MIT systems group trying to forecast what the world was going to be like. Of course, the approach did not meet the requirements of a thorough statistical exercise: the data for that task were simply not available.

Eventually the discussion subsided, yet the Club of Rome had achieved something significant: namely, it had created a broad-based societal discussion of limited resource issues. This was the first time that global 'limits to growth' had been raised in the public consciousness, creating a degree of legitimacy for the environment movement that would otherwise have been difficult to create. The Club of Rome report achieved what one may expect from a good scenario exercise: it challenged people to give priority and time to thinking through important issues that had otherwise escaped their agenda. The quality of the model upon which the scenarios were based could certainly be questioned but, as a piece of attention management, the project was a resounding success. Perhaps it was a timely wake-up call, since it was followed shortly afterwards by the energy crisis of 1973. This crisis shook the world to the point of making it question the fundamental validity of the 'predict and control' paradigm. It was within an oil company, Royal Dutch/Shell, that scenario planning would be picked up and be further developed in the private sector.

ROYAL DUTCH/SHELL AND THE PROBLEM OF PREDICTABILITY

The first widely documented use of scenarios in business was the experience of the Royal Dutch/Shell Group, which adopted scenario planning as a permanent strategy in 1972. The initial impetus came from a failure of traditional cash flow forecasting. Interestingly, despite its large size, Shell did not have a comprehensive cash flow forecasting system in the early 1960s, that involved all its operating companies. As a result, cash availability oscillated between abundant and tight with alarming regularity. Periods when cash was tight created what was known as a 'cold wind', when operating units were asked to slow down and postpone expenditure to keep the Group in equilibrium. This was unpopular, necessitating the costly renegotiation of existing contracts.

Also, this was the era of predict and control and the 'makeable' world, and in the mid-1960s Shell decided to improve the situation. The objective was to improve long-term forecasting of cash flow, in order to give the company time to take necessary corrective action, thus reducing unnecessary costs. A planning system was installed under the name Unified Planning Machinery (UPM). All operating units were required to make cash flow predictions, which would be collated to provide an overall Group projection. However, after only a few years it was apparent that the results of UPM were not a reliable enough basis for action. The numbers generated in the operating units swung violently from one projection to another. It soon became clear that there were no techniques that could improve the situation. A large and powerful company, steeped in 'predict and control', finding itself unable to accurately predict something as fundamental as its cash position considered itself in a state of mild crisis.

The unit created for adding up the returns from the operating units was called Group Planning. At that time, they employed a Frenchman by the name of Pierre Wack. He had come in from Shell France, where he had spent a few years in marketing and planning. As a Frenchman, he was aware of the French school of scenario planning, mentioned above, although he did not empathize with it, feeling their approach was too technocratic. Instead, he was impressed with Herman Kahn: the idea of 'thinking the unthinkable' appealed to him. When UPM started to create serious problems, he diagnosed the problem as trying to apply statistical techniques on variables that are fundamentally unpredictable. He suggested applying Kahn's technique to the problem to assess its potential use.

Kahn had written his book *The Year 2000* in 1967, inspiring the group to carry out an exploratory study of the year 2000 for the oil industry. In a small unit, they tried to apply the rules set out by Kahn. Kahn had suggested that fundamental uncertainties in the situation needed to be carefully distinguished from what could be predicted, the 'predetermined elements'. So the group started to discuss what was predictable; in this case, the future of the global oil price. Deciding what was predictable and what was uncertain required them to decon- struct the oil price through the analysis of supply and demand.

With global demand for oil having grown consistently by 6% to 8% per annum since 1945, demand was initially assumed to be a predetermined element. This led Wack's team to focus on supply. Given that the engineers assured the group that availability would not be a technical problem, most people in Shell assumed that traditional price trends would continue. However, Pierre Wack was not satisfied. He wanted to know if there could be other factors in supply, besides technical availability, that might be more uncertain. By listing stakeholders in the game, they quickly arrived at host governments. Pierre Wack posed the questions, 'Would they be happy to continue to increase production year on year? Would this be in their interest?' They approached the problem as a mental game. By playing the role of a major host government, they logically analysed the various policy options available. It soon became apparent that it was very unlikely that host governments would always be amenable. Many oil-producing countries did not need the increasing flow of funds. Importantly, an interesting discovery was that the situation could be exploited to Shell's benefit. By only modestly throttling supply in a market of inelastic demand, the loss of volume would be more than compensated for by the income resulting from the sharp price increase. The overwhelming logic for oil-producing countries was to try to reduce supply, as it would give them increased income while conserving their reserves. This became known as the 'backward-sloping supply curve'. It would require the producing countries to come together to decide on this strategy, something that could happen in a newly formed grouping: the Organization of the Petroleum Exporting Countries (OPEC)!

Pierre Wack believed that following the Kahn approach to the future instead of traditional forecasting had given them an insight into a possible future that might have a huge impact. To his dismay, when he presented the information to his superiors, it was not well received. He was told that OPEC was a 'tiger without teeth', that unity among producing countries was absent, that the oil companies were in charge and that they would do whatever was required to get the volumes needed to satisfy the market. Understandably, Wack was disappointed with this 'predict and control' response, and he determined to retain this 'crisis scenario' in the strategic conversation in future rounds. They sharpened the scenario – growth in demand, due to the USA converting from being an exporter to an importer at that time, and a gradual strengthening of the OPEC group of nations fuelled the situation. Gradually, people became accustomed to the notion that the point might be approaching when the oil majors would no longer be in full control of production levels. Opinion was divided: some people started to discuss 'what if' strategies, while others didn't think the crisis scenario had any relevance for them.

Then, the scenario became reality. The 1973 Israeli-Arab conflict, the Yom Kippur War, had a dramatic impact. The political embargo limited the supply of oil to several countries. The logic of limiting supply was not lost on the nations involved: prices rose five-fold.

Fortunately for Shell, Pierre Wack's work had ensured enough preparation to allow them to take strategic action well ahead of the competition. This showed the enormous advantage of being prepared. As a result, Shell's position in the profitability league table of oil companies rose from seventh to second place. *The economic value of being well prepared was calculated to be billions of dollars.* On the other hand, those in Shell that had dismissed the possibilities and potential of a crisis scenario found themselves overwhelmed by

> **For Shell, coping with the aftermath of the 1973 oil price shock, the economic value of being prepared was calculated to be worth *billions* of dollars.**

events – and they never recovered. The difference in performance between scenario planners and those that had ignored the strategic conversation was brought into sharp focus. The conclusion was clear. Scenarios had delivered what UPM would never have been able to: the ability to plan for possible futures, enabling a significant competitive advantage under changing circumstances. (For an account of the background to the development of scenarios in Royal Dutch/Shell, see Kleiner[56].)

The oil crisis not only affected the oil industry, but also had a dramatic global impact. The world entered a period of major economic dislocation where, counter to all perceived logic, stagnation was combined with massive inflation in all Western countries. The dominant idea of the 'makeable' world, the business cycle now under control, had suffered a major setback. The phenomenon of 'stagflation' had taken away one of its major weapons. People asked: 'How was it possible that something so fundamental as the 1973 oil crisis, with all its unpredictable consequences, could come without warning?' The 'predict and control' paradigm was heavily criticized.

THE DEVELOPMENT OF SCENARIOS AND STRATEGY DURING THE 1980s

Scenarios are a relatively recent phenomenon in business. Studies of European companies by Malaska and others[57] clearly indicate that, in Europe, scenario planning was not widely used until after the first oil crisis in 1973. After this, the number of adopters of scenario planning almost doubled. Also, there was another surge of adoption in the period between 1976 and 1978. This led Malaska to conclude that the adoption of scenario planning 'is associated with the increasing unpredictability of the corporate environment that took place in the 1970s'.

There were similar findings in the USA. Studies by Linneman and Klein[58] found that only a few businesses used scenario-planning techniques prior to 1974. This contrasted with the two-year period (1974–1975) following the first oil crisis, when the number of adopters doubled, increasing more than two-fold again in the period between 1977 and 1981. They estimated that, in the early 1980s, almost half of all US Fortune 1000 industrial firms, US Fortune 300 non-industrial firms and Fortune Foreign 500 industrial firms were actively using scenario techniques in their planning processes. The quality of this work was not assessed. Like Malaska, Linneman and Klein contend that there is a correlation between the adoption of scenario planning and environmental discontinuities and instability.

Factors Affecting the Use of Scenario Techniques in Business

The 1981 US-based survey evidence of Linneman and Klein also revealed that the use of scenarios was not uniform among various industry groupings, and that the adoption of scenario techniques in business appears to be related to three factors.

The size of the company

By 1981, 46% of the Fortune 1000 industrials reportedly used scenarios. Among the largest of the Fortune 1000, the Fortune 100, the reported usage was in excess of 75% of the companies surveyed.

The length of its planning horizons

Seventy-two per cent of companies using scenarios had planning horizons of at least ten years.

Capital intensity

The majority of scenario users tended to be in capital-intensive industries such as aerospace, chemicals and petroleum refining. In Europe, the 1981 Malaska survey results were revealing a similar picture. The highest proportion of scenario users were large companies operating in capital-intensive industries with long strategic planning horizons, chiefly oil companies, vehicle manufacturers, electricity suppliers and transport companies. The finding that scenarios are used predominantly by large companies is hardly surprising. Large companies have both the resources and the inclination to experiment with new planning models.

The research clearly indicated a substantial growth in the adoption of scenario techniques throughout the 1970s, although by 1981 the rate of adoption of scenarios in the USA was markedly higher than it was in Europe. However, one thing was becoming apparent: the perceived usefulness of a technique, and ultimately its adoption, is directly proportional to the effort and the sophistication required in its implementation.

Scenarios Become Popular

The 1980s saw the publication of Michael Porter's book *Competitive Strategy*[59]. Long before World War II, books had addressed the area of management and decision-making, but in a fragmented manner. *Competitive Strategy* earned its distinction by writing about business strategy in a holistic way; it brought strategy together and treated its study as a discipline. This was not the first book on the subject. Others had gone before, such as Richard Normann's *Management for Growth,* in 1975[60], but Porter was the first to put the area of strategy on the mental map of every executive.

Porter's timing was fortuitous. His book followed the take-off of the strategy consultancy profession, dating back to 1968, when the Boston Consulting Group had been created. Initially, the Boston Consulting Group was a small organization, based on Henderson's ideas of the 'experience curve' and of portfolio management. By the end of the 1970s, the organization was broadening and rapidly growing. Strategy work in business organizations now elicited considerable interest. In addition, traditional accountancy firms were discovering the value of strategy consulting. Demand for business school MBA courses exploded, with many new MBA graduates securing well-paid jobs in the new consulting firms.

What was driving this development? The world had changed after the energy crisis of 1973. Things did not seem so predictable any more: there was more competition, life was less secure and it was a time of accelerating change. People were looking for new ideas that would provide a competitive edge, and scenario planning was well positioned to fill the vacuum. What was the secret of success? Could specific ideas be discovered and used to the advantage of one or a few firms? But if that were possible, would it not be a short-lived phenomenon, as competitors would acquire the skills and erode any advantage? This was a dynamic race and successful companies had to know how to stay ahead.

Scenario Planning and Other Strategic Approaches

Scenario planners were thinking about how their discipline related to the new field of strategy and competitive positioning. It was felt that scenarios would lead to superior strategy. Pierre Wack suggested that using scenarios and competitive positioning together would lead to a *strategic vision*, in turn pointing to various strategic options, one of which would prove to be the preferred option, on the basis of anticipated outcomes and robustness.

> An increasing number of people have come to realize that in confronting questions with many possible answers, the ultimate decision will involve intuition and creativity – it will not result from rational analysis alone.

Scenario planners started to run 'scenario to strategy' workshops. The field had become unwieldy; the clarity of objective that had characterized the 1970s seemed lost in a whirlwind of ideas and recipes. Many were popular one day and gone the next. It was clear that the field had not settled down.

This was part of a bigger scene. As the 1980s unfolded, strategic planners in general suffered an identity crisis: their role and contribution was no longer clear. The founding idea, that strategy development strove to get as close as possible to the one correct answer through increasing investment in off-line analysis, was beginning to crumble. Some people suggested that the speed of change, the level of uncertainty and the dynamics involved in any contemporary strategic situation were inconsistent with the idea of optimization of the makeable world. In addition, the mindset of the people inside organizations was emerging as a major variable in strategy development, indicating the need for managers themselves to be more involved in the strategy process. As a result, the view emerged that planning was more about facilitating a strategy *process*; that strategy had to be developed and owned by the managers, not the planners, and that the job of strategizing could not be delegated to a staff function. While these new ideas were developing, the strategy consultants were experiencing considerable growth, indicating that rationalistic 'predict and control' still dominated the business world. It would take time for new paradigms to break through.

The effect in the scenario planning community was to highlight the bifurcation between two world views. The first view held that, in the final analysis, scenarios were about better prediction, albeit taking into account the irreducible uncertainty in the situation. This school of thought tried to assign probabilities to particular scenarios, if necessary simply on the basis of judgement. This allowed strategic options to be evaluated quantitatively, by means of an algorithm known as Monte Carlo. They did not see a conflict between scenarios expressing uncertainty and optimization. In the 'makeable' world view of the 1960s and the 1970s, this idea prevailed. Managers expected to find the optimal answer, and there were an increasing number of people prepared to give them what they wanted (for a fee!). Unfortunately, the best answer did not always work out, and a shadow was gradually falling over scenario planning, as with the whole area of strategic planning.

For those aware of the history of scenario thinking, they knew that prediction was not its original intention. For example, war games were not about 'predict and control'. Similarly, Alanbrooke, Kahn and Wack did not envision scenario planning as being capable of arriving at one right answer, given the complex situations that they faced. They knew they were confronting questions with many possible answers, and that an ultimate decision was going to involve a lot of intuition and creativity that could not result from rational analysis alone. They used scenarios to make sense of things, to sharpen their perception and to keep an open mind. They also involved the people around them in scenario thinking, by engaging in a multiple perspective strategic conversation. This helped them to circumvent 'business-as-usual' orthodoxies steering decisions. Their purpose could best be characterized by Louis Pasteur's dictum: 'Luck favours the prepared mind'. Scenarios served the purpose of creating prepared minds.

THE 1990s: SCENARIO PLANNING AND ORGANIZATIONAL LEARNING

The Age of Complexity, the Limits of Certainty – and the Rise of Scenario Planning

In 1987, Gleick's book *Chaos*[61] became a worldwide bestseller. For the first time, the new science of complexity was generally accessible. This was a crucial moment in the history of scenario planning. Complexity theory formulated the idea that uncertainty was not only the result of our ignorance, but that complex systems carry a degree of intrinsic unpredictability that cannot be reduced by any amount of analysis.

In the 'makeable' world, there had been a great deal of uncertainty, but this was blamed on our limited knowledge, something that would be reduced with further development of our cognitive apparatus, enabled by ever-improving computers and new science. Optimization made sense, and would be improved over time as we learnt how to better map out the more complex systems. The 'complexity' view suggested that it is fundamentally impossible to predict aspects of the future. Systems, the elements of which could be described in detail, might, as a whole, still perform unpredictably, even in probabilistic terms. The 'makeable' world had been under pressure ever since the oil crisis of 1973. The aftermath of this had emphasized how little we understood

> The growth of scenario planning escalated with the rise of complexity theory, and in particular, the recognition that complex systems carry a degree of intrinsic unpredictability that cannot be reduced by increased analysis.

the behaviour of the systems making up society. The big questions of our time – poverty, war, environmental degradation, overpopulation, globalization, sustainability, technological development and others – had been raised, yet remained unanswered. Also, central planning had come to nothing. This was spectacularly demonstrated when the centrally planned economies of Eastern Europe collapsed in the early 1990s. The trend towards privatization, globalization and the reduction of state control of the economy gained momentum. If we could not predict the behaviour of the system, it seemed better to distribute economic power as widely as possible to reduce the effect of a single adverse event.

After excursions into the rationalist world of predict and control during the 1960s and 1970s, scenario planning found itself back in its traditional territory – that of making sense of developments, and inspiring 'out-of-the-box' thinking

Organizational Learning

In 1988, Arie de Geus published his seminal article entitled *Planning as Learning*[62]. In it, he developed the idea that planners had to give up their self-image of off-line strategic think-tanks. They had to go out into the world of management, as facilitators of the corporate strategic thinking process embodied in the strategic conversation. Strategy could not be developed away from the point of action, but managers dealing with strategic decisions could be helped with better process. From this emerged the notion of organizations as learning systems, raising the question of how this learning process could be understood and improved upon.

Organizational learning was a concept that had been suggested earlier, specifically in Don Michael's book *On Learning to Plan and Planning to Learn*, published in 1973[63]. At that time, this was not mainstream thinking, but by 1985 the world was more receptive to these ideas. Organizational learning became an area of considerable interest. Initially, it was not much more than a concept, and not much was known about how to operationalise it for day-to-day practice. However, the vision was inspirational and

> Pierre Wack believed that unless he changed something in the minds of managers, he had failed. Going one step further, we would argue that unless something tangible happens we have wasted our time.

generated a great deal of activity to flesh out the ideas. So far, most of the work in this area is somewhat inward looking. It is considered axiomatic that certain practices are 'good things', such as systems thinking (looking at the whole system rather than isolated parts of it), effective and open internal communications, and knowledge management. Most of the literature concentrates on how these organizational features can be created and improved upon. Yet, the perspective remains limited with respect to the outside world in which the organization lives. There is still much to do in this area, and it will be a while until organizational learning can be considered a field in its own right.

Scenario planners intuitively feel comfortable with the idea of organizational learning in the wider sense of a process of adaptation based on action, perception and sensemaking. The main line of scenario tradition has always been about perception and bounded thinking. Organizational learning adds the link between thinking and action. There cannot be learning without action. Without organizational learning, we cannot judge the validity of our theories and recipes. This link with action was a focus for attention for scenario planners during the 1990s.

In decision-making, this has focused attention on the group rather than the individual thinker. Most decisions and actions in organizations are the result of group processes, rather than individuals taking decisions in isolation. Group processes have an important impact on thinking by individuals in the group, and scenario work benefits from considering these.

The World of Identity, Experience and Change

The ability of members of the group to identify (in varying degrees) with the organization illustrates this important dynamic in group thinking. Identity can either be defined from the outside (how the organization is viewed by non-members) or from the inside. Scenario planners are particularly interested in the latter. Identity is the shared view of the members of the organization about what the organization stands for, what it is good or bad at and, therefore, what activities it should or should not engage in. As we saw in Chapter 3, identity expresses itself in the form of stories, real or otherwise, that members relay about the history of the organization. This leads to a shared view on the learned recipes that cause success and avoid failure, and the consequent direction of the organization. If events in the real world confirm the recipes, the identity is strengthened. If events contradict the recipes, members engage in conversation to make sense of the new situation, and adjust their identity until congruence with perceptions is regained. Scenario planners need to focus on the strategic conversation in this cycle, where effective interventions can be made to upgrade the effectiveness of the learning process as a whole.

The organizational learning perspective suggests that scenario work has to start with the existing identity and experience of the organization. Without this connection, relevance is lost and energy to act will be quickly eroded. The productive moment comes when the group starts looking at the world from this vantage point but with a wider perspective than the current orthodoxy. Making this transition is the main objective of the scenario project. This

> **In planning and discussing different scenarios, it is the *process* that matters, not the stories that emerge.**

means that scenario work is customized, and there is little organizational learning value in general purpose scenarios. The process is what matters; the stories are only a tool. What we are doing for our insights, surprises, reflection, emergence of issues, etc. in the specific situation we are in. It requires a customizsed project.

Looking at scenarios as a process of organizational learning has returned us firmly to a long line of tradition in scenario work that started with war games many centuries ago, and was brought into the organizational domain by people such as Kahn and Wack.

Currently, there is an unprecedented feeling of uncertainty within organizations. This anxiety is pervasive and straddles many cultural boundaries. In this respect, there is no difference between the private and the public sector; wherever people are trying to consider the future, the same feeling of uncertainty pervades. The game seems to have changed, and we don't seem to have caught on to the new rules yet. What is more, this is perceived negatively, as powerlessness and a threat, instead of as an opportunity. At this juncture, most people seem to dislike change. In our scenario practice, we find that futures with a lot of change are given negatively associated names, while futures that emphasize 'more of the same' attract favourable annotations.

The remarkable growth in interest in scenario planning over the last 10 years can be understood in this context. More people are realizing that they have to face up to irreducible uncertainty in considering their future. Following the failure of 'predict and control', the scenario planning business is booming. Both the private and public sectors are rapidly returning to this way of looking at the future, which, after all, is the way in which individuals naturally deal with the future in everyday life.

This is reflected in the prolific numbers of publications on the subject. The number of articles about scenario thinking has recently risen dramatically, and there does not seem to be any saturation in sight. Consequently, scenario planning, as a service provision, is coming to the fore. It is increasingly adopted by large mainstream consultancies as an important business tool; but those that embrace scenarios quickly find that this is different from traditional consultant tools. This is first and foremost about delivering process within the client organization, with content developed by the client through the use of this process.

SUMMARY: THE BENEFITS OF SCENARIO PLANNING

What can we learn from this long history that will help us in our daily management roles? History contains many examples of the organizational benefits of scenarios. Most of these can be grouped under the following main headings.

Enhanced perception

Scenario techniques enhance individual and corporate perception, as they provide a framework for managers to understand and evaluate trends and events *as they occur*, which cannot be provided by the business-as-usual perspective. Scenarios help managers to make explicit their implicit assumptions about the future, and to think beyond the confines of conventional wisdom. At the same time, managers involved in scenario exercises become more insightful observers of the business environment, capable of recognizing and understanding change and uncertainty, rather than overlooking or denying it. In addition, scenarios challenge conventional wisdom and complacency by shifting the 'perceptual anchors' from which people view the future. This reduces the likelihood of managers and organizations being caught unaware and making mistakes.

Integration of corporate planning

Scenario techniques provide a useful middle ground between total reliance on informal and intuitive planning approaches, and being bound by the methodological constraints of more formal, quantitative techniques. Broader company participation and a greater variety of information can be incorporated into the forecasting and planning process when scenario planning is used. As a result, scenarios can combine seemingly disparate environmental factors into a framework for judgement, in a way that no other planning models can. We will discuss this process in action in Chapter 6.

Making people think

Scenarios provide a politically safe team-learning environment and a rich learning process that stimulates creativity. As models of future business environments, scenarios provide a vehicle for mental experimentation in terms of formulating strategic options and examining their consequences in a range of future environments. By articulating their assumptions in a scenario exercise, managers can identify inconsistencies in their own thinking and that of their colleagues, in a non-threatening environment. People feel motivated to think. Scenario exercises require detailed consideration of environmental driving forces and a fundamental analysis of causal relationships. In this thinking process, people examine their perceptions, expand their mental models and develop a shared view of uncertainty. This leads to increased confidence in decision-making, encouraging the organization to become a learning organization.

A structure for dealing with complexity

Scenarios provide a structure for thinking aimed at attacking complexity. This is accomplished by allowing managers to deal more openly and explicitly with acknowledged uncertainty, to arrive at a deeper realization of what is significant versus ephemeral. By underlining the fact that there is a range of possible futures, scenarios reduce the bias for underestimating uncertainties. Scenario thinking also stimulates managers to think in a disciplined and systematic way and to specifically address uncertainty through examining patterns and structure, based on cause and effect. Additionally, unlike sensitivity analysis, scenarios allow the consideration of related simultaneous movement of multiple variables when considering major system shocks or structural changes.

A communications tool

The communications qualities of the scenario approach are powerful, as it provides a framework for rational discussion on the basis of alternative views, emerging inside or outside the organization. In traditional organizational conversation, when the search is on for the 'one right answer', people try to make their own view prevail, which puts them in an advocacy mode of thinking and listening. In a scenario-based conversation, alternative views are intrinsic and valued rather than squashed. It puts the participants in a totally different and much more open frame of mind. Much of the collegiality that emerges in scenario planning exercises does not evaporate once the scenario exercise is complete, and people involved in the exercise often have new ongoing relationships.

A management tool

In Shell, scenarios emerged as a powerful management tool by which senior executives were able to influence decision-making at all levels throughout the organization. Following the introduction of scenarios in the company, it became apparent that influence could be exercised from the top without becoming directly involved in the process or minutiae of the decisions. This was achieved when the scenarios became the set *context* for any key strategic decisions proposed to management. The discovery of this powerful tool then reinforced the interest of senior management in the scenario process and locked in the scenario culture in the company.

These benefits emerged over time, as the scenario approach evolved with changing needs. The world of scenario planning made progressive discoveries in the use of scenario analysis: not all the benefits discussed here were immediately visible; rather, they unfolded gradually as the scenario method evolved, almost in a hierarchy of meaning, where the benefits that were achieved became progressively more profound. The summary checklist below will help to reflect on how the scenario approach fits with individual and organizational approaches.

Summary Checklist – Building an Understanding of Scenario Thinking in Your Organization

Issue	Key points
1. **People – the natural scenario planners** • Do you recognize the fact that much of your thinking is equivalent to 'spinning scenarios of the future'? • Do you lack confidence in your ability to engage in strategic debate?	Recognize those situations where your thinking is equivalent to 'spinning scenarios of the future'.
2. **Perception** • Do you recognize how your thinking affects what you see and read? • Is the quality of your strategic thinking limited, narrow and uninspired?	Understand that your current thinking affects what you see and read and, in turn, how you can process this information to strategically guide and enrich decision-making.

Issue	Key points
3. Knowledge • Do you believe your organization has developed a good balance between intuition and planning, as well as between overview and detail? • Is your organizational planning uncertain and lacking clear direction, with areas of weakness destabilizing its strengths?	Develop a conscious and effective balance between intuition and planning, as well as between overview and detail.
4. Challenge • Are you aware of the recipes you and your organization are using to make decisions? • Would you benefit from challenging these more explicitly? • Do the strategic approaches imply traditional, 'business-as-usual' thinking?	Examine how your company could benefit from challenging these mindsets.
5. Creativity • How good is your organization in 'thinking outside the box'? • Is strategy lacklustre, with routine policies delivering unremarkable results?	Consider how you could promote 'thinking outside the box' to reveal more successful possibilities.
6. Open-mindedness • In your decision-making process do you, as a matter of routine, always consider multiple options before you decide? • Is the decision-making process typically dominated by a single option, consequently underperforming?	Ensure multiple options are explored before reaching a conclusion.
7. Uncertainty • Is your organization afraid of uncertainty, or does it enjoy thinking about it? Do people see it as a threat or as an opportunity? Is it recognized as a potential source of competitive advantage?	Recognize uncertainty as the ultimate opportunity: it is the ultimate source of competitive advantage.
8. Communication Consider the following conversation: Question: 'How will the Internet change our supply chain?' Answer: 'Well, if we build our website on a dynamic SQL server then we can interface with our existing profile database and customize the user experience. That would change the game!' Do you recognize this sort of 'language' problem? Are you addressing it head-on?	Address the language problem, ensuring that the language used creates real communication and an effective strategic conversation.

In the next chapter, we will explore in detail what the scenario approach entails, outlining the process and assessing how it achieves these benefits. In explaining the scenario process, we will show how it overcomes the flaws of traditional decision-making approaches, facilitates organizational learning and delivers a responsive, intelligent and effective strategy.

In this chapter, we have considered how people are natural scenario planners, and how we can trace a long history in which people have used scenarios to overcome personal and institutional flaws in decision making. We have seen how we have emerged from a period when planning activities were seen as 'predict and control' in a makeable world, towards a future in which scenarios serve institutional perception, reflection, sensemaking and action, creating superior adaptation and organizational learning in a world too complex for the deterministic design of strategy based on forecasts.

Developing the Skills for Long-term Survival and Success: Principles of the Scenario Process

Complexity and uncertainty are unavoidable, and are the main challenges faced by organizations. As we have seen in previous chapters, to deal with complexity and uncertainty, individuals, organizations and communities develop thinking approaches that are often flawed. However, awareness that the future cannot be predicted is the starting point for overcoming these flaws. What is essential to long-term survival is the ability to recognize and react to change *before your competitors*. In this chapter, we will demonstrate how scenario thinking can be used to develop these survival skills.

Overview

Previous chapters have highlighted how decision-making flaws and cultural assumptions affect decisions. In Chapter 5, we saw how, over time, people have viewed scenarios as a tool to overcome these problems. In this chapter, we will outline the principles of scenario thinking, and explain how they can be applied to overcome the thinking flaws that characterize decision-making and action in the face of complexity and uncertainty.

CONTINUED... **Overview**

Competition requires the winning organization to become aware of and react to change in its business environment before its competitors. It needs to develop superior organizational learning skills. In particular, we will show how scenario thinking provides people with a purposeful organizational learning and adaptation approach, helping them to safely navigate the shifting business landscape.

This chapter introduces and explains the specific principles, components and concepts that are the essential tools of scenario planning. This will be achieved by:

- Highlighting how the ability to recognize and react to change as it happens, before competitors do, is the key ingredient of survival. This is an approach known as *adaptive organizational learning*.
- Demonstrating how scenarios overcome the common flaws in traditional strategic thinking. For example, how the scenario approach breaks through the business-as-usual approach that holds back organizations. How scenario planning is the most powerful tool countering the many barriers to learning in the organization, and how it promotes adaptive organizational learning.
- Highlighting the importance to scenario thinking of the key resource of any organization: people. People are the source of creativity and innovation. The challenge for management is to empower and harness the skills, knowledge and experience of their people. A scenario process can help with this.

THE NEED FOR A SCENARIO PROCESS

In previous chapters, we have highlighted a range of innate cognitive limits, in terms of recipes and biases, rationality, filters and cultural assumptions, which impact the effectiveness of human reasoning and judgement, at both individual and group levels. As can be seen from the earlier examples, these cognitive limits result in managers seeking single-track answers to complex business problems, making choices and decisions using limited information processed with simple, abbreviated techniques. In addition, we have seen how organizations get locked into counterproductive behavioural characteristics, such as group-think and fragmentation, which they are often unable to control. It is little wonder that organizational strategies developed in those circumstances invariably lead to strategic failure against competitors who manage to avoid some of these problems. In times of high environmental uncertainty, these cognitive and behavioural limits are even more dangerous, in that they may conveniently suppress awareness of uncertainty in the environment so that it appears to be more certain in the minds of managers, propelling them to act on simplistic, usually incorrect, interpretations of reality.

How, then, is it possible to re-engineer strategic decision-making in organizations to overcome these limits? The answer is to develop a process which:

- surfaces and challenges managerial assumptions and mindsets in a constructive and creative way;
- recognizes uncertainty and makes it explicit;
- provides a way of making sense of an overabundance of information;
- facilitates the development of new insights that would not result from conventional planning methods;
- ensures that all of this is achieved as an organization in which individuals align on coherent action;
- integrates thinking, planning and key future investments to exploit the scarcity landscape (see Chapter 6).

Scenario planning creates space for excellence in managerial thinking, using a structured process to tackle issues in a non-confrontational way, away from the pressure of immediate decision-making. Our perspective is not one of a traditional consultant, thinking out the problem for the client. Only managers of an organization can successfully complete scenario planning, with other professionals contributing nothing more than good process and facilitation. The emphasis is on empowering managers, rather than on off-line planning work and content solutions developed by consultants. The manager is the scenario planner.

This chapter will develop the logic for this scenario approach, helping organizations to better understand their context and therefore manage their success more effectively. In doing so, we will refer back to the flaws that prevent organizations from achieving their goals, as exposed in Chapters 2, 3 and 4, and demonstrate how planners can overcome these. As we saw in Chapter 5, scenarios have long been considered a powerful tool for overcoming these problems. Scenario planning, in this age of accelerating change, is one of the most useful and productive approaches available for individual and collective learning in organizations.

SCENARIOS AND SCENARIO-BASED ORGANIZATIONAL LEARNING

We will discuss how scenarios can be of help in overcoming the problems identified, by reference to a number of fundamental concepts relevant to organizational learning. These include rationalistic decision making, cause and effect thinking, systems thinking, mental models and recipes, and the strategic conversation. By discussing the material in these terms, a framework will emerge that demonstrates the impact of the most up-to-date scenario approach. We will start with rationalistic decision-making.

Rationalistic Decision-making

Most managers operate unconsciously in a rationalistic mode of decision-making. This involves a series of sequential steps, based on the assumptions that:

- there is only one best answer to the strategy question.
- everyone thinking rationally on behalf of the organization will arrive at the same conclusion; and
- implementation follows discovery of strategy. (The challenge of implementation is to make people see the underlying logic, and to motivate them to act accordingly.)

Based on these assumptions, the rationalist approach was formalized in organizational strategy in the early 1960s, through the pioneering work of Ansoff, Chandler and Sloan, and subsequently popularized at the Harvard Business School. It is widely used as the template for developing business strategy. However, this rationalistic paradigm presupposes a relatively stable business environment. Therefore, the less certain the future, the less valid the assumptions underpinning the paradigm are likely to be. This is worsened by the fact that the rationalist approach to dealing with uncertainty is to:

- ignore it, on the basis that there is little point in thinking about inherently uncertain situations.
- use sensitivity analysis, in which the effects of the likely movements in a specific, uncertain variable are examined one by one; or

- generate a range of alternative futures, attaching probabilities to the futures and then focusing attention on the future with the highest probability of occurrence.

All three approaches to uncertainty are problematic.

The problem of ignoring uncertainty

Both empirical evidence and casual observation show that uncertainty causes individuals anxiety, even in relatively simple situations, because we find it difficult to think about risk/benefit conflicts. This is shown, for example, by Borsch's findings that corporate managers tend to get annoyed when consultants present them with the probabilities of certain events, rather than specifying precisely what will happen.[66] In order to reduce this anxiety, individuals actively search for certainty, by denying or ignoring uncertainty. Unfortunately, all strategic decisions are affected by uncertainty and the further one peers into the future, the greater the uncertainty impacting decisions. Appealing as it may be, uncertainty cannot be ignored in the hope that it is anomalous and that normality will soon be resumed. Uncertainty is not, according to Pierre Wack, 'just an occasional, temporary deviation from a reasonable predictability; it is a basic structural feature of the business environment'[65]. There can be no competitive advantage or strategy without uncertainty. The only solution according to Wack, is to: 'accept uncertainty, try to understand it and make it part of your reasoning', which is essentially what scenario planning attempts to do.

Difficulties with sensitivity analysis

Although it may simplify the problem, sensitivity analysis is not usually an appropriate method of dealing with uncertainty in the context of strategy, as it focuses artificially on examining the changes in a single variable, while all other variables are held constant. This may make sense for small changes, but in the real world, things are generally far more complex: variables seldom change in isolation, and changes in one or more variables often have an impact on seemingly unrelated variables, prompting further unexpected changes. Clearly, sensitivity analysis considers situations that will never occur in real life, thus limiting its value. Adopting a scenario approach brings structure to such complexity, enabling managers to take a broader, systemic view of the business environment, leading to a more sophisticated and useful understanding of environmental uncertainty.

The limits of probabilities

Attaching probabilities to a range of alternative futures eliminates the need to confront a broad spectrum of uncertainty, by focusing attention only on the future situations that are most likely to occur. However, there are serious problems with this approach. For example, assigning probability to unique future events is a problematic notion. Objective probability methods, such as the 'classical' and 'relative frequency' approaches, are of no value in dealing with strategic problems, because probability theory relates to situations that belong to sets of events with known statistical characteristics – usually based on accumulating past data. When dealing with unique events, the only viable option is to resort to subjective approaches, in which probability is an expression of an individual's belief that a particular event will or will not occur. Even 'experts' cannot assign probabilities to events which have not been encountered before. In this case, assignments are usually arbitrary, with no predictive value. They may give the illusion of certainty based on questionable mathematical precision, but in fact they cannot be tested and are therefore meaningless. The probability approach to uncertainty is an attempt to introduce optimization and 'find the one right answer' in a situation where fundamental uncertainty makes the idea of the 'best answer' illusory. Given that competitive advantage, in the final analysis, results from uncertainty (without uncertainty there can be no competitive advantage), this seems a less than attractive approach to strategizing.

Limitations of the rational approach

It is now apparent that a rationalist approach to strategic decision-making is incompatible with scenario thinking. They are significantly different thinking paradigms. The rationalist approach assumes that strategy is a one-off decision, and that there is a single, winning answer to every strategic issue that can be arrived at through sequential analysis. The appeal of this approach arises from the fact that individuals tend to be satisfied with a single interpretation of a situation, and are predisposed, at the outset of the decision process, to focus on a single outcome and a single alternative for achieving that outcome, partly to reduce uncertainty[66]. As we saw in Chapter 2, having arrived at the 'answer', individuals develop an inappropriate overconfidence in their judgement because of a failure to recognize the tenuous assumptions upon which their judgements are based. At the same time, the preoccupation with a single outcome generally leads to 'bolstering', where individuals magnify the attractiveness of favoured alternatives over other, non-preferred options.

The scenario approach assumes that strategy is not a unique decision event, but an ongoing and iterative process in which decisions result from an evolving compromise that needs to be periodically revisited and tested in the light of unfolding events. The scenario approach also recognizes that there is no enduring, single 'best' answer to every strategic question; what may appear 'best' today may not be in the future. Scenario planners acknowledge that their knowledge of the future is limited and that additional analysis will not always provide further insights. Also, managers cannot delay making decisions until they feel certain about the future; they must accept that the future is inherently uncertain and unpredictable. Managers need to embrace uncertainty, to think creatively yet systemically about possible future events. In doing so, scenario planners focus not on predicting single future outcomes, but rather on managing uncertainty in a number of alternative projections, a range of plausible future outcomes, which will encompass the main dimensions of uncertainty spanning a particular decision domain.

Fundamentally, the objective of scenario planning is to take management beyond trying to find the best strategy, to developing the best strategy process – an iterative process of adjustment and adaptation that is sufficiently robust to ensure that the organization is able to deal with a range of potential business environments. The primary task of the process is to provoke a strategic conversation within the organization as a foundation for better decisions about the future; the cornerstone of the process is *systemic thinking*. Systemic thinking is a crucial skill of the successful manager who wants to be a scenario planner. We will discuss this subject in detail below, but before we do, we need to consider the nature of 'cause and effect thinking' upon which it is based.

Cause and Effect Thinking

Systems thinking is based on the implicit assumption of causality. Well-known researchers in behavioural psychology such as Tversky and Kahneman suggest that individuals make sense of the world by organizing and interpreting events in terms of cause and effect reasoning[67]. The assumption of causality is one of the most fundamental structural features the human mind imposes on reality in order to make sense of it. We are predisposed to causal reasoning: a causal schema feels natural. Causes logically flow forward into consequences, while causal knowledge is easily transferable from one situation to another. Several researchers have established that people exhibit a high propensity to engage in causal reasoning when faced with important, unusual or surprising events[68]. These events create uncertainty that triggers the search for a causal agent, in the hope that, by finding the causal agent, control over the situation is re-established[69].

However, if causal thinking does not acknowledge more complex, systemic relationships it may lead to simplistic conclusions that underpin many of the thinking flaws described in earlier chapters. For example:

- Cause and effect are separate, with effects following the causes. This supposition stands in the way of a proper appreciation of the counterintuitive behaviour of closed cause and effect loops, where the effects and the causes are not so easy to identify.
- Effects follow causes. There are invariably delays in systems, and effects may appear in different parts of the system. Therefore, looking for a cause close to the effect may lead to false conclusions.
- Effect is proportional to cause. While this may be true of physical processes, it does not necessarily apply to living systems. For example, a variable that is known to normally create an effect may fail to do so in systems with thresholds where a stimulus is too small to produce a reaction or effect.

Despite these fallacies, individuals are comfortable with causal reasoning because cause and effect appear simple and have a strong, albeit often false, resonance of logic. We make up causal statements all the time. For example, 'cigarette smoking causes lung cancer' or 'repeated exposure to violence in television programmes promotes violent behaviour in children'. Although these causal statements may be confirmed in the majority of cases, they may not be valid in every case, as there may be other, less visible factors at work. However, having discovered a single, easily identifiable cause for a particular problem, individuals often neglect to search for alternative explanations.

Systems Thinking

The scenario process readily addresses the problems of causal thinking. Scenario thinking relies on diagnostic processes that highlight causal inferences and explain the influencing factors. Because scenario processes are grounded in systems thinking, it is recognized that causality should refer to relationships between system elements that reflect the structure of the total system. The result is that the scenario process avoids the oversimplified thinking often inherent in causal thinking. This is achieved by systematically examining a *range* of possible causes and structural relationships that can give rise to a particular situation. The recognition of time delays and loops acting in the system is particularly important to understand and anticipate behaviour. In doing so, nothing is taken for granted, and although conventional wisdom may hold that 'A causes B', the scenario process takes this not as an end point, but a starting point, in the investigation of influencing systems and structural relationships. Challenging conventional wisdom increases the likelihood of discovering possible discontinuities, and previously unseen or undervalued linkages with other areas of the business environment. This results in greater understanding and new conceptualizations of complex issues that can differ sharply from conventional views. Most significant is the fact that none of this could have been achieved with conventional planning systems.

Not everyone subscribes to the view that major, unprecedented structural changes are taking place today. Some people contend that the world has always been changing; that the changes today are no more or less rapid than those experienced by our grandparents and by their forebears. Others suggest that it is not the amount of change that is significant, but the accelerating speed of change. Whichever view one takes is hardly important; what matters is that we acknowledge that we live in an increasingly interconnected world in which change spreads around faster and wider, making change continual rather than exceptional. This being the case, trying to understand and make sense of what is going on in the world today and how the current situation may unfold into the future using a linear, event-based mode of thinking, is unlikely to be of much use. What is required is a way of thinking known as 'systems' or 'systemic' thinking.

Many of the cognitive flaws identified in earlier chapters have their roots in a lack of systemic thinking. Systems thinking leads to seeing *beyond* isolated incidents or trends to deeper patterns, arriving ultimately at insights about the interconnectedness and structural patterns of events. This way of thinking is founded on the premise that no event or incident ever stands entirely in isolation: every event or incident is part of a system that maintains its existence and functions as a whole through the interactions of its parts. Therefore, if we really wish to understand a situation, we need to take a wider view that compels us to identify and examine in depth the system in which the situation is embedded, rather than look at the events in isolation. This is central to the scenario process, and it allows one to look deeper and see further, to arrive at an understanding of the context which gives rise to events. Armed with this understanding, we are then able to act with a greater degree of confidence, and make better business decisions

STEEP analysis

A common approach to thinking about the business environment in terms of developing strategy is what is colloquially known as STEEP analysis – the analysis of the Societal, Technological, Economic, Ecological and Political vari ables (or subsets) which combine to form the overall contextual environment. (This analysis may also include legal or regulatory variables as well.) Most managers are aware of the tool, and use it for developing long-term organizational plans. However, the analysis of individual variables, such as political or economic developments, as if they were discrete, stand-alone elements, is problematic. Because of interconnections, this approach results in long lists of factors that are difficult to deal with. What is missing is integration, or systemic insights. The consequence is that STEEP analysis does not help to move thinking forward, and is of limited practical value in strategy development.

For example, two MNCs (multinational corporations) that we have recently worked with had small 'business environment scanning units', comprising two individuals who spent their time collecting, summarizing and periodically reporting on happenings in the business environment, with particular emphasis on economic, technological and political developments. Societal and ecological developments were largely ignored, on the basis that they supposedly had 'very little impact on our organization'. In examining the work of these departments, it was found that:

- each of the environmental variables was monitored and reported on as if they were discrete and isolated variables. There was little or no attempt to identify the causal relationships and interactions between them;
- much of the work of the scanning units revolved around extrapolation of current and past trends, without any attempt to explore new and unexpected forces creating trend breaks;
- it appeared that the work of these units played no role in the development of strategic plans, other than the fact that both units provided forecasts of base rate indices to be used in the plans, such as interest rates and cost escalation rates.

As a result, although the reports produced were circulated to all senior managers, few actually read the reports. Those that did were unsure of what to do with the information, the typical reaction being 'interesting, but so what?' The reports only added to the sea of paper flowing towards the managers, and there was nothing in the reports directing their attention to the important elements of the reports.

This situation is not unique. Analysing the context is not an easy task: often we do not know which variables are key and which are not, and we usually have only the vaguest idea of the inter-relations among variables. It is only by adopting a systems approach – examining the variables and the interconnections between them – that we can gain a basic understanding of the underlying structure, relationships and characteristics of a particular situation. At the same time, to be of use to managers in developing strategy, environmental analysis needs to capture the essence of uncertainty about the future, in a way that is understandable and useful. In complex and 'choice-rich' systems, this is achieved by considering several possible scenarios, reflecting the systemic relationships but also the irreducible uncertainty in the relevant domain.

> The more that managers work with scenarios, the more they develop a tolerance for working with uncertainty, ambiguity and complexity. This is in turn produces greater potential for breakthroughs in thinking, which can be translated into action for competitive advantage on behalf of the organization.

These scenarios provide the context in which to assess the impact of environmental factors on the organization.

Interestingly, when the firms discussed above decided to introduce scenario development projects, societal issues which had been ignored by the business environment units, proved to be significant drivers of the scenarios developed. Conversely, technology, which occupied much of the business environment units' attention, did not play a central role in any of the scenarios developed. The reason for this was that, on examining technological issues in the scenario workshops, the scenario team determined that although technological developments would undoubtedly have a significant impact on their organizations, there was little uncertainty in this area, relative to the other environmental variables. In retrospect, this made perfect sense – both organizations are in long lead-time industries and the technology in these industries does not change overnight. At the same time, both organizations are at the forefront of technology in their areas, and it is unlikely that there would be any technology advances in their domains in the next five years that the organizations were not already aware of.

This situation is not unique. It is often the case that we focus our attention on things we know well; the things that we know we know. However, it is the factors we know very little about that take us by surprise, often leading to strategic failure. We are not looking for them because they are not prominent in our mental models and therefore do not become part of the conversations within the organization. Nevertheless, those factors could potentially undermine the organization's ability to survive. The power of scenarios is that they challenge management thinking to develop a more holistic understanding beyond a business-as-usual mindset. This typically emerges in the scenario process by focusing on questions such as:

- What is driving this particular situation?
- What is happening now in the environment that matters or could matter in the future?
- What are other ways of looking at the situation?
- What are the implicit assumptions in our current thinking that we need to question?
- What are we not looking at that we should be looking at?
- What do we need to see that is now invisible and that no one else is seeing?

The process of answering these questions generates unstructured ideas across a broad spectrum, shifting attention from things and events that we know well to those things that *we don't know we know*. The result is an understanding of the causal interconnectedness of seemingly random data and multiple trends, leading to an understanding of the unseen underlying structure that ultimately drives events. As a result, the systemic approach results in managers becoming better observers of their business environment, benefiting from new insights and perspectives that would not otherwise have surfaced. It results in a reshaping of mental models of how the world works, and makes people contemplate changes that would normally have remained outside their frames of reference.

Mental Models and their Limitations

Throughout this book, we talk about mental models; those deep-rooted recipes, assumptions and guiding ideas that exist in our minds that determine how we interpret events going on around us, that predispose us to expect certain results, and ultimately, that guide our actions. In essence, the human brain is a pattern recognition system. Our brains store thinking in patterns of experience (see Chapter 5), and these patterns become our mental models that 'do our thinking for us'. When something triggers this pattern, our brains play out the script and we react accordingly.

At the same time, these mental models give rise to the cognitive filters, recipes and biases discussed earlier. For example, in Chapter 2 we discussed an experiment in which people were given triples (sets of three integers), and asked to discern the rule applied in generating them. In this and many other similar experiments, the research respondents were confident that they had discovered the sequence, even though they were looking at random sequences, to the extent that they could not see how it could be random. This demonstrates how easily our mental models construct plausible explanations and mistake connections made in the mind with reality.

Although one generally discusses mental models at the individual level, they also exist metaphorically at organizational and community levels. Organizational mental models develop and become embedded in people belonging to the same organization. As management teams work together and share experiences, it is inevitable that they begin to develop consensual views of the future, based on what worked for the organization in the past – and what did not. In general, the older, larger and more successful the organization, the more defined and deeply entrenched is its mental model. In Chapter 3, we highlighted the lock-in process driving this, as models mature and managers within the organization begin to see and interpret events in the world through a common set of lenses, creating a shared mental model of how the future will unfold. The lock-in happens because what they know determines what they see, and what they see determines what they know. Over time, these experiences combine to form the dominant shared mental model in the organization.

The model is thus reinforced, particularly in well-integrated organizations. Those that do not subscribe to the common view complicate matters and are branded as mavericks and ostracized. Organizations hire and promote those individuals who outwardly support the model. At the industry level, interactions between organizations within an industry can institutionalize a shared framework or mental model through which constituents in that industry collectively view and interpret events. Organizational mental models lead to what has earlier been described as managerial recipes, or commonly accepted rules, on how that organization conducts itself and does business. Most of these 'rules' are not explicitly stated in any manual within the organization; they constitute *intuitive managerial knowledge.* Everyone knows what they are, and they are constantly reinforced by managerial actions. Although the recipes introduce an element of efficiency in managing large organizations, they become problematic if they are not periodically challenged.

These ideas can be illustrated by a trivial example from a recent project. The business in question is a medium-sized organization that had embarked on a comprehensive change management programme. In interviewing the management team, several of the managers alluded to the fact that much of the organization's recipe was built on 'rules' that had once functioned well, but had become obsolete. For example, one particular factor that surfaced repeatedly was the policy regarding expense accounts; in particular, the rule regarding how much could be spent on lunch with customers. In the interview process, it was discovered that there was, in fact, no formal rule defining the limits of lunch expenses. In discussing the issues, it transpired that at least 10 years earlier, a previous CEO had chastised a manager for having spent what he regarded as an exorbitant amount on a customer lunch and had arbitrarily reduced the individual's expense claim. Thereafter, this amount entered the organization's managerial recipe as the upper expenditure limit for lunch and had persisted for 10 years, even though it was never formally established! In the context of strategy, the question is what other, more strategic elements of the organization's recipe may have become dangerously obsolete, but continue to drive the organization unchallenged?

This example, trivial as it may be, confirms an important point about mental models: once established, whether at the individual, organization or industry level, they do not change easily or quickly. The reason for this was described in Chapter 2. We saw how initial beliefs, once formed, are not only difficult to dislodge, but they tend to structure the way in which subsequent evidence is interpreted. This arises from the fact that new evidence supporting initial beliefs is judged to be reliable, whereas evidence contradicting the beliefs is dismissed as being unreliable or erroneous (the confirmation bias). Having formed a belief, individuals then fail to test the limits of validity of their theories, leading to the hazard of overconfidence.

Mental models are the mechanism through which the human mind works. Without mental models, there would be no learning and we would have to think out every situation from scratch. However, they also cause the actions of organizations to be anchored in current thinking about what the future is likely to be. Therefore, it is imperative that the hidden assumptions underpinning these mental models are periodically surfaced and examined, to ensure that they have not become obsolete.

The Strategic Conversation

The strategy process is best viewed as essentially a *strategic conversation* with two parts[70]. The first is the formal, well-defined part designed by the managers, which revolves largely around the planning and budget cycles and quantitative information. The second is the informal part, the casual conversations that people engage in at the coffee machine, in corridors, or over lunch. This part is not designed or controlled by the managers, and is usually qualitative and anecdotal in nature. It is nevertheless extremely important because *it determines where people's attention is focused. These conversations are influenced by the mental models which* have developed over time, and which determine how individuals see the world, how they interpret events, how they decide what is important and what is not.

Conversations influencing mental models that in turn influence conversations constitute a system that is locked in, predetermining the attention span of the organization. There are a number of problems associated with these processes and systems.

First, the models are seldom exposed and subjected to scrutiny. This may not be a problem in times of relative stability in the business environment, as there may be a reasonably good match between the mental model of decision-makers and unfolding reality. However, in times of rapid change the mental models become 'a dangerously mixed bag; rich detail and understanding can coexist with dubious assumptions and selective inattention to alternative interpretations of evidence, and projections that are pretence'[71].

Biases ensure that the models are enduring. Individuals and firms tend to stick with their initial theories and assumptions about the outside world, about customers, markets and competition. If these are not periodically rethought, retested and reintroduced, they can very quickly condemn the business to obsolescence.

There may be excessive integration of mental models, leading to group-think. In this situation, individuals forming part of a cohesive group tend to suppress any ideas that do not accord with the ideas favoured by the group. As we saw in Chapter 3, this leads to group-think: critical ideas are inhibited and only those courses of action perceived as being preferred by the group are examined.

Alternatively, there can exist a complete fragmentation of mental models, in which case there is little or no sharing of ideas in the organization and it cannot function or act as a cohesive team. The consequence is that there are so many factions that it becomes impossible to start a coherent strategic conversation in the organization, and paralysis takes hold.

The models include expectations as to what will happen in a given situation, the sequence in which things will happen, possible alternative courses of action, and the information required to decide. Because of these assumptions, the models develop within a limited and rigid information domain and, as we have seen in Chapter 2, the effects of such intuitive framing biases make it difficult to integrate new information into the information set, particularly when this information is at odds with the existing mental models of the decision-makers.

An effective strategic conversation requires that:

- mental models are made explicit;
- there is a balance between commonality and variety of models within the organization;
- a wide range of quantitative and qualitative information is introduced into the conversation.

This is where scenario planning can provide effective intervention, as it requires managers to confront uncertainty by developing a set of plausible, but by no means certain, future conditions. In doing so, the scenario process provides a framework for combining the formal and informal elements of the strategic conversation. It stimulates management teams to think together in a more disciplined and systemic manner. The process forces managers to examine a wide range of information, to articulate and argue the logic of their understanding of the present, and to expose their assumptions as to how and why the future may evolve in particular ways. The result of the scenario process is the creation of a language for a sophisticated strategic conversation that would not otherwise occur. This facilitates the realignment of the recipes or mental models of managers to create a shared, often new, understanding of the situation at a higher level of richness. In the context of strategy, this shared understanding provides a platform for more effective organizational decision-making.

HOW SCENARIOS TACKLE THE PROBLEMS OF ORGANIZATIONAL THINKING

We will now use the organizational learning categories introduced in this chapter to discuss *how* scenarios overcome thinking flaws, by considering the principal activities involved. These include:

- surfacing mental models;
- eliciting the agenda;
- activating and integrating intuitive knowledge;
- analyzing driving forces;
- scenario telling.

Surfacing Mental Models

The first activity involves the surfacing of mental models. Mental models play a central role in this discussion, as they ultimately determine what happens. Mental models are largely intuitive. In order to make the organization more skilful in formulating strategy we will need to highlight mental models, making them explicit and working on them to improve their relationship with reality.

In the scenario process, mental models are initially surfaced at the 'client interview' stage of the project. As we explain in Chapter 7, the first requirement of any good scenario project is that a client should be identified who acts as arbiter on important agenda decisions, providing a focus for scenario development and a reference point to ensure relevance. In many cases, the client comprises the senior management of the organization. As we mentioned earlier, we assume that the client – the manager – is the scenario planner; if a professional supports him we refer to this person as the scenario facilitator.

One of the first steps in the scenario process is for the facilitator to interview the client group. These interviews serve a number of purposes: they provide the opportunity to introduce the scenario facilitators to the clients; they provide a platform to discuss the scenario process and set expectations; and they determine how far into the future the client needs to look. However, the primary purpose of the interviews is to unearth the elements in the current and future business environment that are of concern to the client. The broad, independent themes at the forefront of the client's mental models are extracted through analysis of the interview transcripts, and then summarized as the *scenario agenda*. This is then fed back to senior management to confirm the focus for subsequent scenario development.

In addition to establishing the scenario agenda, asking interviewees the appropriate questions can identify the current thinking and recipes in the organization. As will be discussed in Chapter 7, we favour open-ended interviews based on the so-called *seven questions*, a set of trigger questions developed at the Institute of the

Future and subsequently added to by scenario facilitators in Shell and Strathclyde (see Chapter 7 for details). In answering these questions, interviewees unwittingly reveal what they regard as the main uncertainties in the business environment, their hopes and fears, their in-built assumptions and emotional attachments. Surfacing these allows individual and organizational mental models to be mapped and understood.

Eliciting the Agenda

Managers inevitably have different views on the business, depending on their role and area of responsibility. These different views are often rooted in a functional perspective, for example, people in the marketing division of the organization tend to ground their understanding of events in a marketing perspective, people from production divisions are usually predisposed to view events from an operations perspective, and so on. In Chapter 4, we called this *professional culture*. At the same time, managers are busy people and it is usually difficult to arrange for them to meet on a frequent basis, formally or informally, simply to share views about what is happening in the environment. Whenever such conversations happen, they will take place in the context of a management decision to be taken, forcing individual managers into their own functional corner from where they defend their view on the issue at hand. This is not a situation in which an open exchange of views tends to take place. Consequently, managers are often surprised at the diversity of views surfaced within their management team on strategy and longer-term issues during feedback sessions.

One might be tempted to think that this is perhaps less evident in smaller organizations, given that there is usually more functional coordination, with managers meeting on a regular basis. Our experience in working with both large and small organizations is that there is little discernible difference between the two. Management teams may perhaps meet more frequently in smaller companies but, as with large companies, when they do meet, conversations inevitably revolve around day-to-day operational and tactical problems – and issues of a strategic nature rarely make it to the agenda. Consequently, interviewing management teams to establish the scenario agenda is a useful exercise in its own right. It results in:

- managers becoming aware, perhaps for the first time, that there is in fact a diversity of views held in the management team of the organization;

- confronting managers with the views of their colleagues about a particular situation that does not accord with their own views and understanding of that situation. It forces these managers to make their mental model explicit by having to articulate their assumptions, beliefs and opinions. In doing so, the process often identifies knowledge gaps – areas that management identify as being critical to the future of the business, but about which there is little knowledge in the organization;
- the creation of a shared feeling of identity among the management team, ultimately helping to improve the dynamics of the strategic conversation.

This was vividly demonstrated in a project that we undertook several years ago. The client was a medium-sized but fragmented and geographically scattered multinational. They contracted for a five-day scenario project workshop, with the management team of 20 people as the participants. Interviewing the team required visits to several locations around the world. Summarizing the transcripts in the usual way proved to be revealing, as it was immediately apparent that there was a wide diversity of opinions within the team. The interview summary was then transferred to flipcharts in preparation for the workshop, again a significant task in that over 50 flipcharts were required to list the feedback (whereas normally 10–15 flipcharts suffice in an exercise of this type).

The initial workshop agenda envisioned that the first morning session of the workshop would be given over to the interview feedback, after which the remainder of the workshop would be devoted to developing scenarios and strategy. As it turned out, the management team was surprised at the views, many of them conflicting, which had been expressed by their colleagues in the interview process. The feedback session initiated such a useful, constructive dialogue on the purpose of the organization, the essence of its success formula and its continued relevance that the decision was made to put the scenario exercise on hold, and the remainder of the workshop was spent discussing and exploring the feedback in depth.

It transpired that because the organization was so geographically dispersed, this was the first time that the management team had sat together and aired their views on strategic issues and the organization's future. The workshop became an exercise in unbundling mental models and creating, for the first time, a shared view within the management team. This focused on what was most important for the organization's success formula, where the priorities for action lay, and what needed to be done at the strategic level. By the end of the workshop, the management team had taken a giant step towards establishing a well-articulated and shared platform from which to move forward; they were able to develop an ongoing strategic conversation in the organization. Some other form of intervention may have achieved the same result, but in this case, the initial steps in the scenario process uncovered the management team's divergent views, and which then provided a non-threatening forum to discuss and reconcile their differences.

> A key objective of developing scenarios is to challenge the prevailing organizational and individual mindsets. This is achieved by high-lighting the uncertain aspects of the future, and by expanding the range of future outcomes that managers need to consider when developing strategic plans.

In addition to providing a reference point for scenario development and a sounding board for opinions within the organization, the agenda elicitation process serves to establish exactly what managers in the organization believe is relevant and important in the strategic context. This allows understanding of the dominant mental model in the organization.

Activating and Integrating Intuitive Knowledge

Knowledge can be conveniently divided into two categories:

- codified knowledge, which is well articulated, understood and integrated, and of direct use in decision-making; and
- intuitive knowledge, comprising isolated observations that appear to have meaning and importance, but are not well articulated and remain unconnected with the codified knowledge.

Scaffolding

Connecting and integrating intuitive knowledge into a wider body of codified knowledge does not happen on its own and can be helped by an outside intervention: 'this usually takes the form of an outside agent confronting our unconnected knowledge with the knowledge structure in the wider group or society[72].' This process of building connections between isolated observations and insights is known as *scaffolding*, a term coined by Vygotsky, a Russian psychologist. Vygotsky suggested that (metaphorically) surrounding our body of codified knowledge was something he called 'the zone of proximal development' in which unconnected random, intuitive knowledge resides. By asking questions

and making suggestions, outside agents enable individuals to discover the linkages between intuitive and codified knowledge, thereby codifying it and making
it actionable, and in the process also increasing overall knowledge structure.

At its core, the scenario process is essentially about developing knowledge of
the contextual environment, by scaffolding elements of knowledge in the zone of
proximal development into codified knowledge within the organization. All
scenario exercises begin with a base of codified knowledge, representing the
business-as-usual view of the world. Working with this view alone defeats the
purpose of the exercise, as the scenarios developed in this way replicate knowledge that already exists in the organization, and fail to provide productive
insights for use in strategy development. At the same time, introducing new
knowledge or insights outside the zone of proximal development is equally
ineffective, as this results in information that is experienced as irrelevant and
cannot be readily integrated into the existing base of codified knowledge, and
scenarios that are experienced as implausible and therefore not meaningful to the
organization in terms of strategy development. Developing scenarios requires a
careful balance between moving away from business-as-usual and remaining
relevant to managers and decision-makers.

Scaffolding is brought about in the scenario process in several ways:

- **Good facilitation and process design.** The zone of proximal development
  is specific to the organization, and experienced scenario facilitators know how
  to recognize and delineate the zone in a particular exercise, guiding the
  scenario process in ways that will be productive in exploring the zone. Some
  of this will come from analysis of the client interviews, some will come from
  the interaction between the scenario team members, and some will come
  from the facilitator's experience gained working on previous scenario
  exercises.
- **Scenario team composition.** Ideally, scenario teams should comprise as
  wide a variation of perspectives as possible in terms of age, qualifications and
  work experience. This reduces the potential for group-think and, perhaps
  more importantly, the more diverse the composition of the team, the greater
  the chances that new and unexpected questions may be asked within the
  scenario team. This will in turn trigger previously unseen connections
  between intuitive and codified knowledge.
- **The use of remarkable people (RPs)** who may be defined as intensely
  curious but sharp observers, who understand the way the world works and

have their finger on the pulse of change. The concept of RPs, institutionalised in the Shell scenario process, is founded on the principle that the search for innovative thinking needs to take place from outside the organization. This is achieved by identifying individuals who are not part of the normal ongoing strategic conversation within the organization, but are conversant with the industry structure, language, driving forces and key uncertainties, and whose structured knowledge overlaps areas where the client's knowledge is fragmented and unstructured. Such people are able to think 'out of the box', triggering scenario teams to surface intuitive knowledge and to then integrate this into existing cognitive structures. Therefore, more important than their particular expertise is the *relevance* of their knowledge, both to the zone of proximal development and the existing codified knowledge in the organization.

RPs can often help to reframe a problem, enabling the scenario team to develop a completely new, sophisticated understanding of the problem, which they would almost certainly not have arrived at alone. For example, in one of the scenario workshops we held during a project with a paper company, the RP introduced the concepts of 'configuration', 'reconfiguration', 'prime movers', 'invaders', 'path breakers' and 'reframers'. These concepts were not part of the typical language heard in day-to-day business conversations within the organization. When this language was translated to particular situations within the organization, the workshop participants were able to redefine the traditional industry value chain, moving from the conventional industry notions of pulp, paper and publishing, to content provider, service provider and infrastructure. This enabled management to develop a new, shared and higher-level understanding of those actors and factors outside the organization that could redefine their industry in the future; consequently, they discovered new strategic options available to them.

Although team composition and RPs are essential components of a good scenario process, this is not all that is needed to ensure that scaffolding takes place. Our experience suggests that nothing much happens without good facilitation and process design. We have worked with scenario teams that were not ideal in terms of size or composition, and have not always been able to engage with RPs, but with good facilitation and process design, they have managed to achieve significant and memorable breakthroughs in thinking, leading to meaningful and integrated structural insights. Conversely, in analysing a number of failed scenario projects, it was apparent that much of the failure of these projects could be attributed to poor facilitation and process design.

Analysing Driving Forces

Developing scenarios is a social, conversational process, in which individuals in a scenario team collaborate to build – or scaffold – the unconnected insights of their intuitive knowledge into coherent structures. However, this does not happen spontaneously; it requires an appropriate process led by a facilitator experienced in the dynamics of social interaction, and who understands how to best explore the zone of proximal development. As we saw earlier in this chapter, central to good process design is a systems approach to analysing the driving forces of the contextual environment.

Iceberg analysis

Use can be made of a systems approach known as *iceberg analysis*, which breaks down knowledge into different categories. At the peak of the iceberg (the part of the iceberg that is visible above the waterline), are observable *events*. However, as discussed earlier, the scenario process is concerned with much more than events; it assumes that events are not usually random but related to one another through an underlying structure of causal relationships. These give rise to multiple and inter-related *trends* and *patterns* in the events observed. Trends and patterns are below the waterline of the iceberg, in that they are not immediately visible, but require our mental processing of series of visible events before they become apparent. As one digs deeper into the iceberg, events appear to display organized behaviour, and become trends; dig deeper still and it becomes possible to start seeing patterns in terms of relationships between multiple trends. The awareness of these patterns makes us ask, why are there inter-related trends? At the bottom of the iceberg, we construct the underlying *systemic structure* driving patterns, trends and visible events. We cannot see these structures, but we know of their existence through their manifestation in the events we can observe. They drive the situation as it unfolds.

However, as there may be more than one explanation of why things happen, we normally need to articulate more than one possible causal structure. Different members of the team may, from their various perspectives, suggest different ways of scaffolding the trends and patterns observed, representing the fundamental and irreducible uncertainty in the situation. Having determined the underlying driving forces, one can then begin to project future behaviour, with multiple structures leading to multiple scenarios.

The power of scaffolding is that it provides the means by which our unstructured insights and knowledge are given clarity and meaning. They can become integrated into our codified knowledge, enriching our mental maps. This makes scenario projects something that participants experience as positive and exciting. We are creating order out of chaos, organizing seemingly disparate events and happenings in the contextual environment; events that we intuitively know to be important but which hitherto we have been unable to articulate why this is so. Disparate issues are placed in a coherent framework, enabling integration of knowledge and giant leaps in understanding. In the process, we are using all of this knowledge and insight to develop competitive advantage through developing winning strategic plans.

Scenario Telling

While the scenario process is concerned with articulating and then integrating intuitive knowledge through a scaffolding process, the *writing and dissemination of scenario stories* may be considered as the process of formally codifying knowledge for a wider group.

One widely accepted theory of scaffolding, combining the theories of Vygotsky and Ingvar, is that knowledge is stored and organized in the brain in the form of a *cognitive schema* or *script*, consisting of memories of the future (Ingvar, Chapter 5), comprising the total of our experiences in the form of temporarily organized stories[73]. As we saw in Chapter 5, when faced with a disparate stream of facts and events, individuals attempt to understand the situation by auto-matically applying the schema that most closely resembles the situation. This script essentially guides the individual's understanding of the situation and his behaviour, by preparing him for the next scene in the sequence of expected events[74]. Understanding disparate information in this way implies expectations as to what should happen, the sequence in which things should happen, what alternatives exist, and what further information is required.

In thinking about the future, individuals need to construct new patterns of events, inter-relationships and structures that they have not seen or experienced before. In such situations, they cannot apply their existing schemata in the normal way, but the discoveries and new knowledge gathered through the scenario process provide the basis for them to develop a store of new schemata through which subsequent events will be translated. The advantage of the new schemata is that this effectively results in a widening of the situational understanding, in terms of new conceptualizations of the viable options and solutions to problems.

Having developed new knowledge and ideas through the scaffolding process, this is then codified by embedding it in a limited number of scenario storylines that can be spread throughout the organization. As van der Heijden notes, stories are 'one of the most powerful means of packaging a complex set of seemingly unrelated events and relationships into something that is cognitively coherent and manageable'[75]. Because of this, people refer to them as *umbrella concepts*; in this way,

> The scenario process must move people away from their existing schemas and guide them to explore new territory. This is one of the reasons why good process is so important.

and an effective base for communicating complex, sometimes paradoxical, conditions and events. Scenario stories that are original, compelling, provocative, memorable and that elicit a rich imagery, help to engage the minds of individuals and initiate a strategic conversation within the organization. The same material dryly presented in tabular form may not come across so easily. At the same time, because scenarios are usually developed in sets of two, three or four in which each scenario represents an equally plausible alternative future, the scenario stories have the power to break old stereotypes. This forces decision-makers to question their broadest assumptions about the way the world works

ORGANIZATIONAL LEARNING

So far, we have discussed the principal steps in the scenario process, and how these address the problems and concerns explained in Chapters 2, 3 and 4. We have focused on the cognitive aspects of problems and how the cognitive scenario process overcomes some of the flaws identified.

We now need to widen the discussion by asking why is it important to be concerned about thinking flaws? Why should we be working on trying to overcome these? The ultimate aim is to ensure the survival and well-being of the organization. This is not assured and requires active management intervention. The business environment is subject to change, and the organization that adapts first will have the best chance in the competitive marketplace. The reason why we need to overcome thinking flaws is that they stand in the way of proper observation and adaptation. So far, our discourse has been heavily cognition-oriented. Recognizing that the ultimate aim is *adaptation* moves the discussion beyond cognition into the world of action. Cognition is not the same thing as action, and investing in understanding without realizing the organizational behavioural implications is a waste of time and energy. Unless scenarios have the potential of changing behaviour, they do not deserve our attention.

The Process of Organizational Learning

In this part of the discussion, we will make use of the concept that best connects cognition and action, known as *adaptive organizational learning*, to which our attention now turns. The term organizational learning is currently in vogue, and much has been written presenting it as a powerful tool to improve the performance of organizations, especially in turbulent times. In business, 'learning' is generally used in the context of attempts on the part of organizations to improve their efficiency, effectiveness and innovation in uncertain market conditions. The greater the uncertainty in the environment, the greater the need for learning. This is to enable quicker and more effective responses to the challenges faced. Testimony to this comes from numerous studies suggesting that the majority of large corporations suffer from learning disabilities that slow down adaptation to meet changing environmental conditions. In analyzing the findings of one of these studies, Arie de Geus, a former head of Group Planning in Shell, suggested that over the long run survival depends on sensitivity to the environment and adaptation of actions. This is embodied in the organization's ability to learn, to experiment, to continually explore new opportunities to create new sources of growth and wealth, and to change its behaviour to fit what is happening around it.

According to David Kolb, one of the foremost writers on the cycle of learning, the learning process consists of four stages: concrete experiences, reflective observation, abstract conceptualization and active experimentation, as detailed in Figure 6.1. The process is an iterative one: learning begins with observing what has occurred, we reflect on what has been observed and how it can be conceptualized, we make an assessment as to the underlying structures that drive the behaviour we observed and, from this, we develop a theory as to what is happening. This theory then influences the development of a response leading to the implementation of suitable and appropriate actions in the form of new patterns of behaviour. These actions set an expectation. However, invariably reality will deviate, drawing our attention to what is different from our expectation. This starts the next iteration of the learning cycle, with reflection, conceptualization and mental model-building. This learning is not an episodic event, but a continuous and ongoing process. Reflection and action work together to produce learning; without action there can be no learning, since all that one can then reflect on is one's previous reflections.

Organizational learning occurs when the learning cycle is performed collectively in an organization. This is when individuals come together to reflect on their experiences, collectively developing new theories based on observation and then acting together. In the process of joint reflection, there is a unbundling and sharing of individual world views, leading to a shared understanding of situations and an alignment of mental models. 'If a critical level of alignment of mental models takes place within the organization, planning effectively becomes a joint activity, and experiences will be common, leading to joint reflection in the group and reinforcement of a shared metal model[75]'. Therefore without joint action, organizational learning cannot occur.

In Chapter 3, we talked briefly about single- and double-loop learning. We can now reinterpret this in the light of the learning cycle. The traditional view of organizational learning, associated with the rationalistic view of decision-making, is based on single-loop learning. With single-loop learning, organizations adapt to change in environmental conditions within the confines of a

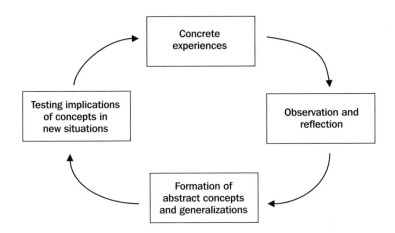

Figure 6.1 The cycle of learning. From D. Kolb (1984) *Experiential Learning as a Source of Learning and Development.* Reproduced by permission of Prentice-Hall.

clearly detailed goal structure, which limits room for manoeuvre in the box 'Formation of abstract concepts and generalizations' in Figure 6.1. Consequently, only incremental improvements are made, but the fundamental assumptions underlying the existing organizational recipes are not questioned. According to Peter Senge[76], this is only the first stage in organizational learning. Learning in its complete sense is achieved only when the organization engages in double-loop learning, by opening up all aspects of its generalizations for questioning. Double-loop learning involves radically altering all organizational rules and recipes that no longer fit experiences. This necessitates a reflective process of continuous experimentation and feedback, in which organizations act to grasp the systemic source underpinning events, ultimately arriving at new ways of looking at the world. Action is a fundamental part of this type of learning, which we have called adaptive organizational learning. As we have already seen, scenario planning is one such process.

Scenario Planning as a Way Towards Adaptive Organizational Learning

Organizational learning introduces a number of interesting notions and observations into the discussion. For example, Edgar Schein suggests that to learn means, among other things, to:

- recognize that we do not possess all the answers;
- concede that we often do not know what to do;
- question the basic assumptions we have long held.

This requires that we make ourselves vulnerable and, as most individuals are reluctant to do this, Schein suggests that we go to extraordinary lengths *not* to learn. The benefit that the scenario process has in relation to this is that it provides a structured process that helps participants to articulate their concerns, and an environment in which it is legitimate and therefore safe to acknowledge quandary, and to question individual and organizational assumptions. In essence, scenario planning is a setting that fosters and is conducive to individual and group learning.

A similar observation comes from Henry Mintzberg, who noted, 'study after study has shown that managers work at an unrelenting pace, that their activities are characterized by brevity, variety, and discontinuity, and that they are strongly oriented to action and dislike reflective activities'[77]. While there is much empirical evidence that supports this view, it is also true that the orientation to action and dislike of reflective activities is largely due to the fact that the reward systems in organizations actively encourage action, and work against managers' ability to pause and reflect. Therefore, an action orientation does not necessarily mean that, given the opportunity, people will not willingly engage in and enjoy reflective learning processes such as scenario planning. As Edward Deming pointed out, 'people are born with intrinsic motivation, self-esteem, dignity, curiosity to learn, and joy in learning'[78]. We are innately curious, designed for learning, and we enjoy sharing our ideas, thoughts, insights, fears and theories of how the world works. Certainly it has been our experience that although the scenario process is cognitively demanding, tiring and, at times, extremely frustrating, most if not all of the teams we have worked with have found the process to be exciting, intellectually stimulating, satisfying and enjoyable.

> Even if they see and understand the disharmony, more immediate pressures will often prevent managers from putting it on the agenda for discussion.

Finally, scenario planning is not a fad. As we outlined in Chapter 5, it has been in continuous use in the military for hundreds of years and in organizations such as Shell since the 1960s. It has therefore stood the test of time. Scenario planning is not an episodic activity or a new management system, it is a way of thinking that should permeate the entire organization and impact all activity within it. As such, it does not require a significant investment in organizational and process restructuring, unlike most other popular management initiatives. What scenario planning *does* require is an investment in time and commitment from management to take people away from their daily operational activities and allow them to come together to reflect and learn.

Memories of the Future – Creating the Jolt

Visit any major bookshop and you will see shelves full of books by well-known writers offering advice on how to manage organizations in the so-called 'new' or 'knowledge' economy. They all suggest that in order to survive, companies need to be more agile, flexible, proactive and strategic in their thinking. Few, however, suggest exactly *how* this can be achieved. More importantly, agility and strategic flexibility alone are insufficient in a world in which much of the future is inherently unknowable. What is required is an ability to understand what is happening before others do, to detect the early signs of change and then convince others in the organization of the change.

There are times when everything an organization is doing seems right – its structure, products or services, marketing and operations and people management are all in harmony with the world around it. However, in a world of continuous structural change, there comes a point at which something about the organization, its products or services is no longer in accord with its environment. If this dissonance makes itself felt, then changes are required to avert strategic failure. The problem is that organizations often do not see (or they see but do not understand) what is happening in their environment. This is not because the managers in the organization are lazy or lack intelligence, but because what is happening lies outside their mental models. At the same time, they are usually so heavily engaged in day-to-day fire-fighting activities in their companies that they believe they do not have the time to pause, reflect and build a perspective on the future.

Psychologists suggest that the only way to overcome organizational resistance to change is for the organization to experience a painful crisis. Only when the organization's survival is at stake will managers begin to make changes. There is much anecdotal evidence to support this, and it is not uncommon to hear managers say, 'We need a good crisis in this organization to force us to re-examine what we do and how we do it'. However, waiting until a crisis arrives before one is able to initiate change is unsatisfactory. So, how does one get the organization to change *in anticipation of events*, rather than as a reaction?

To begin with, one needs to get the organization to see and understand the changes in the environment by experiencing them. This is the forte of scenarios and their ability to create organizational 'memories of the future'. The motivation to change results from the discovery that one of these futures will seriously shake the organization, because it is not what the organization had anticipated. We call this discovery the 'jolt'. It leads to anticipative, rather than reactive, change. The jolt takes the form of a scenario set containing unforeseen exogenous 'shocks', which seriously challenge business-as-usual assumptions and existing organizational recipes. Once manage-

> **In essence, the scenario process is about enabling managers to visit and experience the future ahead of time, thereby creating memories of the future. These 'visits' to anticipated futures are remembered, creating a matrix in the minds of managers and serving as subconscious guides to make sense of incoming environmental signals and to act on them.**

ment have understood and internalized these shocks, they require little convincing that further strategic thinking is required.

Testimony to this point comes from a scenario project completed in Asia. The client in this case was a multinational corporation, which had grown from modest beginnings as a small national business 25 years ago, to a highly profitable multinational today. Although the organization had been remarkably successful, there was some disquiet in the mind of the CEO regarding the future of the organization. The reasons for this were that:

- The organization had expanded internationally and grown exponentially in the last five years, with the result that management ranks, notably middle management, had been stretched in terms of substance and experience.
- Because of past successes, the CEO felt that many of the managers in the organization were no longer thinking; they had become too comfortable and too complacent.
- The industry in which the organization was a player had recently undergone significant changes in terms of consolidations and mergers, and the organization was still trying to make sense of these changes.

As a consequence, the CEO commissioned a corporate scenario project, the objective being to create a process which would stimulate managers to think, and lead to a better understanding of the imperatives driving recent changes in industry structure. A scenario team was established, and developed a set of three scenarios. In examining the implications for the organization across and within each of the scenarios, it was apparent that although the organization could survive in all three scenarios, it could not continue to achieve the success it had already accomplished with its existing business idea in any of them. The fact that all three scenarios delivered the same message, albeit for different reasons, was the natural and inevitable outcome of the process – there had been no deliberate attempt to manipulate the scenarios to arrive at such a situation.

The 'jolt' in this case was that on considering the scenarios, there was a realization within the senior management team that their success formula – which had served them well for 20 years – was unlikely to generate the same success in the future. It did not matter much which scenario one looked at; there were a number of changes in the contextual environment which they had not previously heeded, and which made it unlikely that the organization could continue to succeed in the future without fundamental rethinking taking place in the organization.

In this case, there was no need to wait until a crisis occurred for the management team to contemplate change; they were able to experience the pain of a crisis by proxy through internalizing the scenarios. As in all scenario projects, not all of the management team were immediately convinced by the scenarios. However, a sufficiently large group were, including the CEO, and this created the critical mass to ensure that change was firmly placed on the organization's agenda.

From Scenarios to Adaptive Behaviour

If the ability to learn faster than your competitors is the only truly sustainable competitive advantage, then organizational learning is not a luxury, it is a necessity. It should be a continuous process, enabling managers to discover the future of their companies by assessing changes in their organization, markets, competitors and industry. One of the most appropriate vehicles to achieve this is the scenario planning process. However, as we have already seen, new insights often fail to be implemented because they conflict with deeply held, tacit mental models of how the world works. Consequently, when developing scenarios at Shell, Pierre Wack and his team realized that their task as scenario planners was not so much to produce documented views of a range of plausible futures as to address the 'microcosms' of the decision-makers by designing scenarios such that the decision-makers would question their own models of reality and change them if necessary. Wack uses the term 'microcosm' here to distinguish between a manager's mental model of reality, and reality itself.

At the beginning of this section, we explained that without action there can be no adaptive organizational learning, and that organizational learning is a joint, ongoing activity. Although these are axioms of learning, the linkages between experience, reflection, conceptualization and action may not always be as clear-cut and contiguous as the Kolb model suggests. In addition, there are different interpretations of what constitutes 'joint and ongoing activity'. An example of this comes from an organization, a Scandinavian MNC that we have worked with for many years. Each year the organization brings together a group of its managers from across the globe to engage in a five-day scenario workshop. During the week, the participants work in teams, each team tasked with developing rough-cut scenarios around a particular 'live' issue in the organization. On the last day of the workshop, the teams present the scenarios they have developed to a senior executive from the head office, usually the CEO.

The organization regards these workshops as part of its organizational learning activities, but to an outside observer the workshops might appear to be nothing more than training workshops, given that there is no immediate, observable action following the presentation of the scenarios. The workshop participants return to their offices and continue with their day-to-day action-oriented activities. Also, the workshops are episodic events; participants work in teams during the workshop but on completion, they return to their functional areas. No formal attempt is made to continue the joint learning process within the organization. The CEO, however, argues that the very fact that the participants have undertaken the workshop will make them more adept and perceptive observers of the business environment – people capable of recognizing change. At the same time, having grappled with uncertainty and tried to make sense of what is going on in the environment, the participants will have gained a deeper, systemic understanding of the factors shaping the business environment, which they will then share with their colleagues on returning to their business units. The combination of the two factors will, the CEO suggests, inevitably filter through and influence strategy development in the business units. Meanwhile, in listening to and discussing the scenarios with the workshop participants, the CEO will himself experience challenges to his mental model. As a result, the consequences of the workshop will therefore be new conceptualizations that will inevitably inform future actions within the organization.

The CEO contends that this is organizational learning, even if the new conceptualizations and future actions may not be immediately associated with the scenario workshops. As Huber[79] suggests, as an entity learns through its processing of information, the range of its potential behaviours is changed. The key to organizational learning, therefore, is how organizations process their managerial experiences into behaviour.

Scenario planning contributes to the learning process at both the individual and the group level, in a number of ways and across a wide range of arenas. At the individual level, the scenario process provides an effective framework for assembling, organizing and making sense of a volume of seemingly disparate pieces of information. This then allows individuals to expand the range of what they see, enriching their mental models. At the same time, the scenario process helps individuals to think through ideas generated in the strategic conversation more effectively. At the organization level, scenarios provide a ready-made language to facilitate the strategic conversation across a spectrum of views in the organization. They serve as a vehicle to align mental models, which in turn enables the organization to develop coherent strategic actions. The process, however, is not an easy or trivial one; scenarios can only help managers when they change their assumptions about how the world works, and then compel them to rearrange their mental models. To do this, scenarios must create a bridge between the new realities of the world and the microcosm of the manager's mind.

Making it Happen

The adaptive organizational learning perspective on scenario planning provides the link between understanding and action. There is no adaptive organizational learning without action. However, in Chapter 3 we discussed how, by itself, changing mental models does not automatically result in realigned action and associated organizational learning. Moving from the old world to the new is not always an easy process. As we saw, Pettigrew and Whipp[80] suggest that intended change requires five conditions to be present in order for the change to take place. These bear repeating here:

1.   Awareness of the environmental imperative for change.
2.   Change leadership.
3.   Strategic change operationalized.
4.   HR base of the organization linked with the change process.
5.   Coherence about the change project from the top.

Scenario planning fits well with this model, because it can contribute to at least four of these factors. For example, it can:

• create wide awareness of the environmental imperative requiring change (the jolt);
• guide the formation of operational plans;
• enlist the people in the organization who have the power to act;
• create coherence in management action through development of a shared view.

In a complex, interconnected world, no matter how intelligent and knowledgeable the senior management of an organization may be, they can no longer be responsible for all the thinking that takes place inside the organization. The organization needs to consider the contributions of all individuals in it, harnessing the skills, experience, curiosity and creativity of all its employees. Liberating insights and creativity will create and sustain competitive advantage for the organization – and, as we have seen from the foregoing discussion, the scenario process has much to offer in this area.

Upframing and the transitional object

Underlying all this is the issue of the *identity* of the organization. In Chapter 3, we saw how an essential condition for change to happen is that the new strategy can be argued from the perspective of the identity of the organization, as expressed in its history and its existing recipes. There must be some solid ground from which the change process can be pushed forward. We need some understanding that can be taken from the old world into the new – not everything can change at the same time. We have called this element of understanding bridging the old and the new world the *transitional object*. The organizational learning facilitator needs to consider how to distill from the conversation such a transitional object and make it available to the team. The approach we suggest is a process called *upframing*. We'll explain this concept using two examples.

The first example concerned the management team of the manufacturing plant of a large conglomerate in the food and drink sector. Their manufacturing division had invited us to facilitate their strategy discussions, in the hope that this would prove to be a great team-building event. Things turned out rather differently. We found that their identity was very much interwoven with the manufacturing process, in which they had developed significant skills. In the industry, they were recognized as front-runners. A key factor in their success was their ability to keep unit costs down by keeping volumes high. They spent a great deal of energy making sure that capacity was always loaded, if necessary working for competing firms. Many companies used them as their swing producer (used to meet peaks in demand), and the plant had been equipped with the flexibility to make that possible. It was apparent at the outset that their recipe for success was making sure their capacity was always loaded.

The scenario project provided a jolt by identifying a number of futures in which life would become rather more difficult than it had traditionally been. A key factor proved to be the degree of control the plant had over its destiny: in some scenarios, this proved distinctly tenuous. As only one player in the supply chain, the manufacturing unit could find itself under severe pressure from both the input and the output side. This was a distinct jolt to the team, and they began to search for a strategy to alleviate the risk identified. One 'maverick' proposal was to remove at least the upstream risk by turning the manufacturing unit into the 'supply division' of the whole group of companies to which it belonged, with full control over its own suppliers. This idea seemed a good one, from the perspective of 'controlling destiny', so we were surprised to see the lukewarm reaction to this idea. There seemed a feeling that this sort of thing was not 'for us'.

We engaged in long conversations with the management group in an attempt to understand the problem. We were told that the manufacturing unit had no knowledge or experience in this area; they didn't know what they were taking on; the risks were too great. It was clear that they considered acquiring the responsibility for the supply chain as a huge change, well outside their self-image. This made it look extremely risky and not worth spending much energy on.

Eventually the problems were overcome through a process of upframing. This starts at the current recipe or success formula, in this case loading the capacity of the plant. We discussed why this seemed a good idea. Eventually everyone agreed that minimizing unit costs had been the reason for going after this 'throughput' recipe. Because of this, they had been efficient and enjoyed a low unit cost, and were popular in the larger organization. Having upframed the goal to a higher level of conceptualization, they could now address the 'bridging' question, as follows: 'If we have always been about low cost, doesn't it make sense to open up new ways of pursuing that goal by gaining direct control over our supplies?' After all, being in control would have the potential of significantly reducing supply costs in some of the scenarios developed. This question caused a distinct change in perspective. If their identity was about minimizing cost instead of maximizing throughput, controlling supply seemed a logical strategy to pursue.

It is worth noting that the upframing exercise had not reduced the downside of the idea; the risk was still present. The difference was that it suddenly seemed more manageable. Risk could be reduced, for example, by transferring people with supply experience from the wider organization. They could learn quickly and even if some mistakes were made, in the long run it seemed the right thing to do. So, we noted a distinct change of heart, caused primarily by a desire to put more thinking and energy into the proposal. Despite initial doubts, they then changed their minds and decided to put the proposal to their head office.

In this case, cost minimization was the transitional object, the firm foundation from which the proposal could be pursued. It linked the old world of throughput maximization with the new world of the supply division. This enabled the proposal to pass the 'for us' filter, and allowed them to start working on it.

Our second example concerns a software organization. From as far back as anyone could remember, this organization had been an IBM house, selling IBM hardware and software as a qualified IBM retailer. Their experience with IBM had been very positive; they felt extremely well supported, and the IBM platform provided an excellent ground from which to develop bespoke software of their own. Their success formula, or recipe, was simple and straightforward: sell as many IBM solutions as possible, and in this way create a large IBM-tied installed base that we can continue to support.

The scenarios once again provided a jolt. It seemed that in one key sector of their business it was feasible that the IBM offering could come under severe competitive pressure, with dire consequences for their own organization. The proposed strategic response was clear: give up sole IBM retailer status and open a Microsoft division. Once again, we were taken aback by the difficulties this seemed to generate. They knew very little about Microsoft software and had no idea about the market or the business side of the proposal. Once again, we proposed an upframing exercise. We asked why it seemed a good idea to sell IBM preferentially into the market. After some discussion, they upframed the recipe (and the underlying goal) as 'We sell IBM because we believe it genuinely enables our customers, through their use of the best and most flexible solutions on the market'. We then posed the bridging question: 'If we have always been about enabling our customers with the best solution available, would it make sense to open up alternative suppliers if IBM cannot any longer supply this?' There is only one answer to this question, and although they still knew as little about Microsoft as before, they realized that consistency with their identity required them to go and find out more about it.

'Making their clients more successful' was the transitional object. This is what they had always done and what they intended to continue doing. Consequently, they cut the knot with IBM and are now a mixed supplier. Once again, it was not that upframing had changed the situation, but it changed their perspective on the situation; something that previously fell outside their span of attention had now entered it. Once they had started along the new road they quickly learned, and things proved much less arduous than anticipated.

If enhanced adaptive organizational learning is the ultimate goal of scenario planning then scenario planners have to become involved in 'making it happen'. This includes involvement in cohesion and consensus building, mobilization of the organization, managing change and the evolving identity of the organization, and surfacing transitional objects, in addition to scenario analysis of the business environment. If insights do not result in action, learning does not take place. If no learning occurs, then the scenario project has not contributed to the well-being of the organization. Facilitators have to become involved in the wider learning context of scenario planning.

SUMMARY: DEVELOPING THE SKILLS OF SURVIVAL

In this chapter, we have demonstrated the ability of scenarios to overcome the common blockages to organizational thinking, creating in the process competitive advantage. Recognizing and understanding changes in the business environment ahead of competitors achieves this.

Scenario planning is about helping decision-makers to enact their environment, exploring possible futures, understanding the change drivers and developing sustainable action. Metaphorically speaking, the scenario process raises the antennae of the organization and focuses attention on those 'dots on the horizon' that are the signals of impending change. It institutionalizes the hunt for weak signals in the external environment, forewarning managers of the likely drivers of change. At the same time, it instils a deeper appreciation for and understanding of the myriad factors that combine and interconnect to shape the future, allowing people to refocus, questioning their long and deeply held assumptions about the way the world works, in order to develop a clearer understanding of the world as it is today.

> **Scenario planning allows organizations to rehearse the future, to walk the battlefield before the battle. The result is not, however, a more accurate prediction of the future, but the ability to better distinguish the significant aspects of the future. This, in turn, allows better decisions to be made.**

We have summarized these beneficial effects by suggesting that the aim of scenario planning is enhancement of adaptive organizational learning, which can put the organization ahead of its competitors and in turn ensure its survival and success. The organizational learning perspective suggests the involvement of the scenario planner as facilitator of change processes involving action.

The following chapter provides an in-depth, step-by-step guide to the process of developing scenarios. It brings together the ideas and principles underpinning scenario thinking, exploring the specific processes involved, and helping organizations to overcome many of the problems that limit the development and implementation of an effective strategy.

Scenario Planning in the Organizational Context

CHAPTER 7

Previous chapters have explored the blockages to organizational learning and outlined the philosophy underpinning the scenario approach. This chapter provides a step-by-step guide to the scenario approach, enabling managers to challenge their own cultural perceptions of specific business situations.

Overview

The business world is ambiguous, subtle and complex; recognizing the unpredictability of such a situation is the key strength of an effective scenario process. No other strategic approach is capable of linking cause and effect to seemingly unrelated factors, where the nature of possible futures can dramatically affect organizational success. Scenarios provide unique insights, harnessing knowledge, skills and distinctive competencies to drive organizations forward.

In this chapter, we will outline the structure, context and implications of the scenario planning process by exploring five key areas:

- **Structuring the scenario process**. Adopting the correct approach involves identifying gaps in knowledge, building the team and timing the project.
- **Exploring the scenario context**. Interviewing key players will surface relevant information about the team's current thinking and approach.

CONTINUED ... Overview

Analysing the interviews, feedback and discussion helps to define the scope of the project and set the agenda. The role of the 'remarkable person' is to challenge the team's thinking, preconceptions and pre-programming

- **Building the scenarios.** It is critical to identify the driving forces in the environment. Through testing outcomes, the impact and uncertainty of options can be illuminated. Scoping the scenarios and fully developing coherent stories will highlight the implications for the organization.

- **Stakeholder analysis.** This is valuable as it offers a way of considering the relative positions of different stakeholders, and this can prove useful in several ways during the development of scenario thinking.

- **Impacting organizational thinking and acting.** Scenarios impact on organizational thinking, facilitating an ongoing adaptive learning organization. They promote recognition, understanding and early reaction to the initial jolt of environmental change, to the early indicators necessitating action. Organizational capabilities can be explored, and strategic options can be determined through option planning.

INTRODUCING THE SCENARIO METHOD

A limited viewpoint or the failure to identify potential changes in the business environment, resulting from organizational blockages, severely damages strategic policy. This chapter will detail the steps that organizations need to take to overcome the inertia and pitfalls of traditional thinking. The main feature of this approach is that it *deliberately provokes a high degree of turbulence within the participating group.* It requires participants to accept that there are many different perspectives on complex and ambiguous business problems, whether from different disciplinary bases or from different cultural or ideological standpoints. While not expected to believe in all of the ideas, they are encouraged to accept diversity of opinion, value and belief – to attempt to comprehend *why* others hold their views and, more importantly, *how* these different views might affect the situation considered. By challenging their own view of the world, by looking at it from other perspectives, participants develop a realization of the ambiguous nature and complexity of the world. They also gain an enhanced understanding of the cause and effect linkages between apparently unrelated factors. This understanding enables deeper and broader structural insights into the nature of possible futures and their implications for the organization.

This approach is designed to provide a framework for your own thinking and acting. It should be seen as a method that frees thinking and promotes action, breaking the constraints that beset traditional strategic processes. It is a method that has proven to be effective in supporting organizations of all sizes. These may be facing different opportunities and threats – whether apparent or unnoticed. Opening up the strategic conversations of diverse groups of stakeholders and embracing the complexity and ambiguity of their multiple perspectives promotes a deeper, broader perspective of the business landscape. Further, the approach generates ownership of the process and the scenarios produced by these stakeholders.

In implementing the scenario process, the group must confront the fundamental dilemma: the basic contradiction of objectives. The scenarios must have meaning and relevance to the organization and its members. They must be plausible to the stakeholders, and enable them to imagine themselves in the situations outlined. Yet, the scenarios must challenge the minds of these same members, must be novel and innovative, and must challenge the concept of business-as-usual.

Through case studies and analysis, the following questions will be addressed:

- How do we conduct the scenario planning process with organizations?
- How do we open up the scenario conversation to embrace multiple perspectives on the business problem and its wider context?
- What is the role of the scenario planning facilitator in enabling discussion of complexity and ambiguity among diverse groups of individuals?
- How do we move from the initial divergent thinking to convergence through the construction of three or four internally consistent and coherent scenarios?

As well as being outlined and examined separately, case studies will support the ideas and methods relevant to the different aspects of the scenario process.

While the scenario process is set out in considerable detail in this chapter, we would like to stress that scenario planning is an *art* rather than a science. As such, the process should not be seen as being all-important. Rather, what matters is the quality of the outcomes gained from promoting strategic conversations within and around the organization. So, as you read our detailed process and grapple with its implementation, do not worry about getting it 'right' or 'wrong'

At the end of this chapter, we provide an overview of each of the stages that outlines the process elements and what each is intended to achieve. You may find it helpful to refer to this section as you read the detailed text.

SCENARIOS FOR THE FUTURE OF E-GOVERNMENT AND THE IMPACT OF INFORMATION AND COMMUNICATIONS TECHNOLOGIES (ICT)

The main case study explored in this chapter outlines the scenario method. It involves interaction of the public and private sectors, in a world where the former is driven more and more by the imperatives of the latter: issues such as efficiency, cost-effectiveness and return on investment. At the same time, the private sector is challenged to become more publicly accountable, providing value to the wider body of stakeholders – all those that can affect or can be affected by the organization's strategy and operations – rather than simply maximizing the financial return to shareholders. In the case described here, public and private sectors seek interaction to generate value for themselves, for each other and for their stakeholders.

Background

The project was sponsored by a telecommunications organization that wanted to understand the potential of the application of new information and communications technologies (ICT) for government.

In turn, regional government sought to understand possible future demands upon it, in a market that would be driven not by suppliers, but by central government frameworks and by local business and community demands.

In order to explore these issues, a scenario team comprising members of Northshire Council and its partner organizations, as well as employees of the telecoms company, employed a facilitated scenario approach. In four groups, the team developed scenario outlines for four possible futures for 2006. Each group outlined a storyline progressing from the present day to the stated future date – as shown in their particular quadrant of the scenario matrix. They set out the events characterizing the unfolding scenario history, naming the scenario to catch the attention of the rest of the team, the council, its partner organizations and society. Each group then presented its scenario story to the whole team.

The Story of the 'People's Kailyard'*

In this scenario, the populace was generally active in politics, working with elected representatives and officers, and the democratic process looked healthy. Under pressure from central government, and in response to the demands of citizens and local businesses, the council invested heavily in new ICT. Encouraged by central government, these new technologies were seen as a way of reducing the cost of doing business and driving up efficiency, as well as improving the quality of service. As they allowed for faster and easier communications, it appeared to promote closer relationships between the council, local residents and local businesses. On closer examination, problems emerged. Some considered the process superficial. Central government was seen as controlling, using top-down directive government. Local government fragmented into 'silos', operating in isolation, using 'legacy systems' based upon the historical operational divisions. Eventually, the new technologies appeared as a 'quick fix', as the underlying structural constraints proved more difficult to tackle. Progress slowed and, as service-level improvements failed to materialize, disillusion set in. Also, those lacking access to the full range of new technologies felt excluded from the democratic process.

Initially, relationships with the media had been good in the new culture of openness and involvement, although the council remained cautious over their relationship with the media – if the fragile developments towards greater grass-roots democracy failed, the media would be openly critical. Inevitably, this led to unwillingness to take too many risks, even though there was a demand for increasing change from residents seeking new forms of holistic service delivery. At the same time, the council remained constrained by tight central government control. While the new technologies had opened up the communications channels, not much else had changed – it was business-as-usual!

The scenario arrived at 2006, with grass-roots democracy leading to social inclusion, although 'some are more included than others'. The whole public

---

* 'Kailyard' is an old Scottish term for 'cabbage patch', and was selected by the group members in order to describe a minimum level of subsistence for members of society, despite vast amounts of energy expended.

sector suffered a self-reinforcing lock-in: grand intentions combined with fear over the amplification effect of the media, leading to a desire for quick wins without structural modernization. As a result, the old legacy systems became overloaded, resulting in no real shift in the power base.

The team's response

The scenario team's response was shock, as the developments appeared believable. The current drive for investment in new technologies (to open up access by Internet, telephone and interactive television) could enjoy short-term success, without being sustainable. Clearly, a failure to overcome the institutionalised and fragmented departmental structure was a major block to adding value for residents and businesses. The fragility of the relationship between local and central government was highlighted, as was the council's current inability to deliver services demanded by the newly involved citizens. The sponsoring telecommunications organization realized that short-term market exploitation could prove unsustainable in the long term, with investment viewed as ineffective in satisfying customer demand and client needs. The other three scenarios gave alternative futures. During the process, the organizations identified clear directions for action, in order to guide the future.

We will return later in the chapter to the other scenarios developed during this process, but first we shall examine how the process was structured and developed.

STAGE 1: STRUCTURING THE SCENARIO PROCESS

Identifying Knowledge Gaps

The starting point for all scenario projects is the identification of a key gap in organizational knowledge. Some scenario approaches and outcomes are based on generalized ideas and considerations. Strathclyde Business School in Glasgow, Scotland, has developed a scenario approach based on focused consideration of particular organizational problems, such as: 'How will new technologies impact our service delivery?' or 'How will we attract high-level graduates in a competitive market?' At the organizational level, the knowledge gaps are likely to be of a strategic nature, while at a departmental or business-unit level, they may be more technical and operational in focus. The common factor, however, is identification of an issue known to have a critical impact on the organization and its business, where there is uncertainty over what that impact will be over time.

Problems may be readily identified in general terms; however, management needs to identify those issues that will have an impact upon the organization, which can then be researched in further detail and with greater focus. Without this degree of focus on specific issues, strategic advances will be based on incomplete and possibly erroneous knowledge. The application of structured analysis, known as a STEEP analysis (see Chapter 6), provides a useful framework to assist management in considering the following factors that impact on the business landscape:

- *Social* – demographics, education, tastes;
- *Technological* – IT, telecommunications, logistics, transport;
- *Economic* – growth, markets, fiscal policies, taxation;
- *Ecological* – materials, resources, climate, pollution;
- *Political* – structures, activities, leadership, policies.

Furthermore, to this list can be added legal frameworks, legislation, rights and protection. Significantly, these headings are neither intended to act as a checklist nor do they represent discrete subject areas. Rather, they are simply a way of structuring thinking. However, STEEP can only provide a first idea about the situation. As we saw in Chapter 6, the analysis is superficial, and does not sufficiently account for interaction between variables. For this, a full-blown scenario project is required. From a first identification of the basic driving forces that affect the business problem, the next step is to identify the key themes and issues that encapsulate current thinking about the organization's past, present and future, and use these as the agenda for a scenario project.

Building the Scenario Team

Common mistakes

Scenario projects are often conducted entirely by internal groups within organizations. This can be problematic, for a number of reasons. First, without the separation of facilitation and participation in the process, the exercise may lack focus in particular key areas. People responsible for producing inputs and managing their own and others' ideas may be distracted, thus reducing their personal effectiveness in both areas.

Second, if the facilitation role is separated and is conducted by people from the organization who are not part of the scenario generation group, there are different risks involved. For example, members hold an interest in the business problem, leading them to adopt both participation and facilitation modes. Again, this blurring leads to distraction and reduced effectiveness. Also, internal facilitators outside the interest group within the organization risk being seen by participating members as disinterested insiders – as organizational members with organizational roles – rather than as scenario experts. Clearly, they may not command the necessary authority to administer the facilitation role effectively.

The role of external facilitators

External facilitators have the advantage of being seen as neutral experts, taking on the roles of chair, moderator, timekeeper, recorder and *agent provocateur* but never adopting a stance of expert in relation to the organization, its business, strategy or operation. Being independent of internal power relationships, political activities and influencing strategies ensures the correct environment for open, blame free and creative thinking, facilitating the consideration and development of effective and focused scenarios. Also, during the initial agenda-setting interviews, external facilitators can reorder and present the interview content in an issue-focused and non-attributable format. This guarantees anonymity for participants; separating the idea from the individual leads to a free and frank discussion of ideas. The openness of the interview process, therefore, surfaces a wide range of views, opinions and inputs.

Timing for the Scenario Project

Scenario projects can be undertaken over any period. They can be undertaken on an immediate basis through an instant scenario, in order to surface general issues and options. Within Shell, individual managers will frequently undertake a scenario project within their own minds, even if they only have a short time to make a decision. This approach depends on a developed mindset that automatically challenges existing norms, creating and exploring a range of strategic options, rather than simply preconceiving one 'right answer' and then rationalizing the justification for pursuing this, post-event.

Short, sharp scenarios may be appropriate in some circumstances. In major projects, however, a scenario project would take at least 10 weeks. This extended period allows for compilation and presentation of the various interim reports – covering interviews, scenario agenda and generation workshops and option generation. More importantly, it allows group members time to critically reflect on the content, to undertake further research on the issues raised and to engage in formal and informal discussions, with one another and with other interested parties. Figure 7.1 shows the timescales involved.

STAGE 2: EXPLORING THE SCENARIO CONTEXT

Interviewing Key Players and Widening the Conversation

Many scenario projects begin with an introduction based on the organization's prior identification of the business problem to be addressed. This does not provide the best opening to the process, as it immediately sets constraints upon thinking. Instead, the starting point should aim to open up the conversation, enabling the widest possible exploration of the issues. The initial step explores the context of the scenario exercise. This is best achieved through a series of in-depth, semi-structured interviews with key members of the organization. This group should include top management involved in strategic decisions. It should also include key knowledge holders in the relevant fields of operational decision-making and implementation. If delivery of the solution to the business problem requires collaborative working with external partners, they should be involved at the earliest stages.

The interviews enable key players in the organization to explore and surface their personal perceptions on a wide range of aspects of the business and its operating environment. They provide personal insights into the organization's current business idea, its competencies and strategies, and how it perceives itself as adding value for its customers. More importantly, this initial exercise elicits these key players' perceptions on the future of the organization, on how they see it

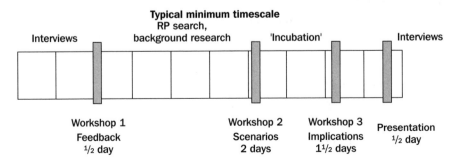

Figure 7.1 Scenario project programme.

aligning with the outside world over time. It raises questions about the fundamental changes individuals regard as inevitable and over the critical uncertainties they see lying ahead. These interviews should last for a minimum of one hour. In order to focus the conversation on both the future and external environment, the framework questions are set in a specific format. The questions start from the external, future environment, working back to the present internal conditions, concluding with a consideration of how recent organizational history has resulted in the current situation. The set we recommend are known as the 'seven questions' (although the real number will depend on the questioning style of the interviewer).

Starting questions – the future

The starting questions surface the interviewees' perceptions of what the external world, in which the organization operates, will be like in the future (for example, in five years).

- What will be the key characteristics that will define the future external environment for the organization?
- What will be the key uncertainties providing threats and opportunities facing the organization?
- What would you personally want to leave behind?

These are determined by asking the interviewee to describe what would constitute both a positive and a negative scenario. This has two benefits: first, it elicits views on the uncertainties. Second, it introduces the term 'scenario', enabling members to think of future worlds outside the organization.

Questions about the present

Discussions of the organization and its present situation can only commence after the discussion of possible futures beyond the organization has been completed. Key questions here include:

- What are the main decisions to be taken?
- What are the organization's current competencies and resources that will enable it to address the opportunities identified?
- Which competencies and resources does it lack that will constrain its ability to respond?
- What is standing in the way of a good future?

Questions about the past

Finally, in setting a current historical context for the developing scenario project, we then move to a discussion of the organization's recent history.

• What have been the key developments in the past few years that have under-pinned the organization's ability to respond to opportunities?
• What key lessons (positive or negative) should we learn from the past?

Recording the interview

In order to move forward from fragmented discussions with individuals to open discussion with the scenario team, it is essential to record and share the full content of the interviews. The content can be recorded either by audio recording or by comprehensive note-taking. The advantages of audio are that full word-for-word accounts are produced which can then be analysed for content using appropriate computer software programs. The disadvantage is that interviewees may be concerned about confidentiality. Such objections can be overcome by note-taking. Notes need to be both comprehensive and accurate, ensuring that content can be fully analysed. In particular, while ensuring that meaning and content are clearly understood, it is often useful to record interviewees' responses in a single-sentence statement that all members will easily and universally under-stand. If necessary, the statement could be read back to the interviewee to ensure correct meaning.

Instant Scenarios

These can be conducted where the business problem is clearly defined, requiring immediate attention or where time is limited. It is still important to widen the conversation as much as possible, by bringing the team together for a short time. Each member thinks about what the key problem is, and writes this on one piece of paper. Members are also asked to write the key customer expectations and the key organizational competency and resource gaps that are exacerbating the problem on separate pieces of paper. Using a round-robin approach, the individual problem definitions are shared, followed by the different customer expectations and organizational gaps. At this stage, commonality or divergence of opinion should be identified and made apparent and explicit. As with the full interview process, material for further discussion has now been elicited. This is then analysed. Throughout the remainder of this chapter, we will highlight specific ideas and techniques that can be used with instant scenarios.

Grounded analysis of interview transcripts

The purpose of analysing the interview transcripts is to collate the ideas presented to produce an all-inclusive view of the organization and its environment. However, the task can be daunting, possibly involving several thousand statements. Clearly, these must be reduced to a manageable set of key higher-level concepts. This is done by studying the text of the interviews to identify recurring concepts – regardless of conflicting or similar opinions. The concepts are therefore grounded in the interview data itself rather than being predetermined by either the organization or the facilitation team. Identifying these concepts provides the overall framework to reorder the interview statements. Further subsets of more specific themes and issues that fall under each key area are then used to collate the full set of interview statements into an Interview Report. This is both structured, with a manageable number of higher-level concepts forming the section headings, and anonymous, since individuals can no longer be associated with the statements. An outline for the report structure is set out below.

Interview Report Structure

Section Headings

Key higher-level concepts that pervade interview discussions. For example, 'Technology as a driving force for change'.

Sub-headings

Recurring themes that contribute to the overall concept. For example, 'Growth of Internet usage' or '3G mobile phone take-up' or 'Development of interactive television'.

Individual Statements

These are placed under the appropriate sub-heading, where they contribute to the theme.

In analysing the key concepts that will inform the next stage of discussion, it is important to identify the interviewees' perceptions of scarcity-related customer values for the future; in particular, the external key drivers of value generation they consider will be central to organizational success. These customer values, if clearly articulated, will indicate whether organizational future orientation is based around business-as-usual thinking or around challenging both the present and the past.

The process of analysing the content of individual transcripts, identifying common key concepts and reordering the text around these themes, determines the dominant perspective of the group. It also discovers the extent of divergence and conflict among values and beliefs. These are key benefits of the Interview Report. Collating interview content under a relatively small number of concept headings enables participants to better conceptualize the range of issues raised.

Setting the Scenario Agenda

The Interview Report becomes the agenda for a short, intensive workshop with the scenario team, drawn from within the wider organization group. The scenario team must be representative of the organization: its decision-making framework, operations, people and competencies. More importantly, the individuals must be willing and able to attend all the scenario workshops.

Ideally, the Interview Report should be circulated to the scenario team about a week before the first workshop. The first workshop uses the report to open up a wider and more generalized discussion of the systemic factors that will impact the business problem. The areas of convergence and divergence around the key concepts and themes are made explicit and discussed in detail. The first main aim is to check if the clustering of statements and identification of key concepts by the facilitation team is generally accepted, and whether the range of perspectives is accepted as a fair assessment. If completed successfully, this promotes shared ownership of the higher-level concepts and of the full range of perspectives on the relevant issues. By considering the concepts and related issues, the aim is to determine the critical uncertainties in the future external environment that generate internal uncertainties for the present organizational strategy and structure.

By the end of the first workshop, the scenario team should have a common understanding of the following issues (although not necessarily shared views).

- Where do we want to be and need to be in the future?
- Where are we now, and how did we get here?
- How do we get to here from there?
- What are the resource and capability gaps that prevent us from doing this?
- What are the knowledge gaps? What do we *not* know that prevents us answering the previous questions clearly and comprehensively?

It is the small set of critical uncertainties, determined by the organizational members themselves, that prevents them from seeing a clear route from the present to the future. This forms the scenario investigation agenda.

Setting the Scenario Agenda: the Northshire Example

In the Northshire project introduced earlier, there was a diverse group of organizational actors participating in the scenario project, involving the telecommunications industry, Northshire Council and its partner organizations. These included managers from various functional departments of the client organization, along with elected members, salaried officers, voluntary workers and professionals from different disciplinary backgrounds in the the other organizations. In addition, the needs and wishes of the various external stakeholder groups had to be considered – from central government to local businesses and residents. The first task was to ensure that the conversations of the group were focused on the external environment; were future-oriented and concerned with understanding, and responding to, customer values. An initial series of semi-structured, in-depth interviews with 24 senior members of the group was conducted, each lasting between one and one-and-a-half hours. The question format was designed to take the interviewees first into the future and outside the organizational context. They were asked:

- When you look five years ahead, what do you consider most uncertain about where we are heading with local government?
- What would you personally consider a good outcome or a favourable scenario from these uncertainties?
- What do you consider a bad outcome – your nightmare scenario?
- What are the major lessons learned in local government in the past five years that should carry us into the future?
- What are the big decisions that need to be taken in the immediate future that will steer us away from the nightmare scenario?
- What are the main constraints standing in the way of the favourable scenario?
- What would you personally like to be remembered for?

Then they were asked specific questions on the business idea:

- Where are the new scarcities in society? Where can Northshire add value for customers in the future?
- What unique resources and competencies will enable Northshire to do this?
- Where will Northshire make strategic investments that will safeguard its future position?

The responses were then subjected to content analysis, from which the key concepts were identified. These included, 'Partners' agendas', 'Central agencies –

help or hindrance?', 'Management of change' and 'Technology as a driving force'. Following circulation of the Interview Report, the first scenario workshop was held with the scenario team, including representatives of the elected members, senior officers of the council, ICT managers and senior representatives from the partner organizations and the telecoms company. Discussion at this one-day workshop revealed four key categories of critical uncertainties, setting the scenario agenda, as follows:

1. Technology possibilities related to potential solutions.
2. Citizen view of technology solutions, and societal acceptance or rejection.
3. Knowledge management, coordinated, 'joined-up' government, complexity and the citizen experience.
4. Governance in the future

These areas set the agenda for a subsequent investigation of the driving forces that would affect the issues across the full range of environmental fields of investigation.

The Role of the Remarkable Person

Widening perspectives on the future of technology and governance

In exploring e-government futures, we sought to bring into the conversation examples of leading-edge, future-oriented thinking from the arenas of ICT. In addition, we involved critical thinkers on the role of governance in society and on the relationships between governments, businesses and communities. Finally, we sought to expose the group to the implementation of e-government initiatives in other countries – from the USA to Singapore and Australia. These inputs were not intended to show the detail of what was being done in other arenas. Rather, they were intended to open up members' thinking to a wider range of 'limits of the possible' – what might be plausible and feasible in their own context, both now and in the future.

As we saw in Chapter 6, the term 'remarkable person' (RP) is not necessarily applied to those who are expert in the field of investigation. Experts can be so narrowly focused on current best practice that they are embedded in business-as-usual. This process encourages individuals to critically engage with their own cultural programming. The role of the RP in the conversation is to challenge the thinking of the scenario team, their preconceptions and their preperceptions of any situation. To fulfil this role, individuals need to be creative and challenging thinkers, both in and around the field. Specifically, they need to bring insights into futures that are beyond the team's current horizon of thought. It is possible to find such people among those at the leading edge of knowledge development in the field, and among those leading the field in a different context. It is also possible to find RPs in related fields that are, perhaps, at a higher level of development. For instance, if we were seeking RP input into conversations on potential futures in low-cost air travel in Europe, we would consider RPs concerned with the possible futures in high-speed rail travel, governance in the EU (European Union), the changing political environment, and the effects of international terrorism.

> **Instant Scenarios**
> It can be difficult to choose RPs for short-term projects. It will help if you identify individuals either within the organization or from your contacts, that regularly challenge the conventional, party line and business-as-usual attitudes. Their key role is to stop group-think from dominating the decision-making process.

STAGE 3: DEVELOPING THE SCENARIOS

Once the scenario agenda has been determined, based around the critical uncertainties facing the organization, we need to consider the widest range of factors that will impact, to any degree, upon the overall situation. The starting point is to extend the scope of participants' thinking. To this end, the investigation should be set within, but not constrained by, a structured framework that considers factors relating to social, technological, economic, legal, political, ethical and natural environments. These fields act not as discrete and exclusive aspects, but as guides to ensure that every relevant factor is surfaced.

Determining the Driving Forces and Testing the Outcomes

Driving forces are those underlying and impacting factors that set the pattern of events and determine outcomes in the business environment and timescale being considered – the forces that make things happen. To test the validity of ideas for driving forces, each member is asked to briefly propose two possible polar outcomes. These outcomes should relate to the specific context of the project, rather than being vague and generalized. Some driving forces and outcomes may be predictable within one particular context, while being more elusive in another. For example, within a 10-year scenario project for health care in a European country, the driving force of changing demographic profile may have predictable polar outcomes, given that birth and death rates are slow to change and that patterns of disease and illness are steady. For scenarios concerning health care in Sub-Saharan Africa, the issue of HIV/AIDS makes outcomes more uncertain. Furthermore, the RP could suggest other views of the long-term status of European health, resulting from antibiotic-resistant bacteria, the resurgence of tuberculosis and food safety issues.

Polar outcomes are not necessarily direct opposites. For example, a driving force behind world food supply would not necessarily lead to the polar outcomes of shortage and abundance. Shortage may be indicative of famine. However, abundance may indicate food 'mountains' in Europe and grain 'mountains' in North America, while the end result of abundance in Sub-Saharan Africa is still famine. Clearly, polar outcomes are always context dependent. The world does not exist in terms of absolutes, despite the tendency of politicians and the media to present it as such. Scenario planning must consider the world as it really is: multiple shades of grey, blue, red, pink . . .

Practicalities

Where the scenario team comprises 10 or more people, conduct the exercise of identifying driving forces with their polar outcomes by seating the group in a horseshoe around large magnetic boards. The facilitation team works together, with one member chairing a round-robin process that generates the driving forces, facilitating discussion and agreement of the context-specific polar outcomes. The other members record the driving forces on magnetic hexagons, placing them around the edge of the magnetic boards. They also record the two polar outcomes of each driving force on individual stickers, ready for later use. To ensure clarity, a useful way to structure the information is to label the driving forces with whole numbers, such as 1, 2, 3, while labelling their related polar outcomes 1a/1b, 2a/2b, 3a/3b (see Figure 7.2).

Instant Scenarios

Exploring driving forces and polar outcomes need not be a lengthy process, if time is limited. In extreme cases, team members could restrict their time to 15 minutes of individual thinking on driving forces, recording their ideas on separate Post-it® notes. The team could then spend one hour discussing the various driving forces in round-robin style, agreeing and recording polar outcomes on separate notes. This combines the benefits of the methods used in the extended exercise, while coping with urgent or cost-related pressures.

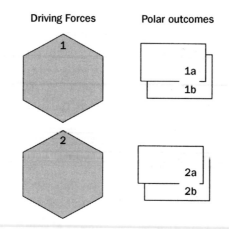

Figure 7.2 Recording driving forces and associated polar outcomes.

The process of surfacing driving forces is not time-constrained. In major projects, this process can last several hours, with upwards of 150 driving forces and 300 polar outcomes being generated. By working with the round-robin approach, all members have an equal say in the conversation and, as each member runs out of ideas, they simply drop out of the round.

Teams can use alternative methods for recording these elements of the process to suit the preferred style and strengths of the group, providing the method adopted allows for manipulation of the individual forces and outcomes. The use of Post-it® notes is feasible, as is the use of computer software packages such as Decision Explorer®. As with the hexagons, the former method has the advantage of allowing all members of the team to see the material and work with it, although it has the disadvantage of requiring a separate means of recording content for later reference. The use of computer software enables real-time recording of content, but makes group viewing and manipulation of the content difficult and cumbersome.

Clustering the Driving Forces: the Northshire Example

For the e-government project with Northshire, nearly two hours generating over 150 driving forces and their associated polar outcomes had left the scenario team mentally and physically exhausted. A short break at this stage ensured that thinking remained fresh, then the task of reducing the complexity to manageability began. Here, the facilitators asked the team to begin moving the hexagons around, to form 'stories' relating to different parts of the overall business environment. Any member could commence a story by bringing together two or more hexagons, briefly explaining his/her reasoning. Other team members then incorporated related hexagons into the story, or started new clusters of reasoning. Within 10 minutes, the whole range of driving forces, apart from two or three stragglers, had been incorporated into nine clusters. The team then discussed each cluster at length, deciding if the forces were related by causality. This discussion resulted in minor readjustment of locations for some hexagons. At the end of the process, however, the team had agreed on the cluster sets, each covered by a short cluster heading (see Figure 7.3).

The aim of the clustering exercise is to reduce the overall number of forces to a small and manageable number of higher level concepts. The large number of driving forces, perhaps several hundred, is impossible to handle effectively without this further structuring. Sense cannot be made of the complexity of the situation, as it is not possible to recognize related forces. Establishing a systemic understanding of the driving forces through clustering will enable the team to exploit degrees of overlap and interdependence. The aim is to produce a set of clusters that are internally related and separate from any other cluster, although some driving forces may sit comfortably in more than one cluster. The content of each cluster should summarize a generalized uncertainty in the environment, making it specific to the themes being addressed.

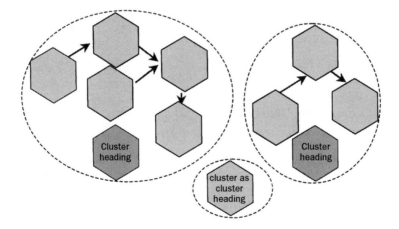

Figure 7.3 Clustering driving forces and naming clusters.

Apart from a general rule of causality, there is no rule to define how clusters should be constructed. Specifically, the clusters should not be based on a disciplinary or single-subject basis, such as technology, politics or economics. After all, the aim is to discuss and set out relationships across fields of interest.

Driving forces can often be gathered together into a single cluster. However, the cluster is only viable if, within the context of the business problem, all the driving forces can be tied together by a single cluster heading. A further test of internal coherence is to draw arrows of causal relationships between individual driving forces. These tests will determine if the content of the cluster can be conceptualized within a single storyline. If a short cluster heading cannot be determined, then the driving forces within the cluster are probably too wide-ranging in scope. If this occurs, it is necessary to break down the super-cluster into coherent stand-alone clusters.

It is important to assure team members that clustering is not simply a means of reducing or eliminating items from discussion. The clusters are only a temporary means of handling the complexity of the 'bigger picture' encapsulated by the full set of driving forces and polar outcomes. At a later stage, the full set of polar outcomes from the driving forces will be reintroduced for constructing the scenarios themselves.

Dealing with Impact and Uncertainty

Having reduced the number of concepts without losing any driving forces, since all are included in the clusters, the next stage is to determine the key areas of critical uncertainty that will form the central themes of our developing scenarios. This stage aims to identify the two general areas believed to have the highest impact on the business problem and the highest level of uncertainty over the potential outcome. This is achieved by preparing a two-dimensional ranking space, depicting high/low impact and high certainty/uncertainty (see Figure 7.4). Team members should then take the complete set of cluster headings and decide on the relative impact each will have on the client organization. There are no scales on the axis: the highest-impact cluster heading should be

Instant Scenarios
In a short exercise, the opposite problem to super-clusters is likely to arise. Since the number of driving forces raised will probably be limited, the number of clusters will be small. A single driving force could constitute a cluster, if no other forces can be logically related to it. The process of clustering and testing for causal linkages should be completed in about 45 minutes.

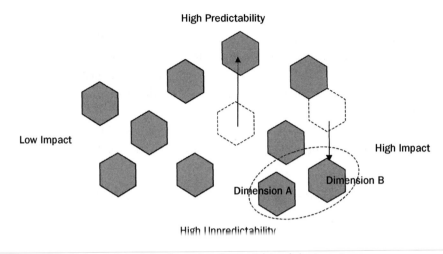

High Predictability

Low Impact

High Impact

Dimension A

Dimension B

High Unpredictability

Figure 7.4 Determining relative impact and uncertainty of cluster outcomes.

placed at the right-hand side of the horizontal axis. The decision is then briefly debated among the team. The cluster heading with the least relative impact is placed on the left-hand side. Again, this is subject to brief discussion. Once the highest and lowest impact headings are decided upon and placed at the extremes of the axis, the team should place the other cluster headings in relative order between them. This normally takes about 10 to 15 minutes, although there can be varying degrees of discussion.

Once all team members are in (reasonable) agreement about the impact relationships, the team should then consider the relative certainty/uncertainty of outcomes for the client organization. At this stage, we stress that the vertical axis must be considered in relation to the outcomes of the cluster, not in relation to the degree of certainty/uncertainty of the events implied by it coming about. That is to say, a cluster may contain driving forces that are indicative of events that we are certain will happen, such as 'growth in use of IT' and 'increasing speed of data processing', but if we are uncertain of the impact that these events will have on the client organization, then they will be moved towards the 'high uncertainty' end of the scale. The cluster headings should be moved in the vertical certainty/uncertainty direction without disturbing their relative order in the horizontal high/low impact direction.

After discussion, the cluster heading where the outcome is considered to have the highest degree of uncertainty should be placed at the bottom of the matrix. The vertical space runs from the highest uncertainty at the bottom to the lowest uncertainty at the top. It should only be moved in a vertical direction. Then, the cluster heading with the highest degree of certainty attached to the outcome should be placed at the top of the matrix. This moving of cluster headings in the vertical direction continues, with discussion among the team, until all the cluster headings are placed in their relative positions on the matrix, as indicated in Figure 7.4.

The next step is to select those cluster headings that are going to form the two scenario dimensions. The choice is made by selecting groups of driving forces that have:

1. the *highest relative impact* on the business problem, combined with
2. the *highest uncertainty* as to the outcomes.

These will be the two cluster headings closest to the bottom right-hand corner of the impact/uncertainty space. In relatively simple scenario exercises, the two clusters may be easily identifiable. However, team members need to assess the two selected headings carefully. Importantly, the two clusters selected must be independent of each other. For example, within classic economic theory, a cluster entitled 'changing rates of unemployment' would be considered to be related to one entitled 'changing rates of economic growth'. However, the reality of the UK economy in the 1980s was the exception that proved the rule. Given this, it is important to allow debate of novel and exceptional suggestions. If the selected cluster headings are related to each other, they should be treated as one cluster, representing the first scenario dimension. The next highest impact/uncertainty cluster should then be selected as the second scenario dimension.

The two dimensions of the scenarios have now been selected, defining the 'limits of the possible' for four possible and plausible futures. At this stage, the team moves from the temporary reduction – designed to make sense of complexity and make the data manageable – to a process of inclusion, where all previous thinking on driving forces and polar events is combined with the thinking developed in the generation of the different 'types of futures'.

Instant Scenarios

In the rapid exercise, the discussion of relative impact and uncertainty should be kept brief. All other factors come back into play in building the scenario storylines, therefore, there is no need for extended discussion and debate over the positions of cluster headings. If agreement is not reached immediately, simply move on, and reconsider the differences in opinion when building up the scenarios. This stage should be completed in about 30 minutes.

Scoping the Scenarios

Before setting the two selected scenario dimensions, A and B, into the four possible futures, the team should brainstorm words and phrases describing the end
states of each dimension at the *limits of possibility* over the scenario timescale.
These terms capture the essence of a world in which this one dimension has
progressed to its extreme (but not implausible) conclusion, with all other factors
in the world being discounted. For example, a scenario dimension of technology
take-up might produce one set of extreme descriptors.

- universal acceptance;
- convergence of technologies;
- low-cost processing;
- high-level broadband installation;
- e-business prevails.

These are independent of any other factors in the environment, such as economic
status, education or social inequalities.

Once the team has brainstormed the two sets of extreme state descriptors for
each of the dimensions individually, it combines these in the four possible
combinations in order to produce the general characteristics of each of the four
possible end states – the four scenarios. As with the separate dimensions, start by
brainstorming the words and phrases that characterize the four futures, recording
them on a 2 × 2 matrix (see Figure 7.5).

For example, the dimension of *technology take-up* could be combined with one of
social inclusion or exclusion. Here, our end states of technology take-up need to be
considered in conjunction with the social context in which we see the limits of
possibility lying between moderate and high levels of social exclusion. In this
case, the best-case outcome of high levels of technology take-up needs to be
tempered by consideration of a best-case outcome of moderate levels of social
exclusion. Clearly, universal acceptance, as an ideal, will no longer be seen as the
reality of the future that we are writing about.

Having conducted the initial brainstorming exercise that describes the four
possible futures in terms of the combination of outcomes from the two scenario
dimensions, all the polar outcomes of all the driving forces originally identified are
brought back into the process. The team places each outcome into the most
appropriate scenario box. For most outcomes, the most plausible box will be
apparent – for example, polar outcomes of high unemployment and high inflation
would not be put within a scenario box defined by descriptors of a stable economic

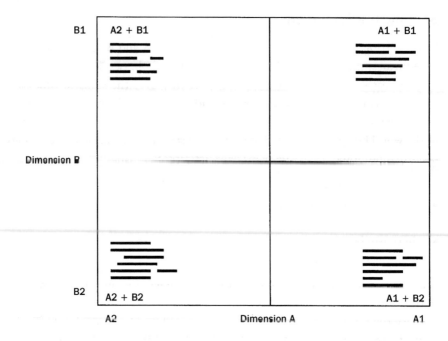

Figure 7.5   Framing the scenarios.

situation with steady growth. Some outcomes will be independent of the scenario dimensions, residing between scenarios. This is normal. A large number of outcomes will inevitably lead to a few that don't seem to fit anywhere. These can be placed to the side of the matrix, for later use in filling in the stories, or placed in any scenario box that lacks sufficient outcomes to bring the story to life. However, this random placing should only be considered as a last resort, after the logic of placing in a particular box has been exhausted. At the end of this process, the team will have developed a scenario matrix with four possible futures set out, each characterized by a set of widely varied descriptors of its end state and what the world will be like at the end of the period under consideration (Figure 7.6).

Setting the 'Limits of Possibility' for Alternative Futures: the Northshire Example

Returning to the e-government scenario exercise, the two scenario dimensions derived from the impact and uncertainty analysis were determined by the team to be:

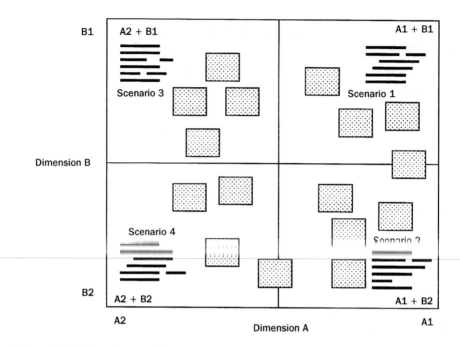

Figure 7.6 Filling the scenario scope.

- **value creation** through the balance of people and technology and the extent of technological development (dimension A);
- **democratic process** and the central/local government power balance (dimension B).

In this case, the team had brought together a number of cluster headings that all had high degrees of impact and uncertainty, but that showed degrees of inter-relatedness. In this event, the related cluster headings were brought together to form the higher-level uncertainties that formed the scenario dimensions. Each of the dimensions was comprised of cluster headings as follows:

- **value creation** – 'balance people/technology', 'technological development' and 'scope for value creation'; and
- **democratic process** – 'democratic process' and 'balance central/local'.

Setting these scenario dimensions in the scenario matrix, the team brainstormed extreme outcomes for each of the dimensions separately. The descriptors for each were listed as follows:

Dimension A – value creation

A1 – Outcomes north	A2 – Outcomes south
Technology delivers growth	Technology creates overload
Responsive institutions	Complexity reducers
Customer driven	Public sector in locked-in fragmentation
Technological inclusion	Rigid, inflexible services
Business network synergy	An information élite as part of new establishment
Quality of life development	
Investments in health care	Slow process for trickling information down the organization hierarchy

Dimension B – democratic process

B1 – Outcomes east	B2 – Outcomes west
Greater participation in public sector organization and in electoral process	Public becomes indifferent, individualism prevails
Community leadership	Emphasis on market solutions and opportunities
Better-informed people wish to be involved	Reduced government and reduced taxation
Power moves to local agencies, with local accountability	Central control increases
Central government limited to setting standards	

These descriptors are then considered in combination (A1/B1; A1/B2; A2/B1; A2/B2) in order to scope out the scenario outlines. Further sets of descriptors are brainstormed to provide more detail of how the two dimensions would operate with each other and to provide a basis for development. Then, the complete set of polar outcomes from the earlier 'driving forces and polar outcomes' workshops is allocated to the most appropriate quadrant of the matrix. Thereafter, the team divides into four groups, each taking the material from one quadrant, and working together to develop the scenario storyline: a five-year 'history of the future' that puts the events into a chronological order, based upon consideration of causal relationships. The aim of each group is to bring to life a plausible and consistent story of the future for the region, its businesses and its citizens.

Fleshing out the Storylines

The final task in scenario development is to turn this list of descriptions and outcomes into a short 'history' of the future. To achieve this, the team must project themselves to the end year of the scenarios, five or ten years into the future, and become future historians, developing the story of how they came to be in the situation they find themselves in.

With the scenarios set out on the matrix, divide the scenario team into four sub-groups, each taking one scenario and developing its story. Allow groups to be self-selecting, so long as they are approximately equal in size, since it is helpful if members have already bought into the 'reality' of the story that they will tell. Each group works with whiteboards, or flipchart sheets, using Post-it® Notes or some other medium that allows manipulation of ideas among the group. The major consideration of the group is 'How did we get to this point?' The group must think of the events that have led to the world as it is to be. The starting point is the set of descriptors and polar outcomes that are given. Largely, the group will be describing the end of the period, but some events will be indicative of events that must happen early on, or of the continuation of trends already identified in society. Other events may already be 'programmed' into history. For example, many countries have elections at fixed periods, while others have a maximum period between them. For many countries, the candidates standing at the next election are probably already known. So, how do the future political landscape and these elections fit into the storyline? Other events may need more creative thinking on the part of group members. Some may be identified by reference to historical precedent, but some may have no precedent. However, in the latter case, there must be a plausible cause-and-effect reasoning chain showing an audit trail from the present to the event.

In turning the scenario scope into a storyline that will grab the attention of others, the group needs to consider the roles of people such as politicians, business leaders, political activists and others (such as stakeholders; see below), whose actions will bring a dimension of reality to the story. The group must also consider how its audience will be brought on board, by setting the starting point of the story firmly in the present. What aspects of the world as it is are critical to starting the scenario – the *pushes*? What events or actions in the near future will be important, in terms of taking the story along this particular path as opposed to that being developed by other groups? The most important aspect of scenario planning, as opposed to mere storytelling, is that the scenarios must have clearly stated implications for the organization. Consider:

- What does this story mean for us?
- How are we implicated in the outcomes of these events?
- What are the impacts on us of our customers behaving in this way?

However, the scenarios themselves should never contain the organization as an actor. That is to say, the organization should not be shown to be having an input and impact on the story, since this risks applying business-as-usual principles in order to guide the future in the desired direction.

Before the group brings their own scenario back into the forum of the scenario team, its members should act as their own devil's advocates, critically questioning their own logic and causal linkages. They should ask:

- Would this event really lead to this outcome?
- Would this individual or group really do this?
- Would this state of affairs really exist to this degree?

For each of these questions they should also consider what alternatives exist, and whether they make sense here, or in one of the other scenarios.

On completion of the individual scenarios within the groups, the scenario team reconvenes and the groups then present their storylines to each other. Here, the wider group acts as devil's advocates, but not in a negatively critical way. Groups must remember that there is no question here of one scenario being better than another, or more likely, no matter whether the future that it describes is considered as being 'better'. The aim of this critical discussion is for the scenario team as a single unit to bring the full set of four stories together in a coherent format, so that each is distinct from the others, yet all four form a related set. Each is independent in telling of a different future, but each is dependent on the others for setting out the limits of possibility for the *real* future that will unfold, barring unforeseen events beyond reasonable expectation.

None of the stories set out will come true, yet all will come true, to some extent. The scenarios certainly must not be seen as the only four possibilities for the future. Rather, they should open up the organization's thinking to the possibility that the future will lie somewhere within the boundaries set by these extremes. They should also provide the members with a continuous research agenda for keeping track of the warning signs that will indicate in which direction the future is heading. Finally, the scenarios should provide models of possible worlds in which to test strategies and options for business development before they are implemented, rather than being prototyped as they unfold in reality!

Instant Scenarios

The development of quick scenario outlines should be undertaken in sub-groups, with each group having about an hour to work up their storyline. Then, the groups present their scenarios to each other, again with the larger group acting as devil's advocates. With limited time spent on the overall exercise, and no interim period for research, it is likely that this type of 'instant' scenario process will be based more upon blue-sky thinking than in-depth research. While members may have reasonable amounts of knowledge and understanding of the subject area from within the organizational context, there may be a fairly narrow view of the external environment. Remember the words of Mark Twain, who wrote: 'The important thing is not how much we don't know, as how wrong we are in what we think we do know.' The scenarios produced in a restricted timescale are likely to be too rough and ready for determining action, but they can be ideal for opening up our minds to our knowledge and information gaps, setting an agenda for further research and investigations. This research could lead into a further, more in-depth and more informed full-scenario iteration.

Beyond the Kailyard

In addition to the group that had outlined the People's Kailyard, the other groups had worked with the scenario scopes as outlined by the combination of descriptors and polar outcomes. The total set of scenarios comprising the Kailyard scenario therefore included three further scenarios: *Forward to the Past*, *Free Enterprise* and *Technology Serves*.

Forward to the past

In this future, centralization dominates over dispersed and local governance, and central government runs the show. There are real barriers to change, with restricted funding for local government, mismatches in the geographical boundaries of councils in relation to areas of wealth and employment, and a reluctance to share accountability across agencies. The adoption of new technologies and the resultant productivity improvement in the public sector has come at the expense of local government, with a drive towards centralization at government level, and to central control or privatization of services at the local level. This future may mark the beginning of the end for local government.

Free enterprise

Here, there is emancipation of the public and a drive away from the paternalism of the old-style bureaucratic governance. The customer rules, and market forces are delivering – but only for some. For those with access to and the capability to use new technologies, there is a public free spirit, with 24/7 access to the new public sector trade. While there are drives towards achieving economies of scale, the concept of one size fits all has been challenged, with a demand for premium services from those who can afford to pay extra for them. There is, however, serious polarization in society, with an 'underclass' being excluded from the new society; those who can either ill-afford, or who are ill-equipped, to use the emerging technologies.

Technology serves

Here, there is a combination of technology facilitating increased access by the citizenry, together with the development of a proactive form of civic governance based upon meaningful dialogue between citizens and government. Elected members and their officers are enabled to act at the local level for all members of society, including the 'invisibles' and the 'excluded'. National government settles the subsidiarity debate in favour of local democracy, and supports trailblazing projects that demonstrate the competence of civic governance, for example in the field of social housing. Here, the new technologies facilitate a new form of joined-up government from the bottom up.

Each of the sub-groups presented their scenario outline to the full participant group, with the key differences between each clearly differentiating the possibilities for a range of plausible futures. In *Forward to the Past*, there is seen to be a downward spiral, a vicious circle towards greater centralization and little or no local autonomy in the future. In *Free Enterprise*, local government is unencumbered by bureaucracy, but there is delivery of 'premium services' for those who are prepared to pay, but with increased polarization and disenfranchisement in society. In the *People's Kailyard*, there is mediocrity and, surrounded by legislation, cross-organizational boundary problems and non-standard protocols. There is much talk of change but a continuous stream of new problems to talk about, so no change. In *Technology Serves*, there is a future in which the group's common aspirations, visions and desires for change are seen to be enabled.

STAGE 4: STAKEHOLDER ANALYSIS

At this point, we will introduce the subject of stakeholder analysis. This tool does not form part of the main scenario approach, but is one that we have found useful for two reasons:

- to test our understanding of the business problem; and
- to test the internal logic of our storylines.

First, however, it is worth declining stakeholder analysis. In contrast to shareholders, who hold a financial interest in an organization, stakeholders are defined as 'those groups or individuals who may affect, or be affected by, any of the strategies, operations or any other activities of the organization.'

It may appear that for many organizations the list of stakeholders can be extremely wide-ranging, bringing in most elements of society. For example, Microsoft's stakeholders include every individual and institutional user of its software products, also, every one of its direct employees, contractors, sub-contractors and suppliers; even those who do not use the organization's products, but whose lives and businesses are in any way impacted upon by it. Finally, it may include anyone who passes by a Microsoft building and is impacted by its aesthetic appeal (or lack of it!).

So, we must find a way of determining those stakeholders who are key to our considerations of external forces impacting the organization's activities. Here, we consider how different groups and individuals fit into the stakeholder framework. This is done by considering the relative degree of interest and power that each has in relation to the business problem, at a particular point in time. Stakeholder analysis is always time- and context-dependent. For example, for many organizations the media can exercise considerable power, but for most this power will be largely dormant, since there is no reason for interest in the organization to be aroused. For some organizations, such as hospitals, this power tends to be exercised when interest is aroused through some dire failure of the normal systems. We might also be tempted in our scenario process to consider the interests of particular groups because they are central to the story of the organization, or out of sympathy; for example, we might be concerned for the plight of children in conducting scenarios on the future of preschool education. But, are the children in any direct way impacting the decision-making process? Completion of the matrix shown in Figure 7.7 helps us to separate reality from emotion, and to think how particular events will change the decision-making hierarchy.

We now have a way of considering the relative positions of different stakeholders, and may use this in one of two ways in the scenario process. First, we may use stakeholder analysis at the outset, in order to test our understanding of the business problem, by asking several necessary questions.

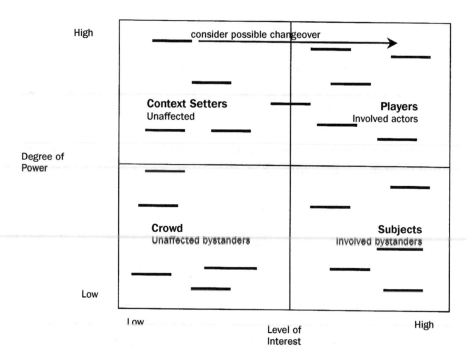

Figure 7.7 Considering the relative positions of different stakeholders.

- Who is key to decision-making at this time?
- What really matters to him, or keeps him awake at night?
- Who are the customers with a high interest in the organization?
- Who are the predatory stakeholders?

This analysis may help us in formulating the scenario agenda. Second, we may use stakeholder analysis at the end of the scenario generation process, in order to test the internal logic of our storylines.

- Who are the players in this scenario?
- Do they stay the same, or do they change?
- Would they really act in this way and make these decisions?

If the answer to the last question is 'no', the scenario is probably fatally flawed through incorrect organizational bias.

One final application of stakeholder analysis is for determining roles for a role-playing exercise by members of the scenario team. One way of trying to move outside your own cultural programming is to try, as far as possible, to put yourself 'in the shoes' of someone else with a key interest in the business problem. Try to understand and adopt their beliefs and values, and critically engage with your own perspective from theirs. Finally, in adopting the devil's advocate role at the end of the scenario-writing process, it can be helpful to critically engage with the storyline from the point of view of specific stakeholders.

- Would we really do that?
- Would we contribute to this situation in this way?

Stakeholder analysis is a tool to be used in parallel with the scenario process, as and when members of the scenario team find it useful.

STAGE 6: SYSTEMS THINKING

Throughout the exercise, the team can positively influence the quality of what they are doing by applying systems thinking. The importance of this was suggested in Chapter 6, where we saw systems thinking at work at various places, for example during the clustering of driving forces. But the role of systems thinking is much wider. At any time during the storytelling phase of the process, teams can ask themselves whether they could identify the underlying causal relationships driving the stories they are putting together. This involves more than just asking whether event A could result in event B. Once the storyline is taking some shape, the teams should pause for a moment and draw an influence diagram (sometimes called a causal loop diagram) of the forces in the story. Prepare by carrying out an iceberg analysis. Describe the events that are taking shape in your story, then specify the trends and patterns that are recognizable. From this identify the deep causal structure by repeatedly asking *why*. Once you feel that the iceberg includes the main features of your story, draw up the causal influence diagram.

This exercise always proves highly enlightening, as it challenges the internal consistency of the storyline. It is particularly important to identify loops in the influence diagram that close in upon themselves, as it is unlikely that the effects of these (for example, lock-in) have yet been accounted for in the story.

In large projects with an adequate budget, there is significant additional value in turning the influence diagrams into system dynamics (SD) models. This value comes from using the models as simulation tools, but even more from an increased understanding of how things hang together, which comes from having to vigorously address the requirements of turning an influence diagram into a quantitative model. SD models are also, of course, of great help in enriching the storylines through simulation, as well as giving teams confidence that their stories cannot be faulted on internal consistency.

STAGE 6: IMPACTING ORGANIZATIONAL THINKING AND ACTION

Looking for the Organizational Jolt

Completion of the scenario generation process is the cue for relaxation and self-congratulation, but what purpose has it so far served? The scenario team may now be aware of a number of different possible and plausible futures, but this will be useless if the outputs of the process are looked at as ends in themselves. The team must now find a way of communicating its work to the organization at large, or at least find a way of putting it in front of key decision makers who have not been party to the process (these should be non-existent or few in number). Key to getting the attention of others is to tell the stories concisely, brought to life in a way that will grab the attention of the audience through the selection of an appropriate medium of presentation. For some organizations, this may best be done by a formal and 'factual' presentation. For others, a mock-up of an article from *The Economist* of June 2011 may be more appropriate.

The crucial aspect of presenting the scenarios, however, is to stimulate the organizational jolt, which may be one of delight, an opportunity presented that had not previously been considered. However, it may also be one of shock, as in the example of the Kailyard, where it was seen that current investment priorities could present a possible threat if they were implemented without considering a wider political agenda.

Identifying the Early Indicators

While scenarios are normally set out over an extended timescale, typically three, five or ten years, they are intended to provide immediate impact on organizational strategic thinking and planning. As such, they must then bring in immediate implications, in terms of early indicators. What are the current issues, trends and developments that impact the business problem? What are the different perspectives on the world as it is that must be taken into account? What are the key indicators showing which of these perspectives is coming to fruition? Has one of the scenarios already started to play out?

For example, consideration of the Singaporean economy for the micro-electronics sector in November 2001 may elicit different views, where:

- There is evidence of a bottoming-out of recession in the US economy, with increased consumer confidence. Retail sales have grown year on year. Wal-Mart had its highest-ever daily sales last week. The US dollar is strengthening against the euro. Unemployment in Singapore has increased, but is now holding steady. Development of new integrated technologies offers potential for growth. Rationalization to date has cut the cost of unit production to most efficient levels ever. New market opportunities are offered by China's WTO (World Trade Organization) entry.

- There is evidence of continuing deflation of prices for electronics. There have been recent signs of a turnaround in the US economy, but this cannot yet be read as a trend. The US economy has contracted during the last quarter. Japanese electronics companies are announcing transfers of production to China, which has recently been admitted to full WTO membership. Efficiency cuts still do not match low-cost economies. Many consumers are holding back from purchasing, waiting for further price cuts.

These different views are not complementary in supporting a unified view of the climate for investment; yet they are not contradictory, in enabling an either/or choice of which is 'right' and which is 'wrong'. In considering the future investment climate, it is necessary to determine the range of early indicators that will show which views and trends are prevailing and which are diminishing. So, any scenario project should show the early indicators that are key to determining which future is unfolding, and the implications for strategic thinking.

Action Planning from the Future to the Present: the Northshire Example

Through discussion of the underlying trends and basic driving forces that underpinned each of the scenarios, Northshire Council derived an initial set of key implications that were seen to be fundamental to their immediate thinking. These were important if the council was to be effective in exerting its influence over the reality of the future that will unfold over the next five years. These key implications were:

- Northshire must lead from the front, and take bold steps in developing an integrated and inclusive approach to technological innovation. The dangers of the small step and short-term approach were highlighted in the Kailyard scenario.
- The council must promote democracy in action by making new technologies serve the people, and by using technology to develop 'civic governance'. It must bring local government closer to the community level, developing a better ability to listen and respond to citizen needs. It must develop transparency and accountability in its deeds and actions, with policies that are meaningful to the public.
- New technologies must be used to demonstrate the competence of local government, achieving public confidence and support through the provision of responsive, community-oriented, more customized services while, at the same time, applying the technologies to support inclusion and reduce inequalities.
- Northshire must use the new technologies in order to promote itself as the 'home for sustainable value creation'.
- The council must proactively promote and lobby for settlement of the subsidiarity debate in favour of governance at the local level.
- Finally, in developing short-term solutions to immediate problems, all players/ agents must ensure that achieving long-term aspirations remains their main aim.

From the outcomes of the scenario project, and the resultant debate within Northshire on these implications, strategic decisions have been focused on supporting local democracy in action; promoting inclusion, quality, best value and sustainability across all operations; fostering the concept of joined-up government, and seeking to foster a better relationship with central government, of whatever political persuasion, while promoting the case for Northshire in the widest political and business arenas. In addition to these strategic decisions, operational actions have been taken in seeking to establish a web-based knowledge and transaction system.

For both public and private sector organizations, participation in the scenario project drove a reframing of their own position in society, through a critical reappraisal of their customers, and the choices and investment decisions available to them in order to leverage value. For the council, it was seen that the local populace and business community are no longer captive markets, and that the previously ignored concepts of choice and value will be key future determinants of whether or not the council will be the preferred supplier in many cases. For the telecommunications company, the implications of the scenario project were to show that technological solutions to socio-political problems cannot be supplier- or technology-driven and cannot be solely generic. They must be based upon context-specific capability, needs and resources. But the project also alerted the company to the fact that government is a customer and, as with all other customers, future investment decisions will be driven by value considerations. These will be informed by critical appraisal of options, in terms of what value will be generated for its own customers, and exploring the value chain.

Option Planning

The development of scenarios, and the consideration of their impact and implications on the value chain that links organizations in complex supplier/customer relationships, should now stimulate strategic thinking. This, in turn, should generate the options that enable exploration of value generation and stimulate action. These options must be based on the starting point of where you are now. What are your organization's core competencies and capabilities, and what are the critical gaps in these that inhibit responses to the range of possible futures presented?

Taking into account current resources, the organization should now develop detailed action plans in response to the original business issue. Once developed, the scenarios serve the further role of vigorously testing these options. The organization can test its proposed options against the environmental conditions set out within each scenario, considering their viability, effectiveness and other issues. This is discussed further in Chapter 8.

SUMMARY: EFFECTIVE SCENARIO PLANNING

It is worth considering that the scenario process is not one of linear implementation, completed once and then laid aside. As a strategic planning tool, the effectiveness of scenarios lies in processes of continuous environmental analysis, scenario generation, option development, scenario testing, selection, refinement and implementation. The implementation process is accompanied by further environmental analysis in order to update the impacts of organizational actions.

Summary Checklist – Implementing a Scenario Planning Process

The following checklist is a guide to conducting an effective and purposeful scenario project.

Stage 1: structuring the scenario process

- *Identify gaps in organizational knowledge.* These will relate specifically to business problems, where there is uncertainty about their impact on the future of the organization.
- *Create a facilitation team.* Ideally, this should be external to the organization and separate from the participants.
- *Decide on the duration of the scenario project.* Instant scenarios can be undertaken where urgency, cost and time are pressing. Allow approximately 10 weeks for a major scenario project.

Stage 2: exploring the scenario context

- *Conduct interviews with the team members.* This will surface insights into customer value, the current success formula, dominant perspectives and the degree of convergence within the team.
  - Starting questions should address the individual's views of the future, present and past (ask in that order).
  - The recording method should be comprehensive and accurate.
- *Collate and analyse the results of the interview process.* Reduce the interview statements to a manageable set of key, higher-level concepts that will structure the Interview Report:
  - Identify and use recurring concepts to structure the findings (this ensures that concepts spring from the participants' ideas and not from the facilitators or other members of the organization).
  - This reordering provides structure and anonymity.
  - Concepts form section heads.
  - Specific themes within the concepts form the sub-headings.
  - Place statements under the appropriate sub-heading.
- *Set the agenda.* The reordered information, in the Interview Report, sets the agenda; the key issues are now ready for further investigation in the first workshop:

    – Circulate the Interview Report one week before the workshop.

    – Open up a wider and more generalized discussion of the systemic factors that will impact on the business problem.

    – Check if the clustering of statements and the key concepts identified are accepted by the team (promoting shared ownership).

    – Identify the critical uncertainties in the future external environment that will generate the current uncertainties.

    – The critical uncertainties, as perceived by the participants, form the scenario investigation agenda.

- *Invite any 'remarkable people', those who can help the team challenge conventional approaches and attitudes.* Choose individuals who are noted for their leading-edge abilities, creative thinking and challenging reputations.

Stage 3: developing the scenarios

- *Identify the driving forces through structured thinking, test the outcomes, and handle complexity.*

    – Ask participants individually to consider driving forces that will impact on the agreed business problem over the scenario period, and to record these on separate Post-it® notes or hexagons, using as few words as possible, but ensuring that they are self-explanatory to others. Number the driving force records 1, 2, etc. for recording purposes.

    – The group should then test the concept of 'driving force' for each proposal by eliciting two polar outcomes that will describe possible end states for this force over the scenario timescale relating to the project. Record these on separate Post-it® notes or hexagons, and label them in relation to the associated driving force, 1a/1b, 2a/2b etc. and reserve them for later use.

    – Cluster the driving forces into groups sharing a higher-level concept – this makes the large number of driving forces manageable and highlights overlap and interdependence.

    – Clusters should include related driving forces, but remain separate from other clusters.

    – Name the clusters, using short titles that encapsulate the full content of driving forces and the higher-level concept.

    – Test the logic and internal consistency of the cluster by linking the driving forces using arrows to show cause and effect relationships. If any driving force cannot be linked in this way, it does not belong within this cluster.

- *Impact and uncertainty.*
  - Prepare a two dimensional ranking space, bounded with high/low impact and high/low uncertainty (of impact). This identifies the two areas that have the highest impact and the greatest uncertainty attached.
  - Make sure the two areas are not related.
  - The two chosen cluster headings form the two scenario dimensions that will be applied to the four scenarios.
- *Scoping the scenarios.*
  - Before setting the two scenario dimensions (A and B) into the four possible futures, the team needs to scope the scenarios, to capture the essence of the end state and to discount irrelevant descriptions.
  - Achieve this by brainstorming words and phrases that describe the end states.
  - Combine the two dimensions to produce general characteristics of the four end states – again, brainstorm words and phrases and record on a 2 × 2 matrix.
  - Place all the original outcomes into the appropriate scenario box on the 2 × 2 matrix. This produces a scenario matrix with four possible futures, each containing end-state descriptions.
- *Fleshing out the storylines.* Aim to produce a short 'history of the future'. Project the team to the end states; each group has to develop the scenario story explaining how that end state was reached.
  - Divide the team into four groups, each choosing one of the scenarios.
  - Each group uses the descriptors and polar outcomes as its starting point. Their task is to produce a logical cause-and-effect reasoning chain that develops the scenario to its conclusion. They should also identify the 'push' that started the scenario.
  - Consider how and why the actions and events unfold in a particular way
  - Keep the story focused on the organization by constantly assessing how the developments specifically impact the organization. (Avoid using the organization as an actor, as this risks business-as-usual thinking distorting conclusions.)
  - Each group should critically question its arguments.
  - Each group then presents its scenario to the whole team.
  - The team critically discusses each scenario. Understand how the four separate accounts are related; when combined, they set the 'limits of possibility' for the future.

— This opens up the team's thinking and makes them alert to signals that suggest a particular direction for organizational development. It also provides models for 'wind tunnel' strategies before implementation.

Stage 4: stakeholder analysis

- *Test your understanding of the business problem* with stakeholders, asking:
  — Who is key to decision-making at this time?
  — What really matters to him, or keeps him awake at night?
  — Who are the customers with a high interest in the organization?
  — Who are the predatory stakeholders?
- *Test the internal logic of your storylines*:
  — Who are the players in this scenario?
  — Do they stay the same, or do they change?
  — Would they really act in this way and make these decisions?

Stage 5: systems check

- Carry out a systems check by drawing an influence diagram of the forces underpinning the scenario story. Ensure that what happens in the scenario is adequately explained through the diagram.

Stage 6: impacting organizational thinking and acting

- *Stimulate the organizational 'jolt'.* This may be an opportunity or a threat, a delight or a shock — but it must motivate people to act.
- *Identify the early indicators*, the events that may be heralding a new future.
  — What are the current issues, trends and developments that impact the business problem?
  — What are the different perspectives on the world as it is that must be taken into account?
  — What are the key indicators showing which of these perspectives is coming to fruition?
- *Action plan from the future to the present.* Derive an immediate set of key implications or findings that are fundamental to the organization's immediate thinking. Also, look for operational actions that will maintain the momentum for change, emphasizing the value and significance of the scenario process.

In this chapter, we have outlined our scenario approach which, as you have seen, includes some options and variations around organizational resources, timescales and other factors. This is not intended to be cast in stone, but is offered as a basis for organizational strategic conversation that will open members' minds to a wider range of 'limits of the possible' for the future business environment. In the next chapter, we move on to consider how these insights into possible futures can contribute to organizational learning, to effective strategic thinking and to considered action in any reasonably foreseeable and plausible future context.

Scenario Planning: Taking Charge of the Future

CHAPTER 8

No other strategic approach satisfies the fundamental business
need for successfully handling external drivers of change
against a background of uncertainty. In this final chapter, we will
show in practical terms how the success of the scenario
approach lies in the continual strengthening of the organization's
capabilities: extending distinctiveness, manipulating and
controlling market opportunities – and delivering better
performance. This chapter is about the wider context in which
scenarios function and deliver.

Overview

In this chapter, we will place scenarios in their wider context of management and strategy. The steps that organizations take to integrate scenario processes and culture into the organization are vital in ensuring a successful future. In this chapter we will:

- Outline different possible aspirations, derived from the need for organizations to be successful, within which the scenario approach makes its contribution. Success in scenarios critically depends on being clear about the purpose of the exercise.
- Outline the action planning necessary to take charge and act on the results of scenario thinking. The need is to understand the drivers of change in the external environmental – and then to act positively upon them.

CONTINUED... Overview

- Discuss four archetypal projects that strengthen organizations by using the scenario approach. These are making sense of a puzzling situation, developing strategy, improving anticipation, and building an adaptive learning organization.
- Show the ultimate value of scenario planning as an ongoing, iterative learning process. Here, sensemaking, through scenario construction, feeds action-oriented strategy and activity, which leads to further experience and sensemaking of experience, promoting a strong organization that survives and prospers in the ever-changing business environment.

THE ENERGETIC PROBLEM SOLVER

Today's business environment has focused attention on problem-solving. Faced with the continuous onslaught of problems, with new difficulties often obscuring old ones before the old ones have been adequately addressed, managers often view themselves as being in the problem-solving business. The *energetic problem solver* is a person who defines his job in those terms, measuring success by the number of problems solved (or dissolved) per unit of time. All his energy goes into sorting out situations as quickly as possible, so that he can move on to the next problem-solving situation.

The downside of this is that problem-solving dominates his mindset; essentially a reactive frame of mind. After all, the world around him determines where and how his time is spent, which in turn determines his attention span. The energetic problem solver becomes trapped in a loop that becomes increasingly difficult to escape from. The problems he finds are diagnosed in terms of the 'business-as-usual' world. Therefore, concentrating on problems causes his attention span and vision to focus on maintaining business as usual. It is

> **In order to perceive external developments that are relevant to long-term success, the manager and the organization need to deliberately step out of the daily routine and turn their attention to the wider environment, becoming sensitive to early indicators of new long-term trends.**

difficult to see much beyond business-as-usual and attending to the unknown dots that may be appearing on the horizon. Similarly, as situations develop and become too large to ignore, the eventual response is often one of panic. As illustrated in the film *Lawrence of Arabia*, mentioned at the very start of this book, panic does not lead to vigilant decisions.

We have seen, in some of the examples explored earlier, that managers vary in their abilities to recognize problems at a distance. While the energetic problem-solving mindset keeps the organization steady in a day-to-day business context, it does not adequately deal with its survival in the longer term. Trend-breaking variables will inevitably destabilize the business environment. In order to perceive developments that are relevant to the longer-term success of the organization, managers need to deliberately step out of the day-to-day routine and turn their attention to the wider environment, and become sensitive to early indicators of new, long-term trends.

Observation – the Cornerstone of Strategic Success

In order to become an effective scenario planner, it is important to hone observational skills. Logically, seeing something is related to understanding it. Understanding an event follows on from locating it in the broader picture. Recall from Chapter 2 how we tend to 'see' adverts about the car that we have just purchased, rather than those describing the virtues of other cars. Imagine it is a Peugeot; you will be surprised to notice how many Peugeots there are on the road. They were probably always there, but you had previously overlooked them. But now you have been in one, test-driving around town. They are now part of your life story; they have become meaningful for you. Their meaningfulness puts you in a position to notice them.

> **The strategic conversation is a team activity to evolve and use knowledge – it should not be viewed as an opportunity for individuals to dominate.**

In Chapter 2, we saw that by focusing on one issue we often fail to see other aspects. Many problems in organizations are due to people focusing on business-as-usual, while failing to see new developments emerging from other angles. There are many examples of how businesses fail when they concentrate on supplying the best possible product from their perspective, to a market that wants something else. The histories of Lego, Yahoo! or Xerox bear this out. Focusing on a small problem area makes one oblivious to wider developments. That applies to each of us as individuals but also, as outlined in Chapter 3, to organizations as a whole.

The solution to these problems lies in disengaging from the business-as-usual world for a while and mentally exploring new territory, new ideas and new conversations existing around us. Becoming a better observer begins with an awareness and appreciation of a wider range of issues. This is the domain of scenarios. In the final analysis, all scenario work is underpinned by the ability to see things earlier and react to them more quickly. This is the general framework for embedding scenario planning in organizational activities to steer these towards success. We will now explore, in more detail, different ways in which scenario work can be incorporated in the general process of deliberations, decision-making and action. We will do this by detailing four projects designed to apply effective scenario planning skills in a wider context in different ways.

Purposeful Scenario Work

The decisive factor between success and failure in scenario work is the degree to which the project is *purposeful*. Much scenario work is undertaken on the basis of weak or non-existing reasoning: 'the situation is uncertain,' 'it has worked for him' or 'it seems the thing to do'. Starting from such a basis is a recipe for failure. Complete clarity concerning what you want to achieve is essential in order to design a process to meet your objectives.

What sort of goals can we distinguish in scenario projects? The story from *Lawrence of Arabia*, explored in the Introduction, highlights the need for, and the potential of, scenario thinking. When faced with unknown variables and an uncertain future, the quest is for a clear vision of the future, an ability to make sense of the dots on the horizon. It suggests a range of generic problems in desperate need of scenario thinking. In general terms, achieving an effective, measured and controlled approach to strategy and action when facing discontinuities in the environment, organizations and individuals need to:

- quickly perceive approaching new realities;
- make sense of new realities earlier;
- understand available manoeuvrability;
- engage in more effective strategic conversations;
- create mental space for powerful strategy;
- articulate the range of options open for action;

- engage the organization in effective experiential learning;
- build accommodation around an action programme;
- know when to act and, just as important, when not to act.

One important point: these objectives are interlinked. For example, perception requires the ability to make sense of the situation, and creating mental space requires an understanding of manoeuvrability. Also, articulating powerful options requires an ability to create mental space, while a learning organization requires a powerful strategic conversation.

Considering the various goals we have met in our scenario practice, we have concluded that the purpose of scenario projects can be expressed along two main dimensions:

- Projects can either serve specific aims (one off problem solving projects) or more general process aims, promoting longer-term survival capability in the organization.
- Projects can either be undertaken to open up a closed organizational mind for exploration or to achieve closure on decisions and action in an organization that is drifting.

Combining these dimensions provides us with four combinations, which show the four main areas of purpose that can be distinguished (see Figure 8.1).

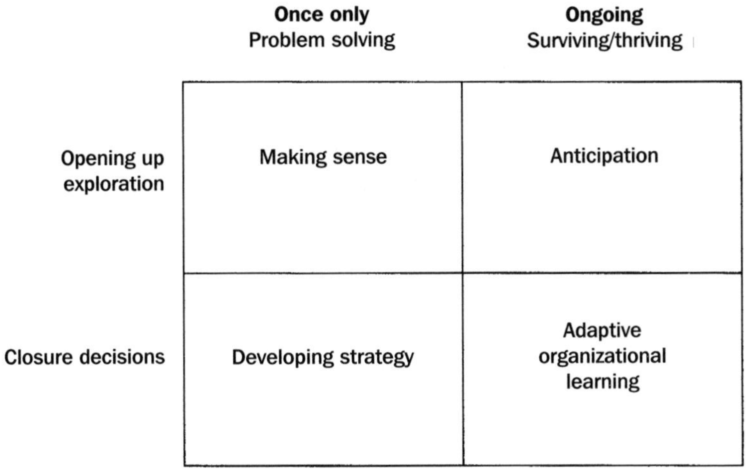

	Once only Problem solving	**Ongoing** Surviving/thriving
Opening up **exploration**	Making sense	Anticipation
Closure decisions	Developing strategy	Adaptive organizational learning

Figure 8.1 Purposes of scenario projects.

Scenario users are advised to clarify where they are (or want to be) in this matrix before embarking on a project. Of course, all four projects in Figure 8.1 pursue desirable aims and have value. However, they involve different process designs and facilitation emphasis; therefore, clarity over which one matches best with user needs is helpful to make the effort effective. In the following pages, we will describe tools for scenario planning, focusing on these four projects, which are designed to be particularly effective in:

1. **Making sense of a puzzling situation** (for example: 'I don't understand what is going on in e-commerce; I have not seen a satisfactory explanation of why the euphoria of the year 2000 has completely evaporated.')
2. **Developing strategy** (for example: 'We need to be able to articulate better to our investors that we, as a management team, are on top of this business.')
3. **Anticipation** (for example: 'We are caught off-guard too often; we must get better at understanding "dots on the horizon" that point towards the future.')
4. **Adaptive organizational learning** (for example: 'We, as a large organization, are too prone to getting stuck in recipes and business-as-usual. We must learn to adapt quickly and become more agile.')

PROJECT 1: MAKING SENSE OF A PUZZLING SITUATION

The Analytical Approach

One response to the need to understand a perplexing situation is to delegate the task to a group charged with developing strategy, plans, budgets, reviews, special studies and so on. This 'think-tank' approach implies that making sense of the future is seen as another problem to be solved through organizational means. This reflects a rationalistic view of organizational survival (see Chapter 6), the underlying assumption being that there is one correct strategic answer that can be revealed through thinking and analysis. Everyone can think on behalf of the whole organization, and the more effort and resources that are expended on this activity, the closer we will get to the correct answer.

The think-tank approach makes the organization think beyond day-to-day problem-solving. This is an important step in the right direction. But knowing where to start can be a daunting question. The natural reaction, at this point, is to think in terms of analysing the situation as it presents itself. The planning department can start with the problems that the organization is currently facing, but instead of taking a problem-solving stance, it should start by exploring the longer-term survival implications. This type of analysis starts with unexplained and puzzling changes in the environment. It seems that business-as-usual expectations are not met as easily as before. For example, demand may be falling, there may be a perceived performance gap that did not exist before, or competitors may suddenly act in an unexpected way. Initially, the problem often manifests itself in declining profitability.

Well-organized companies manage to anticipate these problems by early recognition of signals in the environment. The problem is that there are many environmental signals that could all warn of something significant. Which of these should be analysed?

The Limitations of Analysis

Being able to recognize important and relevant signals, and then being able to assess the implications, is difficult. Sound analysis requires, in the first place, a well-defined research question. The more precise and detailed the question, the more focused and purposeful will be the analysis. Unfortunately, in a situation of puzzlement, there is no precise question! It is not clear what to analyse, where to look and how deep to probe. Analysts use their current understanding of how things hang together to break down the 'puzzlement statement' into a number of questions that can be researched. The weakness of this deconstruction approach is that it implicitly makes use of existing business-as-usual mental models. The problem is tackled with models that refer to the situation of the past, not that of the future. This is exactly where we did not want to be. Business-as-usual may not map with the new situation as it presents itself.

There is no sure way to switch our mental models from the past towards the future. That is exactly why we want to carry out the analysis. We are in a vicious circle, we need the analysis to understand the future, and we need to understand the future in order to define the question we want to analyse. We are imprisoned in a thinking box. We have to find another way to ask ourselves the questions that really matter.

There is no suggestion here that analysis is not extremely important, but it cannot do the job entirely on its own. We need to independently define the important questions to analyse. For this reason, analysis needs to be complemented by intuition. We are looking for an iterative process in which exploiting intuition and asking the right questions alternates with rational thinking to find answers.

Purposeful Analysis and How Scenarios Steer Attention

History is organized – but the present is always a blur

The historian David Hockey observed that while all history seemed to be nicely ordered, the present is always a blur. As events slip into the past, we become able to construct a cause-and-effect structure that provides a logical place for everything we remember. History provides us with the story (or stories if there are multiple interpretations) that explains the dynamics of the world as we remember it.

Scenario planners turn this process into the future. The idea is to give the present a *historical order*, by looking at it from a future vantage point – as if it had already become history. The scenario planner observes from a point in the future, from where the present is considered and explained – as a historian would explain historical facts. A key difference between scenario planning and history is that scenario planners cannot limit themselves to only one story. Because of inherent uncertainty, multiple future vantage points are required. From each position, a different story is told that makes sense of the current 'blur'. Uncertainty ensures that we will always end up with multiple scenarios: each one will be a logical story that interprets and explains what is happening and why.

Storytelling is an intuitive activity. But once the stories have been told, some events have become meaningful, while others prove more difficult to fit in. This raises several important questions. These are the questions historians struggle with; for example, 'Is it reasonable to assume that A has led to B?' or 'How strong is the assumed causal relationship between C and D?' The research questions will have become clear and obvious: purposeful analysis can now follow.

Combining Intuition with Rational Analysis: the Iterative Scenario Approach

In Chapter 7, we discussed the present-day approach to scenario development in some detail. Here, we will consider how the scenario method allows the iterative process of intuitive exploration, alternating with rational analysis, to take place.

Identifying driving forces

All scenario projects start with a group of people brought together to work on the scenarios in a conversational mode. Recall how the selection of the group is aimed at creating a mix of expert knowledge (reflecting the business-as-usual approach) and outside-in thinking. The first task is to identify the forces driving the situation. This is an intuitive process using brainstorming techniques. The definition of driving force is left vague; the field is wide open and participants trigger ideas in each other. In this case, the more open the exercise, the better.

Clustering and modelling driving forces

The next step is to create order in the disparate list of driving forces produced in the first step. Again, this makes use of people's intuitive knowledge, clustering the driving forces that intuitively belong together. Following this, the participants are invited to explain how the clustered driving forces causally depend on each other and portray this, for example, in arrow diagrams, as explained in Chapter 7.

Creating the four end points (the vantage points from where the present is understood)

The team now develops four future vantage points from where the present can be observed. These are called end states at a future point in time. The reason we have four is practical: fewer would not do justice to the many dimensions of uncertainty, while more would make the exercise unwieldy and impractical. The challenge is to select the four vantage points that represent as much of the uncertainty range as possible – they should be as different from each other as possible. The matrix approach, as explained in Chapter 7, has been designed to serve this purpose.

Creating scenarios

Having decided the end states, the team then constructs the four histories of how the currently perceived state of affairs developed into the end states, using historic storytelling techniques, based on causality.

Identifying blind spots and articulating research questions

At this stage, the team is in a better position to define the blind spots in their understanding of the current situation. The modelling and the storytelling phases will have exposed areas lacking in understanding and knowledge. The team may feel uncertain about how to complete the storyline in a few places. Does the way it has linked up elements make sense? Are there other ways of looking at this situation? What actually happened? The search for causality is used to identify gaps in understanding. In a number of areas, the team will have found that it cannot substantiate its intuitive feelings with clear-cut causality statements. Each of these will be the basis of a research question of the form: 'Does A cause B to happen and, if so, what is the relationship?'

Carrying out the research

Having defined the important questions, the system analysis can now take place. Effort is focused, and the results will be directly relevant. Findings will allow a more comprehensive account of the scenario histories, or they will raise the possibility that important driving forces may have been overlooked, necessitating a further iteration.

Facing the Important Questions

Iterating scenario and system analysis raises the important questions. Pierre Wack's first scenario work in Shell was a good example of this process. We saw in Chapter 5 how first-generation scenarios focused attention on the forces controlling the reserves and production decisions in the world of oil. By identifying the stakeholders and noting their relationships, the scenario group considered not only the macro phenomena but also the people behind the decisions. This raised the important research question of what policies the oil-producing governments would follow in supplying the increasing quantities of oil required. Having raised the question, the causal model that was developed (the backward-sloping supply curve) showed how, under certain circumstances, increasing the price of oil would encourage producers to reduce volume rather than increase supply.

> **A combination of scenarios and analysis facilitates the early recognition of, and reaction to, new developments.**

When the crisis scenario became reality, Shell could override the domination of the credible but misguided business-as-usual mindset much sooner than its competitors. Shell had raised the right questions in advance: it recognized the scenario that was playing out and it understood what was happening. Analysis alone would not have given it this advantage; it would have addressed the wrong questions. The scenario approach allowed Shell to use its intuition, together with sound analysis, to expand its mental model of the situation enough to capture the important new variables.

Both elements are vitally important. Analysis without scenarios gives business-as-usual insight. Scenarios without analysis give interesting but superficial stories. Together they have the power to make you see the early indicators of important new developments.

PROJECT 2: DEVELOPING STRATEGY

Defining Strategy

A successful organization is one that continues to survive, based on its environment taking the view that it is making a useful contribution to society. A relevant metaphor is an ecosystem in which many species are involved in a battle for scarce resources. The ones that survive have the best fit with the needs of the environment. However, this is not a constant: it depends on the new species that appear on the scene.

Similarly, society is not a constant environment, it changes. Therefore, the successful organization must also change, adapting to new factors. Good management makes interventions in the organization to make this happen. First, management needs to recognize and understand what is happening in the environment and see changes coming as early as possible. Second, it needs to understand how interventions can be made to ensure that the whole organization evolves in a direction where it remains a successful species within the new ecosystem.

Strategy is related to survival and success. It is an articulated policy framework, used to steer actions towards coherent overall behaviour. Although an individual can have a strategy, here we shall discuss strategy in its organizational sense – that is, as a policy device adopted by multiple layers in an organization, to align the organization's actions in order to create coherent purposeful overall group behaviour.

The Stakeholder Game

In Chapter 1, we defined the management task, in general terms, as balancing the interests of a multitude of stakeholders in and around the business of the organization. Some stakeholders are easily identifiable – customers, employees, competitors, shareholders. Others may be less visible, such as local government, action groups and single-issue organizations, or communities. As we saw, each of these groups has the potential to bring the organization to a halt. It is the most important task of management to ensure that all these stakeholders find it in their interests to stay with, not undermine, the organization. With so many players, this is not an easy task, particularly when the organization is not generating a large surplus and limited resources have to be carefully distributed. In such circumstances, it is worth remembering that stakeholders engage with organizations not only for immediate benefits but also for the promise of future benefits. Stakeholder loyalty can be built not only through physical or financial rewards but also through trust in the future. Mutual trust is extremely important in developing and maintaining relationships between management and stakeholders. Effective communication is thus of the utmost importance.

Creating this complex configuration of connections and trust relationships cannot be based on short-term problem-solving alone. In the final analysis, the whole situation will stand or fall on the level of confidence stakeholders have that a sufficient surplus will be generated in the future. The management task involves generating this surplus for stakeholders, now and in the future. Communicating to all stakeholders the organization's ability to achieve this is a crucial part of this situation.

> **It is the foremost task of top management to ensure that stakeholders find it in their interests to remain with the organization. Developing and maintaining trust, through effective communication, provides a strong foundation for prosperous, long-term relationships between management and stakeholders.**

This task not only entails the building of bridges: it is also necessary to build barriers. Organizational success depends on the existence of friction forces and transaction costs in society. The creation of surplus is due to the organization selectively overcoming some of these forces. It is not in the organization's interest that all friction should disappear. Maintaining bridges and barriers makes the task both complex and subtle.

Strategic Aims

Linking the success of an organization to its ability to foster stakeholder interests can be summarized in the following five points:

1. The the ultimate aim is survival and success for the organization.
2. Survival and success, in the final analysis, derives from the support of the many stakeholders in and around the organization.
3. Stakeholders must perceive it to be advantageous for them to support the organization. Supporting it must be more attractive than disengaging, so stakeholders must derive something worthwhile from the organization.
4. Therefore, the organization must be capable of generating an economic surplus over its immediate operational needs, for the benefit of the stakeholders.
5. If it cannot produce a sufficient surplus today, it needs to offer sufficient promise for the future to convince the stakeholders that it is worth staying.

Good strategy is a policy that, if adhered to by all players, promises enough economic surplus to reward all stakeholders, motivating them to continue supporting the organization.

One final point to remember is that strategy is not the only way to convince stakeholders of the advantages of a continued relationship with the organization. The charisma or reputation of business leaders, for example, can be a powerful stakeholder attractor. It is not always true that the most powerful tool to create trust is strategy. Many great leaders have pointed to the potential danger of strategy: that it can create an organization with a restrictive and set approach, that is less flexible and less able to react to opportunities in its environment.

We will return to the importance of strategic opportunism when we discuss the use of scenarios for organizational learning, later in this chapter. Here, we will address the needs of the organization that has decided it wants to enhance its chances of generating an economic surplus in the future by articulating a strategy.

Gaining the high ground in the scarcity landscape

Strategy is about the future. Specifically, it is concerned with the future ability of the organization to generate an economic surplus. First, we should consider how an organization can generate an economic surplus.

In Chapter 1 we saw how, in a market economy, the possibility of earning a surplus arises in situations of scarcity. If the supply of a good or service is abundant, it does not sustain a surplus for the supplier. Only when there is scarcity and when new competition is held back by barriers will the price be able to rise above its costs, creating a margin or surplus for suppliers who can supply the scarce resource. Profitability requires barriers to entry. Where there are such barriers, the price of a good or service no longer relates directly to its cost of production; rather, it relates to customer value – the alternative costs that buyers would incur if the product were not available. As there may be a considerable margin between customer value and production costs, the situation allows for a profit to be made by the supplier. An example of such a barrier to entry is a patent. In the pharmaceutical industry, the high demand for a product, where no alternative exists, makes production a lucrative proposition.

Understanding barriers to entry is a crucial part of strategy development. However, it is only potentially interesting in the context of goods and service that are in short supply and where the organization can provide something that is in demand, thereby creating a surplus for stakeholders.

The next step is to recognize that this situation is far from constant. Needs evolve over time, and what is in short supply today may be available in abundance tomorrow. However, there will always be scarce resources. The world around us is finite and our appetite for goods and service seems boundless. The economy will always hit limitations and bottlenecks somewhere, and it is at those points in the system that companies will enjoy profit. Strategy is about the future of this ever-moving scarcity landscape, and it involves making assumptions about where the new bottlenecks will appear. It requires that we map out future constraints, and scenario planning is an invaluable tool to achieve such an end.

Mapping the scarcity landscape is not an easy task. The economy is made up of a considerable number of economic actors, all in the business of buying and selling. The complexity of the system is enormous, not only because of the numbers of actors involved, but also because of external changes continually being introduced into the system. For example, one powerful driver of change is technological development. Other change drivers involve culture, demography, politics, economics and so on. All this forms part of the future scarcity landscape that the strategist must consider and anticipate. The field is very large; the strategist needs a device to delineate a more manageable segment. This is the purpose of the organization's *business idea*.

The Business Idea

In Chapter 1, we introduced the notion of the business idea. This is an important tool for the scenario planner, and we will analyse its characteristics in more detail here.

The notion of fit
The scarcity landscape, external to the organization, needs to be studied against the characteristics of the organization itself, in order to develop strategy. A

successful strategy indicates first of all how an organization can provide a scarce resource. This implies that the organization can achieve something that its competitors cannot. It needs to be different and distinctive. If the organization does not have such a distinctive resource or competence, then there are no barriers to entry; others will quickly emulate what it is doing and the resource will not remain scarce for long. This leads us to the second essential element (understanding the scarcity landscape is the first) of sound strategy: an understanding of how the organization can offer its market a unique capability.

A distinctive competence is an essential component of a sound strategy. The full potential of such distinction can only be exploited if it fits well into the scarcity landscape in society. When scarcity and distinctiveness are well-matched, customers, after considering alternatives, are prepared for and pay the higher prices that will leave a surplus with which the organization can buy stakeholder support and future development. The important point to note is that there needs to be enough surplus left after the stakeholders are satisfied to invest in the mainten-

> Offering customers a unique opportunity introduces an effective barrier to entry. Distinctiveness that frustrates competition, is an essential element of good strategy.

ance and development of future distinctiveness. The latter part of the loop is fundamental for longer-term survival, since the organization needs to adjust its distinctive competencies to maintain a good fit with the market during periods of change. Only by paying attention to future distinctiveness will the organization continue to provide scarce resources, creating the surplus needed for survival.

As we saw earlier, the success formula can be described as a self-sustaining loop, with distinctiveness leading to exploitation of scarcity, which leads to the generation of a surplus, which can be invested in maintaining distinctiveness to keep the loop going. This perspective points towards an element of fragility for organizational success: once the loop has been broken, it is almost impossible to resurrect it. Once distinctiveness has gone, exploiting scarcity is no longer possible, which precludes the ability to generate a commensurate surplus. Inevitably, it will be impossible to resurrect the distinctive competencies. With the surplus falling away, the stakeholders will leave, and organizational death is only a matter of time.

If the distinctiveness can be developed in line with the societal scarcity landscape, the organization will survive. However, if the fit is lost, the organization will die. This is the stark message of strategy development. And this is where the scenarios will have to make their contribution in the strategy process.

The scenarios do not have to cover the whole scarcity landscape; only the part that connects with (or could connect with) the organization. The scenario project has a specific agenda, which sets the scope of the exercise by reference to what the organization is uniquely good at. Therefore, before we can think about scenario work, we need to consider distinctiveness and how we can analyse it. It is important for the scenario planner to be familiar with techniques for mapping the distinctiveness of an organization, as this indicates the general area of human endeavour in which the scenarios have to be positioned. We will now develop this concept further, outlining the powerful tool at the scenario planner's disposal to map out a scenario agenda for the organization; the business idea.

Friction Forces and Barriers to Entry

Understanding how distinctiveness arises

How does distinctiveness arise? Common sense suggests that if one organization can do something, then others should be able to follow suit. In most market economics, rules have been established to keep competition and entry of newcomers open and free. Collusion among market participants with the aim of keeping others out can be heavily penalized. On the other hand, there are many examples of firms who exploit a unique feature that others find difficult to copy. For example, Microsoft has been successful at keeping potential competitors at bay and, despite many attempts to copy it, IKEA has retained its distinctiveness. The example of Xerox in Chapter 1 highlighted its unique capabilities, and other businesses such as pharmaceutical companies have powerful barriers to entry around them. Also, small shops seem to be able to survive against competition from the large supermarkets. They must have something going for them.

> Managers know intuitively what their distinctiveness is, but they fail to discuss it explicitly among themselves.

An organization that survives must have an element of distinctiveness in its relations with its customers. As we have just seen, without distinctiveness, a firm cannot survive. Interestingly, managers are often unaware of the true nature of their distinctiveness. Organizations that survive year after year tend to take their distinctiveness for granted, while they concern themselves with day-to-day business. In case study after case study, we have observed that it takes time and effort for the management team to articulate the sources of the distinctiveness of their organization. Notably, we never fail to develop the answer, once they have decided to put energy into its articulation. Managers know intuitively what their distinctiveness is, but they fail to discuss it explicitly among themselves, as part of the strategic conversation. Given the fragility of the survival loop, managers should be aware of the implications of this oversight.

It is important to understanding why competitors are blocked from copying the success of another firm, and how distinctiveness is maintained and protected. There are two broad categories of friction forces underlying barriers to entry and the maintenance of distinctiveness; first, resources or positions owned by the organization; and second, organizational capability. Both of these will now be explored in detail.

Resources or positions owned by the organization

An example of this form of distinctiveness is an organization owning a patent affording it legal protection from emulation. Such companies are granted a monopoly position for a limited period, in order to provide them with an incentive to invest in research and development. Other forms of legal protection exist, such as a concession granting sole exploitation rights. Mining and oil companies are often given such protection. If the organization is lucky, and finds an attractive resource quickly, it will generate a surplus over the costs of production in the market.

For other organizations, developing a strong position in the market can be almost as effective as legal protection. Examples include companies which enjoy a high reputation among their customers or which have a highly developed and well-recognized brand name. Experiments in markets for consumer goods have shown how branded products command a price premium. An obvious example was the New Coke experiment, discussed in Chapter 2. A successful brand is built up over a long period at significant cost, but a brand that is well established, such as Coca-Cola or Nike, is almost impossible to beat; so few organizations will try.

Similarly, the ownership of sizable assets by incumbents in an asset-intensive activity will deter potential competitors. In this connection, how specific or versatile the use of the asset is will determine the strength or weakness of the barrier to entry. The ownership of a general-purpose good, such as an office building, provides less protection than ownership of specific assets. Machinery can often only be used for one purpose. Also, alternative use of brand names is often limited. If investments in assets or brand names are specific to the activity or the product produced, and have no other value, they become a sunk cost and their opportunity cost, if underutilized, will be very low. In such a situation, they will constitute a reason for a powerful defence by the incumbent against invaders. Newcomers will face formidable opponents discouraging their entry into the market.

Organizational capability

It is only recently that organizational knowledge management has become a subject of study in its own right. However, only a small part of organizational knowledge can be mapped. Most of it is intuitive and tacit, embedded in behavioural patterns and non-articulated recipes. If this embedding concerns only one person, the intrinsic value of this knowledge will eventually make rewards gravitate to the individual, not to the organization she belongs to. An example of this is the star football player. Similar effects can be seen in consultancy and software firms, where the basic scarcity is the talent to do the work and surplus generated through personal knowledge ends up largely with individuals, not with the firm. However, more often considerable knowledge remains embedded in the organization and in its knowledge architecture as a whole. Many knowledge workers perform only in the context of their organizational situation and cannot repeat this when they are on their own. In that case, the organization owns the knowledge, the knowledge makes the organization distinctive and it can be used for surplus generation.

Often, such embedded knowledge is not well codified, and for that reason alone, cannot be emulated by a competitor. A major tacit element involves staff motivation – which is notoriously difficult to copy. The reader will recognize this from everyday life: some service providers simply perform better than their competitors, with outsiders unable to explain why.

Developing Distinctiveness

How is distinctiveness developed? Before we analyse sources, it seems useful to remove one source from the list of possibilities. It does not make sense to assume that buying a distinctive competence or resource can create significant surplus generation potential. Once distinctiveness exists, its economic value will represent today's value of all future cash flow it can generate, and one must assume that this value will be expressed in its price. The buyer will not see any surplus deriving from the purchase, as this money was paid out when the distinctive feature was bought. Companies like Microsoft, IKEA and Coca-Cola have created their distinctiveness themselves, either by chance or by design, and the value of this is expressed in their share price.

This does not mean that purchasing resources or capabilities does not make sense. However, they can only become the source of surplus-generating distinctiveness if they *can be combined with distinctiveness that is already present* in the buying organization itself. For example, an organization owning an international patent may decide to acquire a subsidiary with an export capability in order to exploit the value of the patent in foreign markets. The export capability, as such, is not a distinctive feature and can be acquired at a price related to its cost. It becomes a source of surplus revenue only in *combination* with the patent that the organization already owns. This is called *leveraging* and it is the most common and safest approach to organizational survival and development.

Apart from leveraging, distinctiveness can also come from insight or even luck. Newcomers and invaders are often able to move first in a market on the basis of their superior insight into the new needs of the customer or simply by luck (although it is useful to remember Louis Pasteur's view in Chapter 5 that 'luck favours the prepared mind'). Insight or luck can provide what is known as a 'first-mover' advantage. There is a window of opportunity, during which the new entrepreneur enjoys a unique situation in which to generate a surplus. Depending on the friction forces discussed above, this time window may be longer or shorter, but is always of a limited duration. The newcomer needs to use this time to create more permanent distinctiveness, by building new barriers to entry. Without this, competitors will soon learn the secret of the newcomer's success, copy it and erode its advantage.

The Role of the Business Idea in Strategy

Distinctiveness allows an organization to provide the market with a scarce resource, which generates a surplus that can be invested in maintaining and developing distinctiveness for the future. This is the crux of organizational success. Distinctiveness drives success. Future distinctiveness derives from current distinctiveness, through a process of leveraging. The process of strategy development starts with mapping this system, using the device of the business idea that we introduced in Chapter 1. This is a simple diagram showing how the organization uses and maintains its distinctiveness.

Consider the following example that we recently analysed, when the HR manager of an organization involved in engineering contracting approached us.

He had introduced a programme of 'personal and team development' in the organization, which had been positively received by the staff. Unfortunately, the organization had recently encountered new and severe competition, which brought pressures to cut costs. As it was not an immediate operational necessity, the 'personal and team development' programme was a clear target for cost-cutting. The HR manager thought that cutting this programme

> **Distinctiveness allows an organization to provide the market with a scarce resource, which generates a surplus that can be invested in maintaining and developing distinctiveness for the future. This is the crux of organizational success.**

would be a mistake, but had not been able to convince his colleagues in the management team of the strategic value of the programme.

We discovered that the 'personal and team development' programme (which was known as PTD) had not been conceived as part of a comprehensive strategy, but had originated in an isolated initiative from the CEO who believed that it could be useful and important. Under the circumstances, it was not surprising it was now under threat. The urgent requirement now was to show how it could be seen as an integral part of the organization's strategic 'success formula'. We approached the task by using a business idea diagram, with the aim of demonstrating the programme's necessity.

Working closely with the HR manager, we set out to develop the organization's business idea. The organization had not spent a lot of time thinking strategically, and there were no strategy documents available that we could study. However, since this was a case of convincing the management team of the strategic value of personal and team development, it was important to express the business idea in language that would be recognized by the managers as their own. Eventually we discovered that there was a mission statement, and the management team had spent a day together on the longer-term plan, which had been reasonably documented. There was also the company website for further information.

It is typical, but nevertheless surprising, how many strategy documents, such as mission statements, show people often confusing strategy with self-evident truths. For example, a statement that 'we want to be our customers' preferred supplier' does not offer any strategic information. If you are not the preferred supplier, you are out of business. Filtering out such obvious statements from the organization literature and from our interviews with managers, the following list of potentially relevant ideas emerged (in their own words):

- Distinctively different.
- Easy to deal with.

- Employing the top quality in the market.
- Enabled teams.
- Work as one team.
- Embrace uncertainty.

Using their ideas, we could now construct the loop:

1. 'Distinctiveness' leads to the 'supply of scarce resources',
2. . . . which leads to the 'surplus for investment',
3. . . . which leads to future 'distinctiveness'.

The following points should be noted:

- A business idea diagram (see Figure 8.2) is an arrow diagram indicating causality. Nodes are variables.
- It annotates distinctiveness by boxing in relevant nodes.
- It indicates how distinctiveness leads to the generation of a surplus.
- It shows a self-sustaining loop indicating investments in future survival.
- It is simple and can be comprehended as a whole.

In this case, using familiar language, it had been possible to show how personal and team development (PTD) can be projected as central to the future success

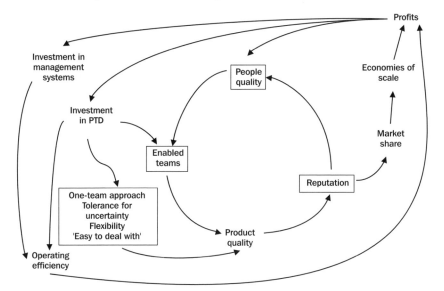

Figure 8.2 Example of a business idea.

loop of the organization. Without it, there didn't seem to be much business idea or sources of distinctiveness left. The diagram vindicated the intuition of the HR manager, providing ammunition for him to get the programme accepted as a high-priority activity in the organization. Today the programme continues as the main strategic thrust of the organization, and their competitive position is starting to show the results. Customers are seeing the difference in approach. Market share is starting to increase, without this having been gained through price slashing.

Business Ideas and Scenarios

Having developed the business idea, we can now ask ourselves whether this is a robust formula to take into the future. Will it stand up as a basis for the organization to maintain distinctiveness, enabling it to continue to generate a surplus? Will it do this in the various future scenarios that we think could develop? It is worth emphasising that whether the activity will remain relevant and whether the indicated distinctiveness will remain a societal scarcity can only be addressed against the multiple business environment futures we can see developing. This is what scenario planning is about.

The strategic thinking process is sometimes compared to the testing of a model aircraft in a wind tunnel. We test the Business Idea for the future (the model aircraft), in various scenarios (conditions in the wind tunnel). If in one scenario the model fails, we need to go back to the drawing board to make it more robust. Strategy development implies the testing of the business idea in a number of relevant scenarios. The technique of scenario development was discussed in Chapters 6 and 7. What needs to be considered here is how we can ensure that the scenario test conditions are relevant to the task. Knowing the object to be tested (the business idea) is important in designing the test conditions. A jet fighter requires different conditions in the wind tunnel than a microlight aircraft. Similarly, we have to use the business idea to develop the scenario agenda.

Identifying stakeholders

The individuals and organizations around our organization that may either have power over what happens, or who are significantly affected by the actions of our organization, need to be identified first. In Chapter 7, we introduced *stakeholder analysis*. Taking account of the powerful players around the organization in our scenarios is obvious, but the powerless are easily overlooked. If they are significantly affected by the actions of the organization, they may well become powerful in the future and are, therefore, worth considering. For example, powerless individuals who feel strongly about an issue may organize themselves and become a new, powerful organization. A current example is the uncertainty around the future development of the anti-globalization movement, giving rise to coalitions that would be considered highly unlikely only a few years ago.

It is obvious that customers need to be considered as major stakeholders in the scenarios. In general, the focus is on scarcity in society. Customers exist as soon as the organization provides a product or a service that is scarce in society and not available from others in the same offering configuration. Scenarios need to explore the future of the specific scarcity addressed, and the scope for others to enter the same field and copy, or even improve on, the distinctiveness the organization exploits.

Consider the Kindercare Organization in the USA, which provides high quality childcare to professional parents. By observing the situation in his own family, Perry Mendel realized how significant value was pent up in society because of the lack of high-quality childcare, which kept mothers at home looking after their young children themselves. He thought that if he could change the perception of childcare from 'parking young children for the day' into 'providing high-calibre education to very young children,' professional mothers would be more willing to leave their children for the day, go to work and generate considerable value to pay for the service. On the basis of this, he developed a unique way of overcoming this bottleneck and went ahead to build a hugely successful childcare business.

Or consider the example of the engineering contractor company we discussed earlier in this chapter. Having identified its business idea, it now needs to consider its robustness for the future. Its scenarios need to address such questions as:

- What is the future of the scarcity it is relieving? What is the scarcity that is being exploited, and how could it change?
- How will customers' value system develop?
- Will it continue to value product quality, including flexibility by the contractor? Why?
- If this remains the secret of success, what is the chance that competitors might catch on and take away its lead?
- Who are the existing and potential competitors, and how are they evolving?

- Will business continue to be conducted as it is today? Probably not, but how will it change?
- Is it possible for new invaders to come in with an alternative product or substitute that will be even more attractive to the customer than the current product?
- Could technology create a breakthrough?
- Could the scarcity of top-calibre people change?

On this last point, the high-quality staff in our business idea would probably have been overlooked in the scenario project if the business idea had not been articulated first. It raises interesting questions around the future of education, labour markets, workers' preferences and general societal value evolution around work and leisure that would otherwise have escaped the attention of the management team.

In this way, the scenario agenda takes shape, by considering the relationship between the organization and the stakeholders, with the business idea in the background. The analysis is important to ensure that the people in the organization regard the scenarios developed as highly relevant.

Consider its scope for growth

Following a review of the possible vulnerability of the business idea, we need to consider its scope for growth. If there is a good chance that our business idea will stand, what do we do in order to expand its exploitation? Should we expand? Imagine we would want to aggressively expand the business; where would we look? In our example, we may conclude that the business has to consider entering other areas of activity. Can we identify any that are also subject to a dearth of quality and reliability where we might be able to use the same business idea formula? Or could we consider other geographical areas?

At the end of this analysis phase, the strategist has developed a good idea of the subjects that need to be addressed in the scenarios. At this point, the scenario generation, as described in Chapter 7, can take off.

The Strategic Journey

Having discussed the important elements of strategy, the next task is to assess *how* a strategy process happens in an organization to make all the strategic factors combine to form a coherent result. Again, everything depends on the purpose of the exercise. For example, strategy may be developed for internal or external purposes. Internally, a strategy may be required in an attempt to test the strength of the organization and to consider how it can be made more robust. The larger the organization, the more such an exercise is required in order to align the actions of all organization members, especially in times when strong coherent action is required to protect the collective interest. This means that in difficult times strategy is required more, not less. In fact, one often sees the opposite happen: in times of crisis, everyone is busy fire-fighting and there is no time for discussing strategy. This may be the practicality of the situation; however, as we saw in Chapter 2, panic is not the best way towards vigilant decisions and successful organizations.

The relevance of business plans

Alternatively, strategy may be developed for external purposes. As we saw, the prime leadership task in any organization is the management of the network of stakeholder relations both inside and outside the organization. The task involves gaining sufficient stakeholder confidence to persuade them to continue to support the organization. This is largely a job of expectation management. Current results play a role, but the ultimate factor is the confidence the stakeholders place in the future, and therefore in the quality of the management. An important question revolves around the degree to which management is in control of its future. A powerful instrument in the conversation between management and stakeholders is the business plan. Drawing up a business plan requires the development of strategy on which the plan can be based. The need for a business plan is an important reason to invest time in good strategy.

A business plan is a one-line prediction of the future and, for this reason alone, is flawed. This begs the question, why make business plans? The business plan is, primarily, a conversational tool. It allows management to engage in a purposeful conversation with stakeholders, in order to demonstrate its understanding and control of the situation at hand and to focus on key questions. Business plans are often the basis of discussions on financing, mergers and acquisitions, collaboration deals, hiring key personnel, negotiations with trades unions and so on. Business plans developed for these purposes can be (in fact, should be) discarded after the intended conversation has taken place.

Some business plans are developed as a means to coordinate the actions of multiple actors in an organizational context. An example is the allocation of budgets on the basis of the plan. Budgets are used for the allocation of resources and, later on, as the basis of post-mortem evaluation, to establish deviations with what has actually happened, for reporting purposes (exception reporting) and to hold people accountable for results.

Stages in strategy development

Many companies develop strategy only when required and on an *ad hoc* basis. If this is the case, the exercise can be carefully designed to suit the specific purpose. Larger organizations find it more effective to develop strategy on an ongoing or periodic basis, for example, embedded in a regular planning cycle. Even if organizing the planning cycle is a task delegated to planners or strategists, management may still take a keen interest in the development process, to ensure that the results fit with its requirements and understanding of the situation.

A typical planning cycle would be annual and involve the following steps:

1. Initial phase, making space for new ideas and outside-in thinking:

    •   interviews with top managers and relevant experts
    •   development of the business idea
    •   development of the scenario agenda
    •   scenario development
    •   articulation of strategic options (throughout the opening-up phase)

2. Convergent phase, making choices:

    •   clustering options into strategies
    •   testing of strategies
    •   articulation of the updated and upframed business idea
    •   development of the strategic plan; search for accommodation
    •   operational planning and budget allocation
    •   cascading down of the process through the organization

3. Retrospectively, inside-out thinking:

    •   review of performance against budget and signing off on accountability
    •   review of assumptions, in preparation for next cycle

With a more *ad hoc* approach, the process can be customized. The more formal process steps, described above, would be the design starting point.

PROJECT 3: IMPROVING ORGANIZATIONAL ANTICIPATION

We now move to the next project. The difference between this and the first two is that we now move from one-off scenario projects to installing an ongoing scenario capability and activity. The reason for considering such a change in emphasis is a shift of focus in the management team from 'specific problem-solving' (understanding a particular phenomenon, developing a particular strategy) to ongoing 'process' (improving perception and decision-making, translating decisions into action). We move on from the 'design thinking' that has underpinned Projects 1 and 2 towards a process-oriented view of management that drives Projects 3 and 4. In Project 3, we focus attention on improving the process of organizational anticipation.

We suggest that this task is important but concerns far more than acting, but from honing the organizational ability to see, perceive and understand what is happening around it. This requires the mobilization of as many resources as possible to observe, perceive, experience, make sense, rationalise, decide and act. Mobilizing these resources for corporate use means effective networking of people and creating a high-quality ongoing strategic conversation in the organization. The objective is the sharing of individual perceptions and sensemaking, such that decision-makers at all levels increase their awareness and develop a wider view.

The strategic conversation is the focus of attention in this project. We will discuss how scenarios can help in that process. But let us first consider what is involved in achieving such a shift in thinking.

Multiple World Views – The Limits of the Rationalistic Approach

We have just seen in Project 2 how a few people, thinking on behalf of the organization, can use a scenario-based analysis to develop insight into a situation at a particular point in time that allows them to consider the next step forward. The project was a one-off; there was a clear end point when the strategic conclusions had been reached and were on the table for decision and action. The use of the scenario process so far (in Projects 1 and 2) has strong rationalistic design overtones, as discussed in Chapter 6. The assumption is that the world works according to 'laws of nature' that can be discovered and acted upon. In principle, there is an objective answer to the question: 'What is our best strategy?' The answer is determined by logic and, provided enough resources and intelligence are applied, anyone can get close to it. Once the answer has been found, it will then be obvious to everyone concerned. Logic will dictate what people will do. Thinking and acting can be separated from each other. The thinkers come up with the best answer, while the 'doers' carry it out, simply because it makes sense. The logic of the one right answer will prevail, whoever has come up with it.

Whether the world works in this fashion is controversial; we'll never know. Even if it was possible to prove that there is one right answer, it may not be all that useful an idea. Even if it exists, complexity and indeterminacy put the one right answer beyond human reach. Moreover, other aspects to organizational life place significant limits on the effectiveness of the rationalist approach (see Chapters 3 and 4).

The notion of the socially constructed reality

As discussed in Chapter 6, different people in the same organization have different world views, causing them to evaluate situations very differently. Their 'right answers' will be different, depending on their starting point. Earlier, we suggested that the prime managerial task was the balancing of stakeholder interests. These interests are made up of expectations, which are based on past performance and confidence in future performance. This is obviously a dynamic situation. At any point in time, while some relationships are moving to the fore others may be slipping into the background. Conversations with stakeholders need to take into account that the parties involved will have very different interpretations of the situation.

We tend to take for granted our own ways of thinking and use of language. It is difficult to imagine how another person would want to pay attention to anything else, or how they define problems and opportunities differently, or have other ideas about what can and should be done. We often assert that our view is just a matter of common sense. Yet it is not so difficult to discover how one person's common sense often is another person's 'non-sense'.

This turmoil increases when we engage in arguments and actions about what should be preserved, what should be changed and who is entitled to do what. Paradoxically, as we saw in Chapter 4, while the world is becoming more inter-connected, human groups are increasingly intent on accentuating their indi-vidual distinctiveness – going their own way. We have learned how to behave in a world that is characterized by independence and diversity, while we largely remain unaware of our accumulating interdependencies. Everywhere, the boun-daries delineating our ideas, territory, means, relationships and status are increas-ingly challenged, defended and changing.

Considered in this way, we can only conclude that the discovery of 'truth' in the social sphere is not possible; instead, each person constructs her own social reality (see Chapter 4). Individuals create and choose among stories that give motive and meaning to social action. We do not necessarily do this consciously – quite the opposite. Some stories use the language and ideas of science; others are built around spiritual beliefs, while others use an economics-based language. Many of these stories claim that they tell the truth about social reality. But if we overview the whole landscape, one can only come to the conclusion that there is no agreed-upon firm ground – there is no 'court of last resort' in our social discourse.

Linking different world views – planning and action

In this situation we find internal conflict, partly the use of power in organising in

a conversation in which all interpretations are held to be worth considering. Within organizations, some people have a degree of legal decision-making power, while others have the power of authority based on knowledge. But no one has the formal power to force people to change their minds. Making decisions is one thing, making things happen is a different matter altogether. The latter requires the collaboration of many – they will need to be brought in line.

The alternative way forward is the conversation. We construct our realities for ourselves and for each other chiefly through language. As they spend time together in an organization, people will compare notes on what they have observed and thought, and their views will gradually align. The process needs to bring the participants from their isolated positions of different interpretations to a point where they are prepared to collaborate on a proposed course of action.

A management team that takes its strategic responsibility seriously cannot delegate this 'life or death' strategy process. The first assumption that has to change is that thinking and action can be organizationally separated. People responsible for execution have insights that are not available to strategists, but their input can be crucial for success or failure. Strategists have analytical insights that people in execution miss and need to be made aware of. There is really only one reasonable position for management to take: to involve both thinkers and doers in the whole process.

The strategic conversation is not a management tool. It is an emerging phenomenon that happens naturally, unavoidably, in any organization. Formal management processes are responsible for only a small part of this strategic conversation. Most of it happens when people have chance conversations. To mobilize the brainpower within an organization, we must mobilize this strategic conversation. The conversation already exists. What management needs to do is to intervene to mobilize it to create a more powerful survival and adaptation process. How can we mobilize these rich resources for long-term survival? How can management intervene in the strategic conversation to make it purposeful, open, wide-ranging and relevant? These are the main questions facing management today.

The scenario method offers a way to shape this conversation. Let us consider an example of a scenario-mediated strategic conversation.

The Mont Fleur Story

Consider the example of the Mont Fleur scenario project[81]. In the early 1990s, developments in South Africa made it possible to imagine that a transition from apartheid could be possible. Nelson Mandela had been released, and talks had started on how to progress. This created a totally new situation for the country, and everyone had to rethink her position and outlook. People who had focused on the fight for freedom suddenly saw the possibility that they might be called upon to participate in government. Parties that had been facing each other in guerrilla warfare suddenly saw a prospect in which they might have to work together. Sworn enemies had to be turned into colleagues – a daunting prospect. Sometimes strategy requires the collaboration of parties from different organizations who are not used to having this 'strategic conversation'. In such a case, it has to be created. This was the situation in South Africa in the early 1990s.

In 1991, Pieter le Roux, an economist at the University of the Western Cape, invited Adam Kahane, a scenario practitioner from Shell, to facilitate a scenario project. Scenarios were well known in South Africa. During the 1980s, a scenario exercise, led by Clem Sunter of the Anglo American Mining Corporation, had played an influential role in building public discussion about the future of the country. These had been analytical, sensemaking scenarios, as discussed above under Project 1. However, this current project would be different. It would address the need for a new strategic conversation between parties who had until then met each other only across the battlefield. This was definitely not a search for the ultimate truth, but an attempt to bring highly divergent views a little closer together. Kahane gave the following account:

> The scenario team included 22 members from across the spectrum of South
> Africa's diverse constituencies. The multiracial group included left-wing
> political activists, officials of the African National Congress (ANC), trade

unionists, mainstream economists and senior corporate executives. Our purpose was to investigate, and hopefully develop, common mental models about the future of the country. When we started, many people in the group were pessimistic; they expected to spend the meetings in endless dispute, unable to agree on anything. In this highly charged political atmosphere I said during the first meeting, 'We're not going to discuss what you would like to happen. We're going to discuss what might happen.' This turned out to be a liberating choice of words. If I had asked what future they wanted, each participant would have pulled out their party platform. In the end, the process did produce a scenario they all preferred, but they would never have got there if we had started by looking for it. Instead, we were looking for a common understanding.

We started with an exercise that made people realize that they couldn't predict what would happen. Dividing them into sub-groups, we asked them to come up with stories of what might happen to South Africa, seen from the vantage point of 30 years in the future. When we recombined in plenary, we had 30 scenarios to consider. During the presentations, no one was allowed to say, 'That's a stupid story,' or, 'You shouldn't be saying that.' I allowed only two types of interruptions: 'Why does that happen?' and 'What happens next?' If the presenter couldn't answer those questions, then they had to sit down; the story was no good.

It turned out that this was a great exercise. People came up with all kinds of wild stories, including stories inimical to their own interests. For example, one left-wing sub-group proposed a story called 'Growth through repression,' suggesting that South Africa might have a tough authoritarian left-wing government. Another story suggested that the Chinese government would provide arms and support for a Communist liberation movement, which would overthrow the government. I don't know whether it was originally proposed seriously, but when people asked, 'Why does that happen?' there was no way to substantiate it. So it fell by the wayside, almost immediately.

The rest of the whole exercise was a narrowing process - pruning our scenarios from 30 down to three or four 'useful' stories. To be useful, they had to be logically consistent and plausible, which are difficult criteria to meet. But the discussion of plausibility and consistency was very good for this politically charged, diverse group. Then we asked, 'Which of these stories is useful to tell to an audience?' In other words, what did participants believe our audience needed to think about? In our plenary group, after much discussion, we narrowed our selection down to four distinct stories, all focused on the nature of the political transition (the most important single uncertainty in the country).

By the standards of Shell . . . these were not very deep scenarios; they had little research or quantification behind them. But their significance came from the fact that they were arrived at collaboratively by a very broad group. All members of the team endorsed all of them – not as desired futures, but as valid mental models for how the future might unfold.

When the team came together, they had no common view on the difficulties of transition. By arguing over the distinctions between the scenarios they came to a common view, on a moderately detailed level, about some of the problems of transition. For example, I'm sure that very few of them, before the meeting, had considered the question of macro-economic constraints on a newly elected government. Now, through the scenarios, they are deeply familiar with it.

You may wonder what keeps people, in these highly charged meetings, from walking out. Conservatives and radicals kept coming back because they felt they were learning a great deal – and enjoying themselves. The advantage of scenarios is that, unlike in a negotiation, people don't have to commit their constituents, but they can see a common language – a common way of understanding the world - emerging fairly early in the process. Once the scenario process is over, that common language should make subsequent negotiations easier to conclude successfully.

The Role of Scenarios in Strategic Conversation

People who were once adversaries participated at Mont Fleur because they could see that under changed circumstances they might together face a new common enemy. Being better able to face an outside enemy by becoming a more perceptive organization is the *raison d'être* of the strategic conversation. This is why organizations need to invest in it and manage it. Powerful scenario-based conversations that make the organization a better observer of weak signals have been created among stakeholders in many areas of human endeavour. Examples we have been involved in include bringing together customers and suppliers, collaboration between government departments and partner groups, and inner-city rehabilitation projects with the involvement of many parties. Other interesting examples from the literature include cooperation between guerrillas and state police (in Colombia and Guatemala).

The Mont Fleur example and other similar projects illustrate how the scenario approach facilitates and streamlines the strategic conversation and adds a number of powerful features to it that make the organization more perceptive and able to see and act on weak signals in the environment. Some of these are discussed next.

Overcoming day-to-day thinking

The main problem in the strategic conversation is preoccupation with day-to-day issues. Everyone is overloaded, there is no time for fancy theories: ensuring that the business runs smoothly is the focus of attention. Short-term orientation can become a culture in the organization, and people have their 'idea killers' ready to hand to target the longer-term thinkers. Which of these have you heard before?

- We have tried that already.
- The boss will never buy that.
- It does not fit with the culture.
- It would be too big a drain on resources.
- It's too risky.
- That's not the way we do things over here.
- The people are not ready for that.
- It's too political.
- You don't understand.
- Things are a lot more complex than that
- I just feel it is wrong.
- We have no time for that sort of thing.
- A good idea, in a few years time.
- If it's not broken, don't fix it.
- You cannot argue with success.
- I am too busy, come back later.
- Let's get on with the business.

An essential enabling condition for the strategic conversation to work is that management sees and understands the crucial importance of mobilizing all resources in the fight for longer-term survival. The enemy is outside, and the shared awareness of this drives the people together to consider, as a team, what can be done. This leads to the strategic conversation which has to be lifted up from the 'here and now' towards building the longer-term strength of the organization. To achieve this, management must step out of a 'problem-solving' mindset from time to time to make space for everyone to consider

> **An organized, scenario-based strategic conversation process will focus attention on longer-term survival and lift the conversation above day-to-day, 'business-as-usual' issues.**

and discuss personal observations, experiences and insights that will together determine longer-term positioning and survival.

Moving from adversarial behaviour to exploratory thinking

The strategic conversation is concerned with the inherently uncertain future. But our norms that define what it is to be competent and powerful require that we convey an image of certainty. Conventionally, we hide our uncertainties in public interactions and we hide the errors that naturally arise from that in a complex and unpredictable world. Consequently, there is often no room in the conversation for different world views, which are attacked or suppressed. The problem here is that bringing stakeholders together can only happen by considering alternative views. This means that a successful strategic conversation can only be based on recognizing and acknowledging multiple perspectives and uncertainty. When uncertainty about the outcome of strategic action is acknowledged, perceived risks and vulnerabilities increase. However, significantly, options and the opportunities for resilience can also increase[82]. As we discussed in Chapter 1, there can be no strategic success without uncertainty.

Adopting the scenario approach signals to participants that it is useful and productive to acknowledge that things are uncertain and that there are various ways of looking at what is happening. It highlights the fact that the group wants to take advantage of its opportunities to learn from uncertainties. Trial and error, inherent in the scenario approach, is a means for alerting participants to opportunities to adjust proactively to each other's views, rather than fighting them.

Overcoming limiting role assumptions

The organization has both an advantage and a handicap compared to the individual manager interested in long-term trends in the outside world. The advantage is that it has not just one but many pairs of eyes, leading them to look at different aspects. Potentially, the range of vision is many times that of one individual. Unfortunately, this capacity is often not used effectively.

The handicap in organizations is that perception by one individual member is not the same as perception by the organization. There are many barriers in the way of people who have an insight. The first, and probably most important, is role assumptions that make people believe that they are not allowed to express their insight. 'I am not in strategy, I implement. It is the job of the strategists to look out for and discover the trends. It is not my role to contribute there.' Or, 'I am only a salesman, what do I know about strategy?' Observations and insights are put away and never reach the surface.

A properly organized scenario process puts all participants at the same level. The process ensures that all views are heard. This needs to be created as an embedded organizational capability.

Mobilizing insights over a wide front

People will talk about the things they see and how these impact the business. As we saw, this takes two forms. First, there is the official organization conversation about the future – the planning cycle, the budget discussions, the annual review meetings, and so on. Second, there are informal conversations that take place when people meet by chance. The two conversations often have little in common. Many people in informal conversations are not participants in the official planning discussions, while those who are often have very little idea of what is being talked about 'down the line'.

The conversations can be bridged by means of the scenario process. It turns unheard observations that are often not much more than intuitive feelings into articulated and tangible insights about the future business environment, that may have a significant impact on the way the organization positions itself.

Providing cognitive organization

When designing the strategic conversation we need to address the dilemma of creating space for important insights coming up through the organization, without overwhelming the system with new ideas.

The answer is that the organization requires a process that allows insights to be surfaced, discussed and then scaffolded (see Chapter 6) into an overall shared mental framework so that they can be understood in context. Without scenarios, we are looking at a very large number of ideas and insights, and it is difficult to see how to deal with them all. There just won't be enough hours in the day to handle this level of complexity. However, scenarios organize a multitude of events, ideas and insights into a limited number of stories that are cognitively manageable.

We influence each other through the stories we tell. The stories that have the strongest influence are those rich in metaphors that elicit feelings of fear, hope, security and threat. They create the jolt needed for action (discussed in Chapter 6). Skilful strategic conversations making use of scenarios provide an opportunity to engender this type of impact,which is necessary to start mental models moving and converging.

Fighting group-think and fragmentation

The need for scenario-based strategic conversations is particularly indicated in organizations needing to overcome the dangers of an internal mindset drift towards fragmentation or 'group-think'. If this is not stopped in time the organization will find its ability to perceive early signals severely impaired. Maintaining a healthy balance, crucial for the organization's ability to read external signals, requires active management intervention. Group-think narrows the range of vision of the organization. Fragmentation kills the process by which perceptions and insights penetrate towards organizational decision-making. A balance needs to be maintained between, first, valuing a range of views and perspectives that will make the organization sensitive to developments over a wide territory and, second, a willingness to exchange views and come to a critical mass of support for the next step.

The scenario-based strategic conversation bridges the conflicting needs of diversity and convergence. It provides space for different world views through the mechanism of multiple stories, but it also makes these the subject of conversations that move views closer together until an accommodation is reached.

Creating the Scenario-based Strategic Conversation

As illustrated in the Mont Fleur story, scenario work in the context of a strategic conversation is less formal than in the 'making sense' and 'strategy development' projects discussed earlier in this chapter. There is more room for manoeuvre in the strategic conversation than when the end goal of the project is the systemic analysis required in the earlier projects. However, experience suggests a few basic principles to adhere to in facilitating successful and purposeful conversation:

- Where we end up is important, but even more important is ensuring that views are expressed and converge.
- Avoid normative thinking. Instead, focus on what might happen.
- Make the group acknowledge uncertainty and different world views.
- Make the group explore – try out new ideas and metaphors.
- Use disasters and crises, not as threats but as learning devices.
- Acknowledge personal vulnerabilities – be aware that some views may be seen as threatening by some people.
- Reduce personal vulnerability by maintaining a sense of fun.
- Don't chair the conversation, but facilitate and use group dynamics.
- Use the scenario method.

Within these principles, every organization will have to find their own way of intervening in the conversation. Some larger organizations set up a formal timetable with groups that straddles the hierarchical reporting lines engaging with scenarios, thus creating a two-way – top-down and bottom-up – conversation. Other organizations use *ad hoc* events, triggered by the need of the moment.

Using the Internet to Enhance the Strategic Conversation

One increasingly powerful option is offered by electronic communication. Using the company intranets or the Internet to develop corporate scenarios for the future is increasingly useful. In Siemens, a group calling itself FutureScape, with members located all over the world, work together on future thinking. Members do this alongside their normal work. Interaction happens mostly through the organization's intranet, but members also occasionally meet in person for workshops. At Nokia, participation in the scenario dialogue includes hundreds of people throughout the organization. Discussion spaces on the corporate intranet focus on building scenarios and matching them to business concepts.

Experience[84] suggests that the following points will enable this process to work effectively:

- base virtual communities on existing real communities;
- diversity (including external people) is strength;
- combine online interaction with occasional face-to-face interaction to build trust;
- aim to *pull* interest rather than *push* information;
- 'fluid' is better than 'final' – think of things as draft versions;
- use a facilitator to link discussions, add insights and create focus;
- separate the open, exploratory spaces from the structured, convergent areas;
- use shared knowledge databases;
- archive everything;
- circulate short interim reports to the wider community.

To summarize, Project 3 is about making the organization a more effective observer of the world around it. This means being better able to read signals, including weak signals (the 'dots on the horizon') and alert the organization to potentially important developments and trends. The way to achieve this is to mobilize all available eyes, ears and brainpower in the organization. This means that all these resources need to be networked together in a way that allows observations and insights to flow into and through the cognitive machinery that underpins strategy-making. The way this is done is through facilitating the (largely informal) strategic conversation. The most powerful intervention tool available for this is scenario methodology. The most important aspects it offers are: first, widening and focusing of the attention span; second, creating room for multiple perspectives and serendipity; and third, creating a process that leads to a cognitively manageable result.

PROJECT 4: BUILDING AN ADAPTIVE LEARNING ORGANIZATION

Action and Experiential Learning

In Chapter 6, we introduced the complexities of organizational life to highlight the limits of the rationalistic view. As Henry Mintzberg observed, most intentional strategy comes to nothing. He suggests that rationalistic organizations have an overwhelming implementation issue in the hustle and bustle of daily life. This problem led us to the position that in many cases a more realistic and effective, albeit more limited, objective might be the sharing of individual perceptions and sensemaking, such that decision-makers at all levels become more aware and develop a wider view. This led to Project 3, the scenario-empowered strategic conversation that facilitates the organization to become a skilful observer of the external world – both in terms of what it sees, and how this knowledge is linked to decisions in the active network of observers and decision-makers.

We now make the next step to Project 4, which moves beyond exploration into action. The introduction of action into the cognitive loop is a crucial further step towards adaptive organizational learning, which we introduced in Chapter 6 as a useful perspective to understand the role of the scenario tool in organizations.

The Strategic Journey of Project 2 Revisited

If scenarios and strategy are intended to lead to action and change to make the organization more robust to cope with developments in the business environment, the traditional 'planning' framework will not take us all the way. We need to move from strategy to an ongoing process of strategizing, beyond a rationalistic thinking process to an organization-wide conversation that leads to action. The adaptive organizational learning framework promotes the use of scenarios to integrate perception, reflection, mental model management, strategy thinking, action planning and experiential learning as essential parts of making a more robust organization. The organizational learning framework moves us from one-off strategy development to ongoing strategizing and experiencing.

Having arrived at this point, it is useful to revisit the strategic trip we made in Project 2. This project is consistent with the activities of a traditional planning cycle – that intense period of managerial activity that requires extensive 'number crunching' and culminates in the generation of the annual budget or business

processes leading to common assumptions constituting organizational identity and recipes. In Chapter 6, we saw how upframing of these 'business-as-usual' assumptions is needed to enable policies and implementation that lead to robust performance.

Upframing addresses the organizational culture and involves the whole, or at least a critical mass, of the people in it. Strategy cannot be left to a specialized group. Top management must lead the process of stepping out of the current orthodoxy and upframing the business definition. This can be achieved only by involving a critical mass of opinion in the organization in a strategic conversation. It is easy to underestimate the degree to which management's own orthodoxy is systemically determined in interactions with the rest of the organization, and it is almost impossible to make anything happen unless the organization's assumptions have developed in sympathy with management's thinking during the development of strategy.

The conclusion is inescapable: if scenarios and strategy are meant to lead to change that makes the organization more robust against external developments, the traditional planning framework will go only part of the way. We need to move from strategy to an ongoing process of strategizing, beyond a rationalistic thinking process to an organization-wide conversation. The organizational learning framework helps us to understand the role of scenario thinking as part of building a more robust organization.

What is Adaptive Organizational Learning?

Organizational learning is a metaphorical analogy of individual learning. Individual learning is an ongoing process. In Chapter 6 we introduced the experiential 'learning loop'. The individual perceives changes in the environment, which she tries to understand using existing knowledge. Having updated her mental model of how the world works, she then plans and acts on the basis of this new understanding. She will then expect the result to be a better fit with the environment. Perception is triggered when the real world deviates from this expectation, and the cycle starts again (see Figure 8.3). Organizational learning is the same process interpreted for an organization.

The organizational learning process contains aspects that are part of any normal planning cycle. This includes both making sense of the business environment and working out a response strategy. There is also a significant difference. In the traditional planning cycle the expectation against which reality is compared comes from outside the loop, in the form of targets or missions which are set by managers or owners external to the planning activity. Traditional planning in which action results from the comparison of performance against externally set goals can be called single-loop learning, as defined in Chapter 3. In the adaptive organizational learning concept, the generation of targets or missions becomes part of the loop itself – a situation known as double-loop learning (see Chapter 3). The loop is now self-contained. It is important to note that this is only possible because action is now included in the learning system.

An illustration of this difference is the conflict between Field Marshal Lord Alanbrooke, the British Chief of the Imperial General Staff during World War II,

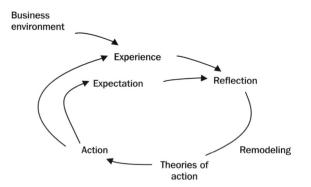

Figure 8.3 The principle of experiential/action learning.

and the Americans concerning the timing of the Allied invasion of the European continent during the war (see Chapter 5). Early in 1943, the Americans were pushing to set a date for the invasion so that their preparations could start. This is the traditional planning approach; set a target and work towards it. If you find you are deviating from the set course, take action to get back on-course (single-loop learning). In 1943, Alanbrooke did not want to set a date. He worked on the basis of a few fundamental 'laws' of the battlefield that did not allow him to make a decision at that time. In the meantime, he studied new intelligence, relied to put himself in the shoes of

> As an aside, compare Alanbrooke's laws of the battlefield (fight the enemy where he is weak, only take calculated risks, always consider the whole system) with the rules underpinning the market place as expressed in the business idea (relieve a scarcity, be distinctive, consider the whole system).

the enemy and had a scenario team testing the various options. Eventually, Alanbrooke decided that Hitler's main weakness was his inability to tactically relinquish any terrain. By opening up other fronts elsewhere, in particular in Italy, German divisions would be pulled out from the west, reducing their defences there and improving Allied chances for the invasion. Alanbrooke eventually convinced the Americans to carry out the Italian campaign before attempting the western invasion.

The Americans were left with the impression that Alanbrooke was indecisive and reluctant to invade – they had misunderstood his approach. The double-loop learning approach always seems indecisive to energetic problem-solving managers, who feel unhappy until the way forward has been laid out in the traditional planning approach, allowing them to move on to the next problem. However, as Mintzberg[77] convincingly argues, the world of the energetic problem-solver is a mental construct that does not overlap well with reality. Organizational learning starts from the premise that strategy, in general, is much more emergent than intentional.

The world cannot be wholly deconstructed: things are too uncertain. This is not changed by managers making goal or mission statements that are based on arbitrary single-line assumptions about how things are, or are going to be. Instead, organizational learning shares the following idea with the scenario approach: it makes a distinction between what we know about the future (the systemic relations and predetermined elements, already in the pipeline) and what is fundamentally unknowable. Adaptive organizational learning implies taking action as justified by our existing knowledge, while observing and perceiving events as they unfold.

The next step is to use this new understanding to develop new knowledge as quickly as possible, providing the basis for further action.

The various uses of the scenario approach discussed so far come together in the concept of adaptive organizational learning. The phases involved are perception, strategic conversation, sensemaking, strategy development, action planning, action, expectation setting, perception. We have argued that the use of scenarios improves sensemaking in puzzling situations. In Project 1 we saw how scenarios can have a major contribution towards sensemaking beyond traditional analysis, in raising really important questions. Furthermore, in Project 2 we saw the value of the scenario approach in strategy development – including the use of the business idea concept – in

> Scenarios have a major contribution to make to adaptive organizational learning. The scenario approach provides the external component of the process. Without it, organizational learning develops into an inwardly focused activity that will ultimately threaten survival chances.

that it allows the full, systemic repercussions of the strategic situation to be taken into account.

However, scenarios do not remove uncertainty. At the moment of action, there is irreducible uncertainty that makes it impossible to say whether we are doing the right thing or not. Only by trying and finding out will that be made clear to us. Therefore, scenarios are most effective as part of an organizational learning model, which includes testing and finding out. In Project 3 we saw how scenarios, in the institutional context, influence the ongoing strategic conversation towards making the organization a more effective observer. In Project 4 we now add the role of scenarios as an enabler of more effective, coherent and consistent institutional action.

Essentially, scenarios are a fundamental part of engaging in the learning loop.

Building a Scenario Culture

In an organization that pursues adaptive organizational learning, scenarios will be familiar, not as an episodic activity but as an ongoing, thinking style that permeates everything that the organization does. In such organizations, people have abandoned the idea that strategy is about finding the one right answer. Instead, they see strategy as a thoughtful process of moving through the business environment, simultaneously applying knowledge gained from experience and from careful perception and observation of what is happening.

People engage in strategic conversations as they do in every organization, but here the process is a conscious one, and interventions are made by management to enable conversations to attain higher levels of effectiveness and reach. As a result, every relevant observation by any member becomes an object that will be scaffolded into the shared picture of how the world is explained and acted upon. Knowing that this is the case, individuals develop a high degree of skill and motivation in looking for signals, especially weak signals that may warn of unexpected developments. The strategic conversation must then address the question of where to go from here.

The larger the organization, the more the process needs to be organized. Typically, the organization chart will show how the activities are allocated to groups of people, all supervised by an overall management team. But this scheme ought to be a flexible one, since adaptation to the realities of the business environment will require groups to be reconstituted as events change over time. However, as scenario-based organizational learning becomes a culture that pervades the whole organization, people are functional immediately in the new group.

Every group has its own management team, with its own business idea, articulating systemically how it services a scarcity that deploys its distinctive competences. The idea is that wherever there is a team there will be a business idea. The team will feel the need to articulate the idea so that the organization can better see what it is doing. The team will regularly engage in scenario thinking to move its thinking into the future. Often, a facilitator will engage the team in a structured conversation lasting a few hours, in which the team updates its understanding of predetermined elements and uncertainties related to its business idea. The discussion is used to incorporate new observations and insights into the mental model of the situation shared by the team, so that activities can adapt to new knowledge.

Top management approach their work in a similar way. Like any other team, they articulate their business idea, known as the *corporate business idea*. It is important that this is built on business ideas at other levels and that subordinate teams are both well briefed on the corporate success formula and in agreement with it. A small staff group will normally be responsible for enabling this two-way conversation, which will result in the alignment of business ideas across the whole organization. In the scenario culture, strategy pervades the conversation up and down the reporting lines, and the line of argument makes use of multiple futures and multiple perspectives. An ongoing concern is to ensure that the business-as-usual model does not gain the upper hand, and that space remains for experience-based divergent views to be considered. Also, the staff group is charged with the responsibilities of making sure that sensemaking is an ongoing activity and ensuring that it does not get stuck in an overwhelming orthodoxy.

The staff group will facilitate scenario discussions in the top team. The resulting scenarios will be considered upon the important questions that they raise. Research will be carried out, to feed future scenario work. While this scenario conversation is open to everyone through the corporate portal, occasionally, the staff group will also consolidate the current understanding in a number of 'corporate' scenarios that will be widely distributed – including any stakeholders in and outside the organization whose support is important for the organization's survival.

> Teams need to be empowered so that they can engage with the learning loop, including making decisions and learning from those decisions. There is not a strong top down line of command; the teams simply pursue their objectives themselves. This brings thinking and acting closer together, enabling a fast learning capability.

The organizational learning culture is based on scenario-based conversations. Whenever a decision needs to be made, people will want to develop a few scenarios around the issues involved – even if there are only a few hours available (see the *instant scenarios* in Chapter 7). They would feel extremely uncomfortable having to make decisions in any other way.

Team Empowerment

The team is the important decision-making unit in the adaptive learning organization. Since the team structure is not constant but adjusts to the needs of the business environment, it is important that individuals have a common understanding of how teams function and that this understanding pervades the whole organization. Self-organizing teams require team skills. While team dynamics and skills lie outside the scope of this book, within the context of organizational learning we shall consider the imperative to turn self-organizing teams into self-strategizing teams. The latter is a self-organizing team that turns its energy towards the strategic task of creating a set of activities that constitute a good fit between its own distinctiveness and the needs of its business environment, which may be outside or inside the organization. The principle is to bring experiential action learning, as portrayed in Figure 6.1, to the daily task of the team. This process of self-strategizing is based on the following principles:

- The team remains in charge – there is no delegation to an outsider.
- Strategy is approached as a team effort.
- Strategy is learned by doing, experiencing and reflecting.
- Over time, the team thinks increasingly strategically.
- As strategy becomes natural, business development emerges as a priority.

Self-strategizing does not develop overnight: implementation requires persistence. An important starting point is providing the team with new tools that will inspire new behaviour. The tools of strategy are well known and mapped out in numerous textbooks. It would be useful for the members of the self-strategizing team to have knowledge of the concepts and language of strategy. But, within the context of organizational learning, the team needs to be able to also actively and operationally discuss its own business idea and scenario thinking. Clearly, it is necessary for the team members to have a working acquaintance with the tools for these activities. These tools include interviewing, cognitive mapping, systems analysis, basic business economics, risk management, scenario facilitation, option planning and operational project planning skills. In addition, the teams can be helped by external process assistance that facilitates the new thinking and supports consistency of effort, particularly in the early stages. Specifically, this external help could include:

- keeping strategy on the agenda;
- introducing conversational tools and techniques to make strategy easier; in particular, the business idea and the scenario approach;
- organising external interaction as required by the team, including expert presentations, learning journeys and other modes of communication;
- guarding the learning process (capturing, feeding back, raising challenging questions, triggering reflection, and so on).

The external help must not interfere with team responsibility, autonomy and decision-making. The team remains in charge, developing strategy and action itself. The external helper is not a consultant, relieving the team from the task of thinking strategically. Rather, he acts as a process facilitator, a servant of the team, whose aim it is to develop over time a genuine self-strategizing capability.

The Across-team Strategic Conversation

Installing a self-strategizing capability in teams is the crucial step towards the goal of empowering adaptive organizational learning. It does not, on its own, ensure that the whole organization acts strategically – the overall process also needs attention. As self-strategizing develops, teams will increasingly endeavour to protect the integrity of their own regulative processes. However, teams also belong to a corporate whole that needs to constrain and steer activities towards the common purpose. Corporate constraints provide the discipline for focused creativity, for reduced detours or dead ends and for shaping reliable behaviour. With adaptive organizational learning, this task of influencing team behaviour falls to the across-team strategic conversation. Creating this is a clear responsibility of the top management team.

Creating the process

There are two aspects to this task: creating the process, and enabling people to participate in it. We have already seen how the scenario approach provides a framework for the process. In addition to the scenario method, the across-team conversation requires a guardian, whose role it is to trigger activity that covers the important aspects of the corporate strategy process. This job includes such activities as facilitating the top team process, organizing events, creating communication channels, capturing conversation, feeding back, moving the process on, raising challenging questions and triggering reflection. As discussed earlier, a larger organization will normally need to organize these activities in a dedicated staff group; this group will often provide external facilitation help to the self-strategizing teams.

Enabling people to participate

The other responsibility of senior management is to create an environment in which people feel able and committed to participate in the learning process. Don Michael[82] suggests the following as minimum requirements:

- Project the extraordinary opportunity for everyone that derives from ongoing learning and change.
- Avoid a culture where competence is projected in 'an image of certainty'. Use facilitators instead of chairpersons (nobody has the full answer).
- Acknowledge uncertainty and avoid a culture where errors are published. Construct attitudes and procedures that embrace error.
- Encourage participative behaviour, by example, storytelling and using appropriate metaphors.
- Make participative behaviour normal.

- Acknowledge personal vulnerability and provide support from the centre. This is particularly important during periods of disruption that accompany the learning process. Create trust that this support will be forthcoming in the future.
- Provide short-term reinforcements and rewards.
- Practice what you preach.

In this type of culture, scenario thinking and strategic conversations will thrive. As a result, people will pull together and accommodate each other's needs and wishes; the corporate needs will surface and be acknowledged. In short, the whole organization will act as a genuine learning organization.

RETHINKING THE FUTURE – THE VALUE OF SCENARIOS IN DEVELOPING COMPETITIVE ADVANTAGE

Throughout this book, we have considered the limits to organizational thinking, including routines such as inertia, biases, stress avoidance, group-think, fragmentation and tacit cultural assumptions, and discussed ways that these may be overcome using scenario-planning techniques. We gradually widened the discussion until we came to see scenario approaches as a fundamental part of the process of adaptive organizational learning that underpins every successful organization.

It is worth emphasizing the importance of scarcity – a point made at the start of the book. Scarcity provides value and competitive advantage: the team with the greatest, rarest talent has the highest value, the best prospects, and often the greatest success. The reason that this is significant is because scenario thinking provides value that is scarce, and as we have seen, does this in two closely related ways. First, it enables managers to understand the present: the business recipes all need to be accurately assessed, measured and managed to deliver success. Whatever the outcome, the starting point for scenario thinking provides this advantage. If your understanding of the present situation is greater than your competitors' understanding, then that is clearly a major resource and source of competitive advantage.

The second advantage, closely linked to the first, is the fact that a clear understanding of the present not only provides a foundation for a better understanding of the future, but also the confidence and process to achieve this. In other words, understanding the present – overcoming business-as-usual thinking – means that an organization can start to develop adaptive organizational learning. While many managers focus on trying to know and control everything, in a world of complex, continuous change, what matters more is the confidence and ability to discern and prepare for those approaching dots on the horizon. It is not simply *what* you know that matters, but *how* you react to what you do not know. The advantage of scenario thinking is not only a greater understanding and insight into present, and hence future, situations; it is also, and most decisively, a capacity to manage the unknown challenges of the future. This point was highlighted in Chapter 5, where the historical development of scenarios was outlined. Royal Dutch/Shell did its organization, and scenario thinking as a whole, a great service by seeking to understand possible future scenarios from the 1960s onwards. The benefits of this were spectacularly highlighted by the energy crisis in the 1970s: as a result of its work, Shell was able to understand what was happening and take action to ensure its continued success ahead of its competitors.

DEVELOPING THE SIXTH SENSE

To help you implement some of these concepts in your organization, it is worth reflecting on a few key issues:

- What sort of manager do you want to be? One that fights for the organization's survival? One that, if the organization is currently prospering, maintains the status quo and business-as-usual – or a manager determined to develop the sixth sense, developing both the current success and potential of the organization?
- Is your understanding of the reasons for your current success accurate, or might it be flawed? For example, do others in the organization share your views?
- Do you understand the dots on the horizon – what they are today, and what they might mean for the future?
- Are you ready and prepared to get involved yourself? (But remember, strategy cannot be easy – if it were, it would not be worth doing.)
- Are you clear about the purpose of your scenario project?

It is worth remembering that the commonly held assumptions of managers preserve organizational coherence, by acting as a filter to signals from the environment. Many of these signals are not recognized, or are routinely ignored or dismissed through alternative, yet plausible, explanations. These limitations result in managerial 'blind spots' that lock management into an obsolete business-as-usual world view, leading to strategic drift. In such circumstances, the organization will gradually become misaligned with the environment and its stakeholders, such as customers.

We have seen, in the cases of Xerox, Motorola, Lego, Yahoo! and others, how strategic inertia in the face of a changing environment impacts dramatically on companies. By focusing strategic energies on assessing multiple futures, and embedding this in a living model of adaptive organizational learning, companies are better placed to gain considerable advantage by the early recognition of, and reaction to, a changing business environment. In an increasingly volatile world, companies ready for the unforeseen will reap the rewards, while their competitors miss the harvest!

Abilene paradox

Written by Jerry B. Harvey, the paradox is essentially about a man suggesting a family trip to the distant town of Abilene on a hot, dry Sunday afternoon. Everyone agrees to go, but only when they are returning from their long, uncomfortable journey do members of the family confess that they were only going because they thought everyone else wanted to. Even the person suggesting the trip did so because he thought, mistakenly, that others would prefer it.

This is highly relevant to the organizational context within which managers work, and shows how organizational structures and characteristics affect, positively or negatively, the number and seriousness of individual thinking flaws. The key issue is the lack of honesty in communicating thoughts and feelings. The Abilene paradox is similar to many organizational paradoxes: choices are validated even though all the individuals concerned have reservations – they just aren't voiced. Individuals avoid conflict because conflict carries risk. In organizational life, confronting the issues carries the risk of loss of face or even one's job.

Adaptive organizational learning

Adaptive organizational learning is the process occurring in organizations that leads to the adaptation of its behaviour to improve fit with the environment and a better performance, especially in turbulent times. 'Learning' happens when organizations improve their efficiency, effectiveness and innovation in uncertain and dynamic market conditions. The greater the uncertainty in the environment, the greater the need for fast learning. This is to enable quicker and more effective responses to the challenges faced. Arie de Geus, former head of Group Planning in Shell, has argued that an organization's ability to learn faster than its competitors is the ultimate source of competitive advantage. Aspects of learning are experimentation at the margin, perception, reflection on experience, sensemaking, development of 'theories of action', and, ultimately, an ability to act on the conclusions reached.

Bolstering (see also *Buck passing* and *Procrastination*)

The conflict theory of decision-making describes *bolstering* as a way in which decision-makers cope with the threats or opportunities that are often part of crucial decisions. Decision-makers tend to defensively avoid the stress of making difficult decisions by adopting coping patterns in their decision behaviour, and one of these approaches is bolstering, along with *buck passing* and *procrastination*.

Bolstering involves uncritically boosting the advantages of the 'least worst' option of those options that are available – often the status quo or business-as-usual option. All three coping patterns lower the stress inherent in facing up to a difficult decision.

Bolstering, especially when accompanied by *escalation of commitment* to the current strategy, can lead to a feeling of perceived organizational invulnerability to events in the business environment. As a result, it typically leads to two common outcomes: an incomplete search for, and evaluation of, incoming information that would bring greater choice, and a lack of contingency planning in the event that the favoured decision or strategy begins to fail.

Buck passing

This is another major coping pattern, together with *bolstering* and *procrastination*. Buck passing entails passing the ultimate responsibility for the decision dilemma to other individuals or groups.

Business idea

An organization's *business idea* (BI) is its success formula, describing its competitiveness, based on its uniqueness in the world. Judging the strength of a business idea means assessing three factors:

1. *How it will create value for stakeholders of the organization.* Value is being created if the idea addresses a scarcity, either by filling it or by alleviating its effect.
2. *How the organization will deliver its unique competitive advantage.* A business idea has to clarify the system of uniqueness that the organization brings to bear on its activities.
3. *How the organization invests on an ongoing basis in its distinctiveness.* This is important because a success formula cannot be effective forever – anything that is unique will eventually be copied, or its value may disappear because people's interests move elsewhere – therefore, an organization must invest in the renewal of its distinctiveness on an ongoing basis.

Business ideas belong to management teams, and exist at all levels in corporations where management teams operate.

Confirmation bias

This is the tendency to seek confirming evidence to justify past decisions. This tendency may also be used to support the continuation of the current favoured strategy – often business-as-usual. *Confirmation bias* may lead managers to fail to evaluate potential weaknesses of existing strategies and overlook important and successful alternative strategies. An example of this is the *waiter's dilemma*.

Decision dilemma

A *decision dilemma* occurs when the decision-maker perceives that continuing with the current course of action – often business-as-usual – carries risks, and that alternative courses of action also carry risks.

Double-loop and single-loop learning

Double-loop learning is when organizational error is detected and corrected in ways that involve the modification of underlying norms, policies and objectives. This process leads to a better fit between the organisation and its environment than single-loop learning, but is difficult for many organizations to achieve.

Single-loop learning is a more common situation encountered in organizations, when the detection and correction of organizational error take place in an attempt to maintain its current policies and objectives. *Escalation of commitment* is a form of single-loop learning. Chris Argyris and Donald Schön[84] have most famously articulated these terms.

Driving forces
Those fundamental forces that bring about change or movement in the patterns and trends that we identify as underpinning observable events in the world. Understanding of the inter-relatedness of these forces will provide insight into the systemic structure of the issue that we are exploring. By surfacing alternative plausible outcomes from the impact of these forces over time, we start to understand the 'limits of the possible' for alternative futures.

Energetic problem solver
A manager who measures success by the number of problems solved each day.

Escalation of commitment
Typically, when decisions or strategy start to fail, the responsible decision-maker commits further resources to turn the situation around. This stems from a need to defend his previous choices. There are many business examples of this situation, notably at Coca-Cola during its launch of New Coke, and in the events surrounding the continuing investment in the Millennium Dome in London. *Escalation of commitment* is similar in observable behaviour to *bolstering* – but the former is characteristic of a manager's need to be proven right, while the latter is characteristic of a manager's subconscious desire to reduce the stress inherent in making a difficult decision.

Facilitation
This is the art of helping teams to achieve high performance in their thinking and decision-making. The process of *facilitation* is similar to catalysis; it assists interactions between people that would otherwise not occur. A facilitator is a person who makes it easier for people to understand each other, reach agreement and take concerted action.

Fragmentation	*Fragmentation* is the opposite of *group-think*, and happens in organizations when individuals or groups disagree with others at the same or higher levels of the organization. Often, the explicit expression of emerging dissent is suppressed, with dissenting opinion present only in the organizational background – for example, in informal exchanges rather than in formal meetings. Each of the fragmented groupings may evidence *confirmation bias* in their evaluation of incoming information – which will tend to support initially held opinions. Fragmentation may be magnified if one grouping's views are dominant. Fragmentation may become locked in and extremely difficult to reverse.
Framing	How an issue or situation is seen or framed is particularly significant in providing the basis for developing an effective strategy. Key points about *framing* include:

- Managers follow managerial recipes for success and see emerging issues through single frames of reference. People's roles influence the way that problems are framed.
- Well-rehearsed and familiar ways of making decisions will be dominant and difficult to change.
- Poor framing may lead managers to solve the wrong problem – decisions may have been reached with little thought, and better options may have been overlooked.
- Organizations can go out of business if their managers fail to change their frame so that it encompasses – and allows valid insight into – changes in the business environment.

Friction forces	*Friction forces* are also known as barriers to entry; factors blocking competitors from copying the success of other organizations. These forces preserve and protect an organization's distinctiveness. There are two types: resources or positions owned by the organization, and organizational capability and competence.

Group-think   *Group-think* is the suppression by a dominant group in an organization of ideas that are critical of the direction in which the group is moving. It is shown by a tendency to concur with the position and views that are perceived as favoured by the group (see also the *Abilene paradox*). Cohesive groups tend to develop rationalizations for the invulnerability of the group's decision or strategy, inhibiting the expression of critical ideas by dissenting members of the group. This is likely to result in an incomplete survey of available options and a failure to examine the risks of preferred decisions.

Group-think may become locked-in and extremely difficult to reverse.

Hindsight bias   This is sometimes called the 'I knew it all along' bias. Research by B. Fischhoff[14] has highlighted the fact that if a named event had occurred, the research group tended to recollect that they had predicted it with a high degree of confidence. If a named event had not occurred, they either claimed that they had not predicted it, or that they had placed a low degree of confidence on the poor prediction. This has become known as the *hindsight bias*.

We believe that our judgements, predictions and choices are well made, but this confidence may be misplaced.

Hygiene factors   *Hygiene factors* are ideas that are so well codified and widely accepted that they become routine, written about in textbooks and embedded into recipes in an industry across all competitors. They result from the fact that organizations have always been trying to discover ways of outsmarting the competition, and while not all ideas are equally effective, some are prominent and clearly successful. Initially, some organizations develop competitive advantage by exploiting these ideas but, over time, others see the beneficial effects and will start to copy the same ideas in their own organizations, with the idea eventually becoming established as 'best in class'. Once an idea reaches this point it has become a *hygiene*

	factor, something that is widely recognized as a starting requirement for running any healthy organization.
Iceberg analysis	In scenario planning, use is made of a systems approach known as *iceberg analysis* which breaks down knowledge into different categories. At the peak of the iceberg (above the water level) are observable events. Observers recognize multiple and interrelated trends and patterns in the events. Trends and patterns are below the waterline of the iceberg in that they are not immediately visible, but require mental processing of series of visible events to become apparent. Deeper into the iceberg, patterns display organized behaviour and become trends; deeper still and it becomes possible to start seeing relationships between multiple trends. The awareness of patterns and relationships makes us ask why they occur. At the bottom of the iceberg, we find our basic understanding of the underlying causal structure, driving patterns, trends and ultimately visible events. Although these structures remain invisible, we know about them through interpretation of the events we can observe.
Organizational inertia	See *strategic inertia*.
Organizational jolt	When presenting scenarios is to be followed by action in the organization, it is vital to establish an *organizational jolt*, a wake-up call for the organization that will make clear its need for action. The jolt may be one of delight, an opportunity presented that had not previously been considered, or it may be one of shock, for example with unforeseen threats – dots on the horizon – gathering or major opportunities missed.
Organizational lock-in and positive feedback loops	*Organizational lock-in* happens when the organization becomes wedded to a particular belief or view of the world to such an extent that it leads to actions that simply reinforces this flawed perception. Underlying lock-in is what is known in systems theory as a *positive feedback loop*. The reason why it is so difficult to deal with organizational flaws is the phenomenon of *lock-in*. Lock-in is a feature of systems that feed back on to themselves.

Both individuals and organizations can be subject to lock-in. The waiter's behaviour (see *Waiter's dilemma*) is an example of individual lock-in. The waiter's belief in his ability to identify good tippers is a typical example of a system feeding back on to itself. His theory of action leads him to do things that produce an experience that then reinforces this theory of action. The waiter cannot escape its flawed conclusions. Significantly, there is a huge difference between this problem occurring at an individual or an organizational level. It is (or should be) possible to explain the problem to the waiter and help him to change his behaviour to escape from the loop. Assuming he is a rational individual, he will get the point and change his approach. Since the feedback loop lives in one individual mind, the person can break the loop and get out of the locked-in position.

Organizational lock-in is considerably more difficult to deal with. *Fragmentation* is an example of such a feedback loop. With the conversation in the group addressing a diminishing slice of reality, mental models become impoverished and gradually people only see what happens in their narrow area of focus. Consequently, the conversation becomes narrower and less comprehensive and meaningful. This also leads to *lock-in*, but the difference with the waiter's situation is that no single individual has the power to step out of it. Even if they potentially understand the problem, they cannot escape, as they are forced to spend most of their time in the narrowly based conversation. They become a victim of circumstances.

Group-think is also a locked-in phenomenon.

Organizational strategy	This is an articulated policy framework that is used to steer actions coherently towards survival and success. Good strategy is a policy that, if adhered to by all players, promises enough economic surplus to reward all stakeholders, motivating them to continue supporting the organization.
Overconfidence bias	Closely-linked to *confirmation bias*, *overconfidence bias* is a well-documented thinking flaw characterized by a

	tendency to have an exaggerated belief in one's ability to understand situations and predict the future.
Procrastination	Along with *bolstering* and *buck passing*, this is the third major coping pattern that decision-makers use to reduce the stress of decision dilemmas. *Procrastination* entails delaying a difficult decision.
Rationalistic planning	*Rationalistic planning* is based on the assumptions that:

- there is only one best answer to the strategy question;
- everyone thinking rationally on behalf of the organization will arrive at the same conclusion; and
- implementation follows discovery of strategy, and action is separate from thinking.

Recipes	Managerial *recipes* are the set of beliefs and rules of thumb that are developed over time from experience and institutionalised to guide managerial thinking and acting. Grinyer *et al.*[2] define recipes as 'those rules of thumb that are generally accepted and shared by competent managers as the common-sense way of doing business'.
Remarkable people (RPs)	*Remarkable people (RPs)* are an essential part of the scenario process. They are valuable because the search for innovative thinking needs to receive an impetus from outside the organization. This is achieved by identifying individuals who are not part of the normal ongoing strategic conversation within the company, but are conversant with the industry structure, language, driving forces and key uncertainties, and whose knowledge overlaps the area where the client's knowledge is fragmented and unstructured. Such people can move thinking 'out of the box', triggering scenario teams to surface intuitive knowledge, and can then scaffold this into existing cognitive structures. They are not necessarily authorities of the official wisdom in a given field. Scenario planners usually prefer RPs who are intensely curious and effective observers, and who have an understanding of the world and the way that it works.
Scaffolding	Connecting and integrating intuitive knowledge into a wider body of codified knowledge is a central part of the

scenario process. It happens when someone from outside the organization intervenes, and confronts our unconnected knowledge with the knowledge structure in the wider group or society. This process of building connections between isolated observations and the general structure of our knowledge is known as *scaffolding*, a term coined by Vygotsky[72], a Russian psychologist. By asking questions and making suggestions, outside agents enable individuals to discover the linkages between intuitive and codified knowledge, thereby codifying it and making it actionable.

At its core, the scenario process is essentially about developing knowledge of the contextual environment, by scaffolding information into codified knowledge within the organization. All scenario exercises begin with a base of codified knowledge, representing the business-as-usual view of the world.

Scaffolding is achieved in the scenario process through good *facilitation* and process design, scenario team composition, and the use of *remarkable people* (RPs).

Scenarios

Scenarios are stories about how the future of the business environment could unfold. Scenarios always come in sets of more than one, to express the uncertainty of the future. Scenarios consist of the description of an end state in a horizon year, a related interpretation of current reality, and an internal consistent account of how the world gets from one state to the other. Good scenarios:

- are plausible;
- are internally consistent;
- are both relevant and challenging.

Scenarios are *not*:

- stories about the strategy of the organisation;
- predictions;
- extrapolations;
- good/bad futures;
- 'science fiction'.

Self-strategizing teams

A *self-strategizing team* proactively turns a significant part of its energy towards the strategic task of creating a set of activities that constitute a good fit between its own distinctiveness and the needs of its business environment, which may be outside or inside the organization to which the team belongs.

Sharpbenders research

This research was conducted by Grinyer *et al.*[2] and highlighted potential problems faced by organizations that are inherently unable to detect or respond to change. The research focused on companies that had been failing (defined in terms of the performance of their stock value against the market average), but that had been able to turn things around. The term 'Sharpbenders' originates from a slipping stock value followed by a recovery.

Having identified such companies from stock market records, the researchers then interviewed many of them, and thus produced what is effectively a list of what can go wrong in organizations. The research highlighted five key causes of decline:

1. Adverse development in market demand or increased competition.
2. High cost structure.
3. Poor financial controls.
4. Failure of big projects.
5. Acquisition problems.

An important insight from this work is that most underperformance is due to ineffective implementation of *hygiene factors* in organizations and management, something that is entirely avoidable.

Stakeholder analysis

Stakeholders are groups or individuals who may affect, or be affected by, any of the strategies, operations or any other activities of the organization.

Stakeholder analysis is a tool to be used in parallel with the scenario process. It is a valuable part of the scenario planning process as it tests understanding of the business problem, as well as testing the internal logic of specific *scenarios*. The key is to identify those stakeholders who influence the organization's activities, and to consider the relative degree of interest and power that each has in relation to the business problem, at a particular point in time. Stakeholder analysis is always time- and context-dependent.

Stakeholder analysis is used at the start of the scenario planning process, in order to test understanding of the scenario agenda. This involves asking several questions, such as.

- Who is key to decision-making at this time?
- What really matters to him, and keeps him awake at night?
- Who are the customers with a high interest in the organization?
- Who are the predatory stakeholders?

Stakeholder analysis may also be used at the end of the scenario process, in order to test the internal logic of storylines:

- Who are the players in this scenario?
- Do they stay the same, or do they change?
- Would they really act in this way, and make these decisions?

If the answer to the last question is 'no', the scenario is probably flawed.

STEEP analysis   This is a common approach to structure thinking about the business environment when developing strategy in the Societal, Technological, Economic, Ecological and Political categories, which combine to form the overall contextual environment.

In developing long-term organizational plans, analysis of individual variables (such as economic developments) as if they were discrete elements leads to problems. This approach results in long lists of factors that are difficult to deal with. What is missing is the integration of interconnections based on systemic insights. The consequence is that the STEEP analysis does not help to move thinking forward, and is of limited practical value in strategy development, except as a checklist of areas to include.

Strategic conversation

The strategy process can be viewed as a *strategic conversation* with two parts: a formal element designed by managers, which usually revolves around planning cycles and quantitative information, and an informal part which is the casual 'corridor' conversations that staff engage in. This part is not designed or controlled by managers, and is usually qualitative and anecdotal in nature, but is extremely important because it determines where people's attention is focused. These conversations influence and are influenced by the mental models which have developed over time, and which determine how individuals see the world, how they interpret events and how they decide what is important and what is not.

Scenario planning is valuable as it provides a framework for combining the formal and informal elements of the strategic conversation. The process forces managers to examine a wide range of information, to articulate and argue the logic of their understanding of the present, and to articulate their assumptions as to how and why the future may evolve in particular ways. The result of the scenario process is the creation of 'space (tolerance) for alternative views', and a new and more sophisticated language that is an essential condition for a high-quality strategic conversation to take place. This process, when the managers' recipes or mental models have been challenged, leads to a shared understanding and accommodation that leads to joint action.

Strategic inertia

Behavioural flaws such as *bolstering*, *procrastination* and *buck passing* are all methods of lowering the stress inherent in decision dilemmas, and are characteristic of decision avoidance. Often, such decision avoidance results in greater adherence to the business-as-usual strategy. Such irrational adherence is termed *strategic inertia*.

Systems thinking   This is achieved by systematically examining a range of possible causes and structural relationships that can give rise to a particular situation. In doing so, nothing is taken for granted. Systems thinkers are particularly interested in time delays and loops acting in the system, leading to counterintuitive systemic behaviour.

Challenging conventional wisdom increases the likelihood of discovering possible discontinuities and previously unseen or undervalued linkages with other areas of the business environment. This results in greater understanding and new conceptualizations of complex issues, which can differ sharply from conventional views.

Types of knowledge: codified knowledge; intuitive knowledge; tacit knowledge   We distinguish between three *types of knowledge: codified, intuitive* and *tacit. Codified knowledge* is well articulated, understood and integrated, and of direct use in decision-making. *Intuitive knowledge* comprises isolated observations that appear to have meaning and importance, but are not well articulated and remain unconnected with our codified knowledge. *Tacit knowledge* is knowledge that cannot be verbally expressed (e.g. knowing how to ride a bicycle).

Waiter's dilemma   This is an example of *confirmation bias*, a thinking flaw that is a self-fulfilling prophecy. It concerns a waiter in a busy restaurant who, unable to give good service to everyone, serves only those people that he believes will tip well. This seems to work well, because those customers that he predicts will tip well, do. However, the waiter fails to realize that the good tip may be the result of his actions – and so might the lack of a tip from the other diners. The only true way that the waiter can test out the quality of his judgement is to give poor service to good tip prospects and excellent service to poor tip prospects. Clearly, the waiter's original judgements could be less valid than he assumes, as he has not put the adequacy of his judgement to the test.

REFERENCES

For readers wishing to expand further their understanding of scenario planning and the issues raised in this book, **The art of the Long View**, written by Peter Schwartz and published by John Wiley & Sons (1997), is one of the most popular and significant works available. We would also recommend **The Living Company**, written by Arie de Geus (Harvard Business School Press, 1997), which focuses in particular on the development of a learning organization. Finally, the Global Business Network provides support for businesses that are keen to harness the potential advantages of scenario planning (see **www.gbn.com**).

INTRODUCTION

1. Arie de Geus (1988) **Planning as learning**. *Harvard Business Review* 66(2): 70–74.

CHAPTER 1

2. P. Grinyer, D. Mayes and P. McKiernan (1989) **Sharpbenders: The Secrets of Unleashing Corporate Potential**, Blackwell: Oxford.
3. Further detailed information and analysis is available in V. Govidorajan and A.K. Gupta (2001) **Strategic innovation: a conceptual roadmap**. *Business Horizons*, p. 3, and D.M. Kelly (1984) **Canon catapults ahead in new copier sales**. *Marketing and Media Decisions* 19: 102.
4. For additional information, see B. Elgin (2001) **Inside Yahoo!** *Business Week*, 21 May.
5. A more detailed analysis of this case is provided by C. Fishman (2001) **Why can't Lego click?** *Fast Company*, September, 50: 144.
6. For additional information, see V. Govidorajan and A.K. Gupta (2001) **Strategic innovation: a conceptual roadmap**. *Business Horizons*, July: 3.
7. This example is described in detail by F. Meeks (1994) **Watch out Motorola**. *Forbes*, 12 September, 192.

CHAPTER 2

8. A.S. Luchins and E.G. Luchins (1959) **Rigidity of Behavior**, University of Oregon Press: Portland, OR; M. Sheerer (1963) **Problem solving**. *Scientific American* 208: 188–128.

9. J.F. Porac, H. Thomas and C. Baden-Fuller (1989) **Competitive groups as cognitive communities: the case of Scottish knitwear manufacturers.** *Journal of Management Studies* 26: 397–416.

10. G.P. Hodgkinson (1997) **Cognitive inertia in a turbulent market: the case of UK residential estate agents.** *Journal of Management Studies* 34: 921–945.

11. P.S. Barr, J.L. Strimpert and A.S. Huff (1992) **Cognitive change, strategic action and organizational renewal.** *Strategic Management Journal* 13: 15–36.

12. See K. Benezra (1998) **Chasing Sergio: how Sergio Zyman picked himself up after the New Coke debacle and became keeper of the brand equity flame at Coca Cola.** *Brandweek*, 30 March, 39: 30.

13. Taken from J. St. B.T. Evans (1987) **Beliefs and expectations as causes of judgemental bias.** In Wright, G. and Ayton, P. (eds) **Judgmental Forecasting**, John Wiley & Sons: Chichester. For a review, see J. Klayman and U-W. Ha (1987) **Confirmation, disconfirmation and information in hypothesis testing.** *Psychological Review* 94: 211–228.

14. B. Fischhoff (1975) **Hindsight and foresight: the effect of outcome knowledge on judgement under uncertainty.** *Journal of Experimental Psychology: Human Perception and Performance* 1: 288–299.

15. B.M. Staw and J. Ross (1978) **Commitment to a policy decision: a multi-theoretical perspective.** *Administrative Science Quarterly* 23. 40–64.

16. M.H. Bazerman, T. Giuliano and A. Appelman (1974) **Escalation in individual and group decision-making.** *Organizational Behavior and Human Decision Processes* 33: 141–152. For a more recent review and linkages to organizational decision-making, see H. Drummond (1994) **Escalation in organizational decision-making: a case of recruiting an incompetent employee.** *Journal of Behavioral Decision-making* 7: 43–56.

17. I.L. Janis and L. Mann (1977) **Decision-making: A Psychological Analysis of Conflict.** Free Press: New York.

18. G.P. Hodgkinson and G. Wright (in press) **Confronting strategic inertia in a top management team: learning from failure.** *Organization Studies.*

19. J.E. Russo and P.J.H. Schoemaker (1989) **Decision Traps.** Doubleday: New York.

20. Adapted from G. Wright and P. Goodwin (1999), **Future-focused thinking: combining decision analysis and scenario planning.** *Journal of Multi-criteria Decision Analysis* 8: 311–321.

CHAPTER 3

21. J.B. Harvey (1974) **The Abilene Paradox: The Management of Agreement.** Organizational Dynamics: San Francisco.

22. I. Janis (1982) **Groupthink.** Houghton-Mifflin: Boston.

23. J.K. Esser and J.S. Lindoerfer (1989) **Groupthink and the space shuttle Challenger accident: Towards a quantitative case analysis.** *Journal of Behavioral Decision Making* 2: 167–177.

24. Adapted from J.B. Harvey, p. 31.
25. C. Argyris (1989) **Overcoming Organizational Defensive Routines**. Prentice-Hall: Hemel Hempstead, UK.
26. G. Morgan (1986) **Images of Organization**. Sage Publications: Beverley Hills, CA.
27. H. Mintzberg (1994) **The Rise and Fall of Strategic Planning**. Free Press: New York.
28. A. Pettigrew and R. Whipp (1991) **Managing Change for Competitive Success**. Blackwell: Oxford, UK.
29. D. Michael (1998) **Barriers and Bridges to Learning in a Turbulent Human Ecology**. Presearch Series, Vol. 2 GBN: Emeryville, CA.

CHAPTER 4

30. E.H. Schein (1992) **Organizational Culture and Leadership** (second edition). Jossey-Bass: San Francisco.
31. C.W. Hill (2000) **International Business – Competing in the Global Marketplace**. McGraw-Hill: New York.
32. R.J. Barnet and J. Cavanagh (1995) **Global Dreams**. Simon & Schuster: New York, p. 33.
33. C.W. Hill, p. 106.
34. C.W. Hill, p. 107.
35. G. Hofstede (1991) **Cultures and Organizations: Software of the Mind**. McGraw-Hill: Maidenhead, UK.
36. G. Hofstede, pp. 11–12.
37. E. Luce (1995) **SE Asia: singularly different**. *The Financial Times*, 4 December, p. 12.
38. G. Hofstede, IKEA example.
39. B. Vlasic and B.A. Sterz (2000) **Taken for a Ride: How Daimler-Benz Drove Off With Chrysler**. William Morrow and Co: New York.
40. H. Simonian (1998) **Head-on Collision**. *Accountancy*, September, 26–28.
41. P. Martin (1998) **The new model Chrysler-Benz**. *The Financial Times*, 7 May, p. 19.
42. H. Simonian, pp. 26–28.
43. R. Khol (1998) **The stereotypes about Germans and Americans are wrong**, *Machine Design*, June: 6.
44. N. Tait (1998) **Car-plant cultures clash and compromise as Daimler takes the road to Tuscaloosa**. *The Financial Times*, 15 July, p. 4.
45. E. H. Schein, p. 364.
46. N. Beech and G. Cairns (2001) **Coping with change: the role of post-dichotomous ontologies**. *Human Relations* 54(10): 1303–1324.
47. A. Belkaoui (1990) **A Judgement in International Accounting: A Theory of Cognition, Cultures, Language and Contracts**. Quorum Books: Westport, CN.
48. P. Armstrong (1989) **Limits and possibilities for HRM in the age of management accountancy**. In J. Storey (ed.) **New Perspectives on Human Resource Management**. Routledge: London.

49. L. Dana (2000) **Culture is the essence in Asia**. *The Financial Times*, 28 November, p. 12.
50. L. Dana.
51. E.H. Schein.

CHAPTER 5

52. D. Ingvar (1985) **Memories of the Future: An Essay on the Temporal Organisation of Conscious Awareness**. *Journal of Human Neurobiology* 4(3): 127–136.
53. H. Kahn (1960) **On Thermonuclear War**. Free Press: New York.
54. H. Kahn and A. J. Wiener (1967) **The Year 2000, a framework for speculation**. Macmillan Publishing: New York.
55. D. Meadows (1972) **Limits to Growth. A Report for the Club of Rome Project on the Predicament of Mankind**. Universe Books. New York.
56. A. Kleiner (1996) **The Age of Heretics: Heroes, Outlaws, and the Forerunners of Corporate Change**. Doubleday: New York.
57. P. Malaska (1985) **Multiple Scenario Approaches in European Companies**. *Strategic Management Journal* 6: 339–355.
58. R. Linneman and H. Klein (1985) **Using Scenarios in Strategic Decision-Making**. *Business Horizons* January–February: 64–74.
59. M. Porter (1980) **Competitive Strategy – techniques for analysing industries and competitors**. Free Press: New York.
60. R. Normann (1975) **Management for Growth**. John Wiley & Sons: Chichester.
61. J. Gleick (1997) **Chaos – The Amazing Science of the Unpredictable** (2nd edition). Minerva: London.
62. Arie de Geus (1988) **Planning as Learning**. *Harvard Business Review* 66(2): 70–74.
63. D. Michael (1973) **On Learning to Plan and Planning to Learn**. Jossey Bass: San Francisco, CA.

CHAPTER 6

64. K. Borsch (1968) **The Economics of Uncertainty**. Princeton University Press: Princeton, NJ.
65. P. Wack (1985) **Scenarios: Uncharted Waters Ahead**. *Harvard Business Review* 63(5): 73–89; and **Scenarios: Shooting the Rapids**. *Harvard Business Review* 63(6): 139–150.
66. This view is supported by researchers such as J. D. Steinbruner (1974) **The Cybernetics Theory of Decisions**. Princeton University Press; Princeton, NJ.
67. A. Tversky and D. Kahneman (1982) **Causal Schemas in Judgements Under Uncertainty**. In D. Kahneman, P. Slovic and A. Tversky (eds) **Judgement Under Uncertainty: Heuristics and Biases**. Cambridge University Press: Cambridge, UK.

68. See, for example, G.A. Kelly (1994) **The Psychology of Personal Constructs** (second edition). Routledge: London.
69. B. Weiner (1985) **Spontaneous Causal Thinking**. *Psychological Bulletin* 97: 74–84.
70. K. van der Heijden (1996) **Scenarios: The Art of Strategic Conversation**. John Wiley & Sons: Chichester.
71. P. Wack (1985) **Scenarios: Uncharted Waters Ahead**. *Harvard Business Review* 63(5): 73–89; and **Scenarios: Shooting the Rapids**. *Harvard Business Review* 63(6): 139–150.
72. L.S. Vygotsky (1986) **Thought and Language**. MIT Press: Boston, MA.
73. See for example, M. Minsky, (1975) **A Framework for Representing Knowledge**. In P. Winston (ed.) **The Psychology of Computer Vision**. McGraw-Hill: NY; D.E. Rumelhart (1984) **Schemata and the Cognitive System**. In R.S. Wyer Jr. and T.K. Srull (eds) **Handbook of Social Cognition**, Vol. 1, Erlbaum; Hillsdale, NJ; R.C. Schank and R.P. Abelson (1977) **Scripts, Plans, Goals and Understanding**, Erlbaum: Hillsdale, NJ.
74. R.P. Abelson (1981) **The Psychological Status of the Script Concept** *American Psychologist* 36: 715–729; R.P. Abelson (1976) **Script Processing in Attitude Formation and Decision Making**. In J.S. Carroll and J.W. Payne (eds) **Cognition and Social Behaviour**. Erlbaum: Hillsdale, NJ; R.C. Schank and R.P. Abelson (1997) **Scripts, Plans, Goals and Understanding**. Erlbaum: Hillsdale, NJ.
75. K. van der Heijden (1996) **Scenarios: The Art of Strategic Conversation**. John Wiley & Sons: Chichester.
76. P. Senge (1990) **The Fifth Discipline: The Art and Practice of the Learning Organization**. Doubleday: New York.
77. H. Mintzberg (1994) **The Rise and Fall of Strategic Planning**. Free Press: New York.
78. W.E. Deming (1982) **Out of the Crisis**. MIT Center for Advanced Engineering Studies: Cambridge, MA.
79. B. Huber (1991) **Images of the Future**. In J. Fowles (ed.) **Handbook of Future Research**. Greenwood Press: Westport, CN.
80. A. Pettigrew and R. Whipp (1991) **Managing Change for Competitive Success**. Blackwell: Oxford.

CHAPTER 8

81. A. Kahane (1991) **The Mont Fleur Scenario**. Deeper News Series, GBN: Emeryville, CA.
82. D. Michael (1998) **Barriers and Bridges to Learning in a Turbulent Human Ecology**. Presearch Series, Vol. 2, GBN: Emeryville, CA.
83. D. Erasmus (1999) **Mastering information management: a common language for strategy**. *The Financial Times*, 5 April.
84. C. Argyris and D. Schön (1978) **Organizational Learning: A Theory of Action Perspective**. Addison-Wesley: Reading, MA.

Index

24/7 concepts 216
Abilene Paradox (Harvey) 71,
    73, 78, 279, 284
abstract conceptualizations
    172–85
accountants 107–9
ачтиинчинчип пиппинтии
across-team conversations
    273–5
action plans 221–3, 227–8,
    257–8, 270–5
actions 3–9, 61–2, 75–85,
    105, 121, 140, 172–85,
    220–3, 232–75
    cognition contrasts 172
    learning processes 172–85,
        266–78
    strategy 239–54
adaptive organizational
    learning
    building methods 266–78
    concepts 2–9, 85, 90–1,
        111–18, 138–62,
        171–85, 233–4, 266–79
    cycles 173–85
    processes 171–85
adversarial attitudes 261–4
agendas, scenarios 163–6,
    199–202, 224–5, 244,
    254, 273
agent provocateurs, concepts
    194
Ala-Pietila, Pekka 33
Alanbrooke, Field Marshal
    Lord 123–4, 138, 268–9
anticipation needs 23–9,
    34–5, 176–85, 220–3,
    232–5, 255–66, 276–8

AOL 23–4
arts 189–90
assumptions 90–115, 152,
    160–1, 164, 174–5,
    254, 262

Пиппипит, Тип ...
Barings Bank 56
barriers to entry, markets
    20–1, 241–54, 283
behavioural issues 3–7,
    13–14, 41–67, 73,
    80–7, 105, 120–1,
    153–78, 233–9, 260–4,
    274–5
benchmarking processes 15
Berger, Gaston 128
'best in class' organizations
    15, 31–2
BI *see* business ideas
biases 3, 41, 46–67, 159–60,
    276, 281, 283–7, 292
blame cultures 55, 90–1,
    274–5
bolstering problems 57–67,
    152, 280, 286
bootstrapping approaches 113
Boston Consulting Group 136
'brain' organizations 81, 266
brains 158–9, 230, 266
brainstorming sessions
    209–10, 237
brand names 21–2, 26–8, 34,
    96–100, 245–54
buck-passing problems
    57–67, 280, 286
budgets 81, 219–20, 254,
    267

Bush, George 52–3
business ideas (BI) 14–28,
    34–9, 241–54, 269–75,
    280–1
    concepts 14–19, 22–3,
        37–9, 242–4, 247–54,
        ... ...
    reaction speeds 22–3,
        32–3, 35–9, 147, 153,
        277–8
    scenarios 250–4
business plans 253–4
business-as-usual tendencies
    7–8, 22–3, 35–75, 149,
    167–77, 189, 201–2,
    230–9, 260–78

Canon 12, 19–23, 34–8
capabilities 15–19, 199–202,
    229–75
capital intensity 135–6
Carlson, Chester 19
cash flows 131–4
causes, effects 153–5,
    169–70, 189, 206, 219,
    236–8
central planning 124–9, 139
certainties 138–9
Challenger space shuttle 72–3
challenging attitudes 35–6,
    61–7, 72–85, 145, 149,
    161–9, 188–90,
    199–228, 255–64
champions 83
change issues 3–28, 44–7,
    75–87, 105, 140–2,
    155, 171–99, 240–2
    constancy needs 75–8

customer needs 25–8, 34,
    36–7, 44–50, 66–7,
    93–100, 277–8
identity limitations 75–8,
    85–6, 140–2, 165,
    181–5, 267
markets 18–28, 34, 36–7,
    48–50
rapidity 155
reaction speeds 22–3,
    32–9, 76–7, 147, 153,
    171–8, 276–8
resistance problems 176
sensors 17, 27–8, 33, 36,
    45, 65, 82, 86
structures 27–8, 155, 176
technological changes 47
Chaos (Gleick) 138
childcare businesses 251
Christiansen, Ole Kirk 26
Chrysler Corporation 103–5
Club of Rome 129–31
clusters, driving forces 204–8,
    225–7, 237, 254
CNN 100
Coca-Cola 26, 47–50, 54,
    245–6, 278
codified knowledge 166–70,
    246, 263, 292
cognition contrasts, actions
    172
cognitive schemas 170–1,
    263, 266–7
collectivist cultures 101–2
commitments, escalation
    problems 55–7, 61–7,
    73, 280–2
communication issues 16–19,
    71–5, 85, 109–15,
    140–6, 161–80, 220–3,
    257–66
community thinking 13–14,
    38, 89–115
company size 135–6
competencies 8, 15–22, 47,
    58, 106–8, 196–202,
    243–4, 271–5

competitive advantages 2–3,
    6, 8–39, 145, 178–85,
    276–8
Canon/Xerox 19–23, 34–8,
    45, 66, 231, 244
concepts 276–8
reaction speeds 22–3,
    32–9, 147, 153, 171–8,
    276–8
Competitive Strategy (Porter)
    133–8
competitors 14, 18–25, 34–9,
    240, 245, 251–2, 278
complexity factors 3–5, 36,
    43–4, 110, 138–9,
    143–85, 188–90
conceptualizations 172–85
confidence dangers 52–3,
    62–7, 152, 160, 286–7
confirmation bias 50–1, 55,
    62–7, 160, 281, 283,
    286–7, 292
conflicts
    cultures 91–115
    decision making 57–8,
        62–7, 71, 73–5, 83–4
    organizations 71, 73–5,
        83–4
consensus decisions 24–5, 35,
    61, 82, 84–5, 159
consensus-style management
    24–5, 35, 82, 84–5,
    159
constancy needs 75–8
contingencies 57–61, 63–7,
    73
continuous improvements
    90–1, 178, 223, 270–5
controls 14, 16–19, 81, 86,
    105–6, 124–34, 139
corporate business ideas
    271–2
corporate planning,
    integration issues
    142–3, 239–41
costs 14, 16–21, 30, 32–5,
    240–2

creativity 9, 136–7, 146,
    181–5, 201–2, 267
crisis situations 121–6,
    133–4, 176–8, 200,
    238–9
culture issues 3–9, 13–14,
    25–39, 55, 89–146,
    164–6, 188–90,
    229–75
    appraisals 110–11
    blame cultures 33, 90–1,
        274–5
    concepts 89–115, 270–5
    conflicts 91–115
    definitions 90–1, 96
    differences 91, 96–115
    environmental effects
        105–6, 111–15,
        229–75
    ethnic minorities 109–10,
        112–13
    gender issues 102
    individualistic/collectivist
        cultures 101–2
    local preferences 98–100,
        109–10
    national cultures 89–115
    possibilities 95–6
    power-distance cultures
        101–2
    professional cultures
        106–15, 164–6
    questions 114–15
    scenario thinking 97–115,
        270–5
    skills 110–11
    stereotypes 108–11
    strategic impacts 89–115,
        229–75
    uncertainty-avoidance
        cultures 101–2, 151,
        276
customers 17–39, 93–6, 192,
    197–9, 211–12,
    217–19, 240, 277–8
    bases 19–23, 34–8, 48–50,
        93–6

changing needs 25–8, 34,
36–7, 44–50, 66–7,
93–100, 277–8
relationships 17–21, 25–8,
94–6, 112, 217–19,
240–1, 245, 250–4,
277–8
segmentation factors
48–50
Tetra Pak 28–32, 34–6
value creation 15–19,
25–37, 192, 198–9,
211–12, 223, 241–2,
276–8

ᴄᴜᴜᴜᴜʋʀ ᴆᴜᴜᴜ ᴜᴜᴧ)
data 1–2, 64–7
de Geus, Arie 2, 139, 172
de Jouvenel, Bertrand 128–9
debriefs 122, 165
decision making 1–9, 24–8,
41–67, 113–14, 143–9,
158–71, 232–75
commitment escalations
55–7, 61–7, 73, 282
confirmation bias 50–1, 55,
62–7, 160, 281, 283,
286–7
conflicts 57–8, 62–7, 71,
73–5, 83–4
decision avoidance 54–63,
276
dilemmas 58–61, 72–5,
85, 281
flaws 13–14, 22–3, 38,
41–87, 119, 147–8,
162–71
guidelines 61–7
managers 41–71, 149–53,
162–71, 180–1, 229–78
organizations 69–87
processes 3–9, 55–67, 69,
84–7, 97–8
rationalistic decision-
making 150–3, 173–4,
234, 236–9, 255–66,
287

responsibility conditions
54–7
stresses 57–8, 62–7, 70,
73–5, 276
team dilemmas 58–61,
72–5, 85, 272–5
war games 121–8, 137–8,
141
Delphi technique 126
Deming, Edward 175
developing-strategy goals
233–4, 239–54
developments
priorities 27
scenario stages 202–16,
,ᴜ,ᴜ ᴜ
devil's advocates 61, 214–16
differences, cultures 91,
96–115
Disney 26, 92–6, 108
dissenting voices 5, 61–7,
72–8, 84–5, 161–9,
188–90, 201–2,
214–16, 256–64
distinctiveness factors, BI
16–19, 37, 229–75, 281
distribution issues 21–3
diversity 5, 61–7, 72–8,
84–115, 146, 161–9,
188–90, 197–228,
256–64
dominant viewpoints 61,
73–5, 159
double-loop learning 81–2,
173–4, 243, 268–70,
281–2
driving forces 169–71, 188,
198–9, 202–16, 225–7,
237, 282
clusters 204–8, 225–7,
237, 254
concepts 169–71, 202–16
Dyson, Brian 48

early indicators 220–3, 227–8
ecological issues 156–8, 193,
290–1

economics 125, 156–8, 193,
208, 221, 241, 249–50,
290–1
effects, causes 153–5, 169–70,
189, 206, 219, 236–8
emergent strategies 80, 269
emotions 164, 263, 275
empowerment benefits, teams
272–5
energetic problem solvers
230–4, 269, 282
Enrico, Roger 54
environmental issues 2–9,
17–19, 61–7, 70, 75–8,
82–7, 142–6, 171–99,
,ᴜᴜ ᴜᴜ
culture effects 105–6,
111–15, 229–75
STEEP analysis 156–8,
193, 290–1
ethnic minorities 109–10,
112–13
events 169–70, 190–1,
213–20, 285
execution problems 80–1
experiences 140–2, 159,
172–3, 181–5, 233,
264–75
experiments 172–85, 245
experts 113, 201–2, 237
exploratory attitudes 261–4

facilitators 149, 163–70,
181–90, 193–4, 224,
264–7, 273–5, 282
failures 2–6, 11–67, 70, 77,
82–5, 139, 231–2
concepts 11–39
'Sharpbenders' research
study 6, 11, 14–19,
36–7, 289
success factors 13–14,
35–6, 82–5, 232–3
fashions 44, 47, 120–1, 175
feedback loops 50, 57, 70,
78–82, 165, 173–4,
243, 268–75, 281–92

Fields, W.C. 55
filter concepts 75–8, 148–9,
    159, 183, 248–9, 277–8
financial controls 14, 16–19
fit concepts 242–4
flaws 13–14, 22–3, 38,
    41–87, 119, 147–8
    managers 41–71, 147–8,
    162–71
    organizations 7–87, 147–8,
    162–71
fleshing-out tasks 213–16,
    226–7
flexibility needs 175–6,
    249–54
Ford 99–100
forecasts 3–4, 53, 63–4,
    124–34, 137–9
formal conversations 161–2,
    164–6, 263–6, 291
forward-to-the-past scenarios
    215–16
Foster Brothers 44, 46, 81,
    278
fragmentation problems 3–4,
    73–5, 80–5, 91, 112,
    161–2, 192, 263–4,
    283–6
frames of reference 76
framing flaws 46–7, 61–2,
    283
free enterprises 215–16
friction forces see barriers to
    entry
Fuji Photo Films 20
future considerations 1–39,
    63–7, 112–15, 119–21,
    196–9, 229–75
    limits of possibility
    209–15
    managers 41–87, 196–9,
    277–8
    memories of the future
    119–21, 170–1,
    175–85, 196–9, 213–16
    organizations 69–87
    preparations 11–39

gamblers 53
game theory 126–7
Gap 44
gender issues, cultures 102
Gleick, J. 138
global markets 30–3, 90–115,
    139, 251
Godet, Michel 128–9
grounded analysis, interviews
    197–9
group-think problems 3–4,
    38, 71–85, 140, 149,
    161–71, 202, 263–4,
    284

Harvard Business School 150
Harvey, Jerry 71, 73, 281
Herbert, Ike 48–9
hindsight bias 51–3, 284
history 236
Hockey, David 236
Hofstede, Geert 96, 101–3,
    105, 112
holistic approaches 4–5
HRM see human resource
    management
Huber, B. 179
Hudson Institute 127–8
human resource management
    (HRM) 108–9, 180–1,
    217–19, 240, 247–52,
    272–5
Hussein, Saddam 52–3
hygiene factors 14–19, 284,
    289

IBM 21, 77–8, 101, 183
iceberg analysis 169–70,
    219–20, 285
identity limitations 75–8,
    85–6, 140–2, 165,
    181–5, 267
IKEA 98–100, 108, 244–6
impact analysis 188, 202–3,
    206–27
individualistic/collectivist
    cultures 101–2

inertia problems 3–7, 23,
    41–3, 61–87, 188–9,
    276–8, 285, 291
influence diagrams 219,
    227
informal conversations 161–2,
    164–6, 263–6, 291
information uses 58, 63–7,
    75–6, 112–15, 148–9,
    162
    see also knowledge
Ingvar, David 119–21, 170
innovations 19–35, 77, 168,
    172–3, 189–90, 245,
    287
Institute of the Future
    163–4
integration issues, corporate
    planning 142–3,
    239–41
Intel 78
intended strategies 80
Internet 145, 190–2, 265
interviews 163–6, 187–228,
    254
    concepts 195–9
    grounded analysis 197–9
    recording needs 197–9
    seven questions 163–4,
    196–9, 237–9
    structures 195–9
intranets 265
intuition 1–2, 136–7, 145,
    159–70, 235–9, 244,
    292
investments 16–23, 25, 37,
    54–5, 243–54
iterative processes 153,
    172–4, 230, 235–9

judgemental forecasts 53, 64

Kahane, Adam 258–9
Kahn, Herman 127–8, 132,
    138, 141
Kairamo, Kari 32
Keynesian economics 125

knowledge 2, 8, 17–28, 86,
 145, 159–70, 192–200,
 231–7, 268–75
 see also information uses
concepts 86, 159–60,
 166–70, 192–4, 246,
 263, 268–75, 292
gaps 192–9, 215
iceberg analysis 169–70,
 219–20, 285
types 86, 159–60, 166–9,
 246, 292
Kolb, David 172–3, 178
Koogle, Timothy 24

[illegible] …
 162, 168, 171, 179–80
Lawrence of Arabia (film) 1, 4,
 231–2
le Roux, Pieter 258–9
leadership issues 4–5, 24–5,
 61, 83–7, 180–1, 241,
 253–4, 277–8
 see also managers
learning processes 172–85,
 266–78
 see also organizational
 learning
Leeson, Nick 56
legacy systems 191–2
legal frameworks 19–23, 193,
 245
Lego 12, 25–8, 36, 38, 45, 231
lessons 27–8, 34–7, 43–4,
 75–6, 94–6, 99–100,
 108, 264
leveraging concepts 247
limits of possibility 209–15
local preferences, global
 markets 98–100,
 109–10
lock-in problems 7, 22–3,
 35–6, 65–9, 78–91,
 149, 159, 260–79,
 287–8
 see also business-as-usual
 tendencies

Lonnberg, Margareta 118–20

McDonald's 100
makeable concepts 124–9,
 137–9
making-sense goals 233–9,
 264, 270–5
Malaska, P. 134–5
Mallet, Jeffrey 24–5
managers 2–9, 14, 41–71,
 149–50, 162–71,
 180–1, 229–78
 see also leadership issues
business-as-usual
 tendencies 7–8, 22–3,
 [illegible]
 189, 201–2, 230–9,
 260–78
consensus-style
 management 24–5, 35,
 82, 84–5, 159
decision making 41–71,
 149–53, 162–71,
 180–1, 229–78
energetic problem solvers
 230–4, 269, 282
flaws 41–71, 147–8,
 162–71
future considerations
 41–87, 196–9, 277–8
immature styles 16–19
mental models 3, 6–7,
 41–67, 158–61,
 163–85, 233–9, 267–75
success/failure tightrope
 12–14, 36–7, 82–5
team dilemmas 58–61,
 72–5, 85, 272–5
thinking processes 3, 6–7,
 41–71, 84–7, 97–8,
 120–1, 143–6, 149–50,
 162–71, 180–1, 220–3,
 233–9, 277–8
tools 144–6, 149, 216–17,
 234, 266–7
training 18, 118–20, 124
Mandela, Nelson 258–9

marketing 18–19
markets 229–75
barriers to entry 20–1,
 241–54, 283
change issues 18–28, 34,
 36–7, 48–50
demands 14, 18–19
global markets 30–3,
 90–115, 139, 251
Nokia 32–5
Massachusetts Institute of
 Technology (MIT) 130
Masse, Pierre 128–9
mature organizations 26–8
memories of the future
 [illegible]
 175–85, 196–9, 213–16
mental models 3, 6–7, 41–67,
 158–61, 163–85,
 233–9, 267–75
mergers and acquisitions 14,
 18, 103–5, 177, 253–4
Michael, Don 139, 274–5
Microsoft 78, 183, 217,
 244–6
migrants 109–10, 112–13
Millennium Dome 56–7
mindguarding concepts 72–3
minority views 61, 65–6,
 72–8, 84–5, 161–2,
 188–90, 256–64
Mintzberg, Henry 80, 174–5,
 266, 269
mission statements 248–9,
 269
MIT *see* Massachusetts
 Institute of Technology
Mitsubishi 104
modern scenario techniques
 117–46, 266–7
Monte Fleur scenario project
 258–60, 264
Monte Carlo algorithm 137
motivation considerations 83,
 85, 175, 246
Motorola 34–5, 66
MTV 100

NASA 72–3
national cultures 89–115
New Coke 47–50, 54, 65
Next 44
Nike 245
Nissan Motor Company 104
Nixon, Richard 52
Nokia 12, 32–5, 265
Normann, Richard 136
Northshire Council 190–1,
    200–1, 204–6, 210–16,
    221–3

observations 172–85, 231–2,
    268–75
oil crisis (1973) 131–4, 136,
    138–9
opportunities 5, 6, 64–7, 81,
    108–9, 119, 172–90,
    196–202, 229–75
option plans 223
organizational learning
    building methods 266–78
    concepts 2–9, 85, 90–1,
        111–18, 138–62,
        171–85, 233–4, 266–80
    cycles 173–85
    processes 172–85
organizations 69–87, 103–15,
    187–275
    business-as-usual
        tendencies 7–8, 22–3,
        35–75, 149, 167–77,
        189, 201–2, 230–9,
        260–78
    charts 271
    company size 135–6
    conflicts 71, 73–5, 83–4
    culture issues 3–9, 13–14,
        25–39, 55, 89–146,
        229–75
    decision making 69–87
    flaws 7–87, 147–8, 162–71
    fragmentation problems
        3–4, 73–5, 80–5, 91,
        112, 161–2, 192,
        263–4, 283–6

future considerations
    69–87, 196–9
group-think problems 3–4,
    38, 71–85, 140, 149,
    161–71, 202, 263–4,
    283–4
identity limitations 75–8,
    85–6, 140–2, 165,
    181–5, 267
jolts 176–85, 220–3,
    227–8, 263, 285
lock-in problems 7, 22–3,
    35–6, 65–9, 78–91,
    149, 159, 260–79,
    285–6
mature organizations 26–8
professional cultures
    106–15, 164–6
success/failure tightrope
    12–14, 82–5, 232–3
successful organizations
    12–19, 36–7, 77, 82–5,
    177, 276–8
systemic loops 69, 79–87,
    173–4, 243, 264,
    268–75, 281–2, 292
thinking problems 3–4, 38,
    71–9, 82, 84–5, 140,
    149, 161–71, 220–3,
    283–4
out-of-the-box thinking 168,
    287
outcomes
    scenario planning 65–7,
        202–23
    tests 202–16, 269–70
overview 6–9

partners 33, 253–4
Pasteur, Louis 138
patents 19–23, 245–7
patterns 158–9, 169–70,
    219–20, 285
the Pentagon 92
'People's Kailyard' 191–2,
    215–16, 220
Pepsi 47–50, 54

perceptions 3–9, 53, 75–8,
    121, 140–6, 195–202,
    255, 270–5
performance issues 2–3, 6,
    12–14, 19–28
perspectives 3–9, 61, 110–11,
    167–8
Peugeot 231
polar outcomes 202–16
politics 96–7, 101–2, 125–6,
    156–0, 190–4, 240,
    257–8, 290–1
Porter, Michael 135–6
positive feedback 287–8,
    292
possibilities 124–9, 209–15
    cultural conflicts 95–6
    limits 209–15
Post-it notes 204, 213, 225
power issues 101–2, 257–8
predictions 3–4, 53, 63–4,
    124–34, 137–9
presentations 220
prices 29–32
priorities, developments 27
privatizations 139
proactive behaviour 230–1
probabilities 137–9, 152
problem solving 3–9,
    113–14, 230–4, 255,
    269, 282
process designs 167–9
process gains 3–9, 69, 84–7
procrastinations 57–67, 153,
    280, 287
products 18–35, 92–6,
    98–100, 243–54
professional cultures 106–15,
    164–6
project management 83, 85,
    180, 194–228
psychological considerations
    3, 6–7, 41–67, 73,
    120–1, 153–78, 233–9,
    260–4
purposeful characteristics
    232–6, 252–4

questioning needs 83–7,
114–15, 163–8, 195–9,
235–9

R&D *see* research and
development
Rand Corporation 126–8
rationalistic decision-making
150–3, 173–4, 234,
236–9, 255–66, 287
Rausing, Gad 29
Rausing, Hans 29
reaction speeds 22–3, 32–9,
76–7, 147, 153, 171–8,
276–8
reacher information see information
realities 111–12, 172–4,
232–3, 256–7, 269
recipe-following dangers 70,
76, 158–60, 174,
181–5, 276, 287
recording needs, interviews
197–9
recruitment decisions 51
reflective observations
172–85, 231–2, 268–75
relationships 17–21, 25–8,
94–6, 112, 217–19,
240–1, 245, 250–2,
277–8
remarkable people (RPs) 113,
167–9, 201–2, 225, 287
reputations 21–2, 26–8, 241,
245–54
research and development
(R&D) 18–19, 54–5
resources 108–9, 180–1,
217–19, 240, 245–55,
272–5
responsibility conditions
54–7
reward systems 175, 275
risks 55–61, 71–5, 181–2,
239–41
robustness needs 65, 92,
120–1, 136–7, 153,
251–2, 266–7

routines 3, 41–87, 159–60,
174, 276, 287
Royal Dutch/Shell 2, 131–4,
144, 164, 168, 172, 175,
178, 238–9, 276–7
RPs *see* remarkable people
rules 3, 41–87, 159–60, 174,
287

scaffolding concepts 166–70,
263, 287–8
scarcities, BI 15–19, 36–9,
149, 198–201, 241–54,
269–78, 281
scenario planning 5–14,
43–9, 64–7, 85–9,
117–46, 162–71,
187–228, 233–77,
288
agendas 163–6, 199–202,
224–5, 244, 254, 273
benefits 63–7, 85–7,
142–6, 174–85, 230,
272–9
BI 250–4
checklists 144–6, 224–8
development stage 202–16,
225–7
fleshing-out tasks 213–16,
226–7
guidelines 187–228
human dimensions 108–9,
118–21, 144–6, 180–1,
217–19, 240, 247–52,
272–5
implementation guidelines
187–228
limits of possibility
209–15
origins 117–46
outcomes 65–7, 202–23
processes 64–7, 84–7,
97–8, 137–8, 141,
147–85, 187–228
scope-setting procedures
209–16, 226, 252
stages 192–228

stakeholder analysis 188,
216–19, 227, 239–41,
250–4, 276–8, 289–90
strategic conversations 3–5,
85–7, 140–5, 161–6,
189–99, 231–7,
255–75, 291
structure considerations
192–9, 224
systems thinking 140,
153–8, 219–20, 227,
292
timing issues 194–5, 203–4
workshops 165–9, 178–80,
199–228
see information lines 110–1
scenario thinking 2–39, 63–7,
92, 114–46, 162–71,
232–4, 276–8, 288
capital intensity 135–6
checklists 144–6, 224–8
company size 135–6
concepts 2–39, 63–7, 92,
114–46, 154–5,
162–71, 232–4, 276–8,
288
culture issues 97–146,
270–5
modern techniques
117–46, 266–7
origins 117–46
reaction speeds 22–3,
32–9, 147, 153, 171–8,
276–8
war games 121–8, 137–8,
141
scenarios, word origins 127
Schein, Edgar 105, 111–12,
174
Schrempp, Jurgen E. 104
scope-setting procedures
209–16, 226, 252
SD *see* system dynamics
models
segmentation factors 48–50
self-strategizing teams 272–5,
289

Senge, Peter 174
sensitivity analysis 151–2
sensors, change issues 17,
    27–8, 33, 36, 45, 65, 82,
    86
seven questions 163–4,
    196–9, 237–9
shareholders 17, 217–19,
    240
'Sharpbenders' research study
    6, 11, 14–19, 36–7,
    289
Shell 2, 131–4, 144, 164,
    168, 172, 175, 178,
    238–9, 276–8
short-term issues 260–1, 275
Siemens 265
simulation models 121–8
single-loop learning 81–2,
    173–4, 268–70, 282
skills 8, 83, 110–11, 147–85
social issues 156–8, 193,
    209–10, 216, 243–4,
    256–7, 290–1
Sony 100
stakeholders 5–19, 65–7,
    188–90, 216–27,
    239–41, 262–4, 276–8,
    289–90
    see also customers
    analysis 188, 216–19, 227,
        239–41, 250–4, 276–8,
        289–90
    BI 15–19, 280–1
    relationships 17–21, 25–8,
        94–6, 112, 217–19,
        240–1, 250–4, 276–8
STEEP analysis 156–8, 193,
    290–1
stereotypes 108–11
story concepts 170–1
strategic conversations 3–5,
    85–7, 140–5, 161–6,
    189–99, 231–7,
    255–75, 291
strategic journeys 252–4,
    266–78

strategy 3–9, 33–7, 41–67,
    135–8, 199, 220–3,
    229–75, 286
    barriers 33–7, 199
    concepts 239–54
    cultural impacts 89–115,
        229–75
    cycles 254
    developing-strategy goals
        233–4, 239–54
    emergent strategies 80,
        269
    processes 252–4
    reviews 18–19
    self-strategizing teams
        272–5, 289
    'Sharpbenders' research
        study 17–19, 36–7,
        289
Strathclyde 164
strengths 13–19, 65–7,
    199–202, 229–75
stresses 57–8, 62–7, 70,
    73–5, 276
structure considerations,
    scenarios 192–9, 224
success factors 3–19, 28–46,
    77, 82–5, 177, 198–9,
    232–41, 276–8
    barriers 34–7, 199
    failures 13–14, 35–6,
        82–5, 232–3
    formulas 44–6, 182–5
    global markets 110–15
    Nokia 32–5
    skills 147–85
    Tetra Pak 28–32, 34–6
    uncertainties 13–14, 32–3,
        55–61, 63–7, 86,
        137–85
successful organizations
    12–19, 36–7, 77, 82–5,
    177, 276–8
suppliers 17, 217–19, 240,
    248–52
system dynamics (SD) models
    219–20

systemic loops 69, 79–87,
    173–4, 243, 264,
    268–75, 281–2, 292
systemic thinking 69, 79–87,
    153–6, 173–4, 264,
    281–2, 292
systems analysis 126
systems engineering 124–5
systems thinking 140, 153–8,
    219–20, 227, 264, 292

tacit cultural assumptions
    90–115
tacit knowledge 86, 159–60,
    166–70, 246, 263
Tamara 106–9
Tandy Corporation 33
Taurus 55–6
teams 143, 167–9, 178–9,
    188–228, 249–54,
    271–5
    across-team conversations
        273–5
    composition considerations
        167–9, 193–4, 237,
        271
    decision dilemmas 58–61,
        72–5, 85, 272–5
    empowerment benefits
        272–5
    group-think problems 3–4,
        38, 71–85, 140, 149,
        161–71, 202, 263–4,
        283–4
    practicalities 203–4
    self-strategizing teams
        272–5, 289
technological changes 47,
    125–8, 138–45, 156–8,
    190–3, 204–23, 265,
    290–1
technology-serves scenarios
    215–16
tests, outcomes 202–16,
    269–70
Tetra Pak 12, 28–32, 34–6
    customers 28–32, 34–6

success factors 28–32, 34–6
think-tank approaches 234–5
thinking processes 2–39,
    41–71, 97–8, 120–1,
    143–85
threats 5, 23, 61–7, 121–31,
    189–90, 196–202
Time Warner 23–4
timing issues, projects 194–5,
    203–4
training 18, 118–20, 124,
    178–9
transitional objects 181–5
trends 64–7, 142–6, 169–70,
    219–23, 230–1, 262,
    283
trust issues 240–1
truth 111–12, 214–15,
    256–7
turbulence issues 5
Twain, Mark 215

umbrella concepts 171
uncertainties 13–14, 32–3,
    55–73, 86, 121–6,
    137–99, 236, 260–78

avoidance cultures 101–2,
    151, 276
concepts 63–7, 121–6,
    145, 206–12, 249–54,
    270–5
uniqueness factors, BI 15–19,
    37, 243–54, 276–8, 281
unknown variables 1–2, 4–5,
    13–14
upframing exercises 78,
    181–5, 254, 267

value chains 223
value creation 15–19, 25–37,
    192, 198–9, 211–12,
    223, 241–2, 256–8
values 89–115, 188–90
    see also culture issues
vision 1–2, 25, 35, 136–40,
    230–3, 262
Vygotsky, L.S. 166, 170, 288

Wack, Pierre 132–3, 136,
    138–9, 141, 151, 178
waiter's dilemma 50, 70, 79,
    281, 286, 292

Wal-Mart 221
Walt Disney Organization *see*
    Disney
war games 121–8, 137–8,
    141
weaknesses 13–14, 24
what-if strategies 133
Wilska, Kari-Pekka 33
winners 12–19, 36–7, 77,
    82–5, 177, 276–8
    see also success...
Woodruff, Robert 49
workshops 165–9, 178–80,
    199–228
World Trade Center 92

Xerox 12, 19–23, 34–8, 45,
    66, 231, 244

Yahoo! 12, 23–5, 34–8, 45,
    66, 231
Yang, Jerry 24